D0949659

Jerry Brown

The Man on the White Horse

Jerry Brown

The Man on the White Horse

BY J. D. LORENZ

HOUGHTON MIFFLIN COMPANY BOSTON 1978

Copyright © 1978 by J. D. Lorenz

All rights reserved. No part of this work may be reproduced
or transmitted in any form by any means, electronic or
mechanical, including photocopying and recording, or by
any information storage or retrieval system, without
permission in writing from the publisher.

Library of Congress Cataloging in Publication Data

Lorenz, James D.
  Jerry Brown, the man on the white horse.
  Includes bibliographical references.
  1. California — Politics and government — 1951–
2. Brown, Edmund Gerald, 1938–   3. Lorenz,
James D.   I. Title.
F866.2.L67   979.4'05'0924   78-952
ISBN 0-395-25767-0

Printed in the United States of America

P 10 9 8 7 6 5 4 3 2 1

FOR MY FATHER, DOUG LORENZ

Contents

in order to Win the Governor's Favor. A Rite of Initiation Is
Scheduled for the Author. The Author Suspects He Has Flunked
the Test.

Introduction

This is a story about magic in politics.

The magic was and is practiced by Jerry Brown, Governor of California and other imaginary places, the finest political sleight-of-hand artist of his generation, a veritable Merlin of the media, symbolist, crowd psychologist, manipulator of the human mind, delicate child of life, disciple of Marshall Mc-Luhan, pretender to the crown of Washington, D.C., and of the Holy American Empire, the once and future king.

The author of the story is a person of no great consequence who was Jerry's research assistant during the 1974 campaign and his employment director for seven months thereafter, and who was fooled by the Governor more times than he likes to admit.

As for the mythical figure of the man on the white horse referred to in the book's title and the genies that are mentioned in the book's first quotation . . . the reader will have to discover for himself what these images represent. For as the author was to learn from the Governor on more than one occasion, a little mystery makes life more interesting.

The author is willing to give the reader a few clues, however.

The first clue is: Don't assume the symbols Jerry invokes are strictly Jerry's creatures. They may also be beings who inhabit the reader's netherworld, imaginings that Jerry plays upon more than he manufactures. Try to remember that when Jerry plays a successful trick on people, he displays not only the genius of his craft, but also demonstrates that people want and need to be hoodwinked.

Which brings me to my second point. A politician seeks to reflect his constituents' hopes and fears far more than he tries to change them. Not so much a reformer as an opportunist, he takes what is given and makes the best of it. If he succeeds and opinion polls say his popularity is high, he can be considered a mirror of public psychology at a point in time. And if, moreover, he gains high office in a powerful land, exercises great influence over his peers in the political arena, and, indeed, expresses a certain, essential mood of the time before others grasp it, he may well become the touchstone for a historical period and the representative figure of his age.

I won't be coy about one of the book's themes. I believe Jerry Brown is the representative American figure of the 1970s. I think he has succeeded in symbolizing the doubt, the detachment, and the escapism of the period as profoundly as Martin Luther King embodied the commitment, the involvement, and the passion of the 1960s.

But perhaps I am claiming too much in a brief preface. For, as Jerry Brown was the first to remind us, the 1970s was a time to "lower our expectations," plant our gardens, look to the self, and subsist on a small scale. Bigness was out in political rhetoric. "Small is beautiful" was in. Anyone who wanted to win a large following had to remember as much. And so this book proceeds likewise. It is not an exhaustive survey of the moods of California politics. Nor is it a full-blown biography. It is simply a story, covering a year's worth of events when Jerry Brown and the author spent some time together.

In order to get across something of Jerry's essence, I have tried to use the same storytelling method that he uses in politics; namely, to stay on a small scale, consider a number of different levels simultaneously, and surprise and amuse. There is really no other way. Too much of Jerry's odd genius gets lost in translation if he is described in a conventional manner. And so I am going to proceed a step at a time, reliving the bizarre little episodes as they occurred, zigging and zagging between seemingly unrelated events until... Open Sesame! You, the reader, will see the connections and know Jerry's secret for the first time: mirrors. It is all mirrors. Jerry is reflecting us. We are reflecting him. He is wearing our hopes, our fears, our values, as if they were his own clothing.

I am speaking metaphorically, of course, using figures of speech. But how appropriate for a man who, on more than one level, has fashioned himself into a figure of speech.

I will give you another clue.

When Jerry says things that don't make sense to you, don't assume what he says is intended to make sense. He may simply be trying to confuse matters.

Now why, you may ask, would he want to do that?

What is he diverting us from? And why is he so concerned? As you try to answer good questions like these, keep in mind the way things were as Jerry operated from 1974 to 1977.

It was a time of uncertainty.

Americans were strung out on too many emergencies.

Although we didn't know what the next one was going to be, we were convinced there was going to be one. There was the Vietnam crisis, the environmental crisis, the stagflation crisis, the Watergate crisis, and so on ad infinitum.

With the end of cheap energy, the assumptions about perpetual material progress went out the window. People had to begin thinking about accepting less, which was not very pleasant, and so they began looking around for somebody to blame.

The politicians came to mind first and very quickly.

In a world where everything was becoming more politicized, the politicos were the natural fall guys. The big corporations and unions were possibilities too, but they were less visible. The politicians, by contrast, were on TV every day and had to run for reelection every so many years.

From 1968 to 1974, when our story begins, political careers were being destroyed like cars in a demolition derby.

Quite understandably, Jerry didn't want to be among the unfortunate, so he devised a little stratagem.

Forget about solving the big problems in the real world. No matter what position you take, you're likely to be clobbered by some interest group. Concentrate on the small stuff. Lighten up. Practice symbolic politics.

The symbols were a way out, you see. And survival was the name of the game.

That was why Jerry emerged as the vanguard politician after the Arab oil embargo, when survival became a big issue for the first time since World War II. Jerry had been dealing with the matter of survival on a personal level for a good many years, and so he was ready. It all fit together. He had been, let us not forget, the Governor's son, a privileged kid, never a very good athlete or one of the popular boys in school, something of an oddball, really; and to make matters worse, people were always after him for favors and were envious of him at the same time.

Jerry had to learn to cope, to fend them off, and he did. By the time he was elected Governor of California, the defensive maneuvers were second nature. He didn't waste a minute. Practically every week of his first two years in office, he diverted people with kooky vignettes about his personal life, asked funny questions, acted mysterious, kept people guessing, and filled up the newspapers with talk about saving whales and exploring outer space and other far-sighted projects he could do absolutely nothing about and therefore couldn't fail at. Most of all he spoke of "lowering expectations," code words for: "Don't blame me if things go wrong."

Everything worked. Jerry's public opinion ratings zoomed upward. The savage beast of the electorate was pacified. The fundamental method was diversion. The underlying motivation was fear. The electorate's attention was displaced from the real and ever so intractable world of the big issues to the imaginary and more malleable arena of symbols. That was what the politics of the mid-1970s turned out to be: symbolic politics, escapist politics.

This is not to suggest that Jerry and other politicians of the time had no contact with or comprehension of the real world of taxes, legislation, and regulation. It was just that this aspect of their stewardship was depublicized.

But now I'm starting to say things that could be better discussed during the course of our story. And so, on with the tale. We are about to take a ride on a flying carpet and survey the wondrous world of Jerry Brown. You may be mystified by some of the incidents I will relate, and, yes, your perspective may be turned topsy-turvy, but I don't think you'll be bored.

J. D. LORENZ

Berkeley, California
October 31, 1977

Jerry Brown

The Man on the White Horse

"Why," said he, "a magician could call up a lot of genies, and they would hash you up like nothing before you could say Jack Robinson. They are as tall as a tree and as big around as a church."

"Well," I says, "s'pose we got some genies to help *us* — can't we lick the other crowd then?"

"How are you going to get them?"

"I don't know. How do *they* get them?"

"Why, they rub an old tin lamp or an iron ring, and then the genies come tearing in, with the thunder and lightning a-ripping around and the smoke a-rolling, and everything they're told to do they up and do it . . ."

"What makes them tear around so?"

"Why, whoever rules the lamp or the ring. They belong to who-ever rules the lamp or the ring, and they've got to do whatever he says. If he tells them to build a palace forty miles long out of di'monds, and fill it full of chewing-gum, or whatever you want, and fetch an emperor's daughter from China for you to marry, they've got to do it . . ."

"Well," says I, "I think they are a pack of flatheads for not keep-ing the palace themselves 'stead of fooling them away like that. And what's more — if I was one of them I would see a man in Jericho before I would drop my business and come to him for the rubbing of an old tin lamp."

"How you talk, Huck Finn. Why, you'd *have* to come when he rubbed it, whether you wanted to or not."

"What! and I as high as a tree and as big as a church? All right, then: I *would* come; but I lay I'd make that man climb the highest tree there was in the country."

"Shucks, it ain't no use to talk to you, Huck Finn. You don't seem to know anything, somehow — perfect saphead."

I thought all this over for two or three days, and then I reckoned I would see if there was anything in it. I got an old tin lamp and an iron ring, and went out in the woods and rubbed and rubbed till I sweat like an Injun, calculating to build a palace and sell it; but it wasn't no use, none of the genies come. So then I judged that all that stuff was only just one of Tom Sawyer's lies.

— Mark Twain, *The Adventures of Huckleberry Finn*

Chapter One

THE GOVERNOR-ELECT ASKS THE AUTHOR TO DRAFT AN
EMPLOYMENT PROGRAM. THE 1974 CAMPAIGN DESCRIBED.
THE AUTHOR SERVES AS AN AUDIENCE FOR THE GOV-
ERNOR-TO-BE. THE AUTHOR'S FIRST ENCOUNTER WITH
THE "BROWNIAN MOVEMENT"

"LORENZ," the Governor-elect of California said to me after
the November 1974 election, "you're supposed to be an in-
novator. See what we can do about this unemployment
problem." I wasn't sure whether he was paying me a compliment or extending a challenge that a normal human being
would have a hard time meeting. Probably he was doing
both. Everybody who dealt with Jerry Brown was kept
slightly off-balance, even his father, Edmund G. "Pat" Brown,
Sr., Governor of California from 1958 to 1966 and victor
over Richard Nixon in 1962. "Some people say I got here because of my father," Jerry announced on election night to
the two thousand people who were celebrating his victory
in the Los Angeles Convention Center. "But actually," he
said, as he turned toward the lady who was standing beside
him on the dais, "it was my mother who was the important
influence." The sentiment and the delivery were typical
Jerry Brown, a build-up that turned into a putdown. Jerry
was an amalgam of attracting and repelling forces, working
all night with his close advisers in a camaraderie that, if
nothing else, was born of common exhaustion and, at the

1

same time, drawing back when anyone tried to touch him on the arm or pat him on the back. Jerry Brown didn't like being touched.

I remember the first day I worked on Jerry's campaign staff, August 3, 1974, Richard Maulin, Jerry's finance director, told me: "Jerry will deal with you as long as he thinks you have more water in your glass than he has in his." Jerry would cajole me, flatter me, be nasty too, but he wouldn't ignore me. And all the while he'd be trying to pour my water into his glass. Richard shrugged. "When he thinks he's succeeded, he'll move on to someone else whose glass hasn't been emptied yet."

Richard seemed to know what he was talking about. But then again, I thought at the time, who could say? Jerry seemed committed. During the campaign, he kept telling me that "jobs, not welfare, are the answer." And in the seven-minute inaugural address he delivered on January 6, 1975, the shortest inaugural in California history, he said that unemployment was the number one problem. There was, of course, the unresolved question of how much a state could do. But Jerry and I were agreed that the Governor could accomplish more than Ronald Reagan, Jerry's predecessor, had done. The Governor could initiate model programs on the state level. He could lobby in Washington. He could build pressure. After all, California had 10 per cent of the country's population and paid 15 per cent of its taxes. If the Governor of California couldn't swing some weight in the great economic debate, then who could?

We didn't expect the people in Washington to come up with many solutions on their own. But then, we weren't making many concrete proposals ourselves during the 1974 campaign.

"Look at McGovern," Jerry said. "He was specific in 1972 and he got clobbered."

Jerry was determined not to fall into the same trap. In the standard speech he delivered in the fall of 1974, he was

2

specific only when he assailed his opponent's record. The rest of the time, he inveighed against the recession and "recycled Reaganism" without indicating what he would do differently, and he talked about a "New Spirit" that was so vague, it wasn't susceptible to attack.

"A little generality goes a long way in this business," Jerry remarked after one performance.

I think it was a month before Jerry's opponent, Houston Flournoy, realized he should stop responding to Jerry's attacks. Good college professor that he was (Flournoy taught political science at Pomona College before running for public office), he was somewhat compulsive about setting the record straight. Jerry was aware of this idiosyncrasy, of course. Jerry was always very adept at figuring out how to exploit an opponent's weakness.

Jerry was also good at following his own advice. In fact, there is only one time I can remember when Jerry lapsed — and even that occurred under extenuating circumstances.

It was the beginning of the fall campaign. Jerry was fed up, restless, bored. He was slightly listless and more than a little impatient and he was squabbling with Richard and with Tom Quinn, the campaign director. It was perfectly obvious what the problem was. He was tired of campaigning, which he had been doing full-tilt for nine months. He was sick of the small talk at the fund raisers and the same speech over and over again and the schedule that required him to move about like a water bug, and most of all, he was tired of having Richard and Tom tell him what to do. And so, in typical Jerry Brown fashion, he rebelled. It was only a little bit at first. He showed up late for a few appointments. He tried to change the schedule without notifying the scheduling department. He balked at making decisions. He lost things. He refused to prepare for the TV debates that were coming up with Flournoy.

Oh, it was a fine how-do-you-do by the first week in September. Jerry was generally uncooperative and Richard pestered him more and Tom went about his business and Jerry wondered whether he was being left out and Jerry delivered several lackadaisical Labor Day speeches and then several days later he gave an interview that was so off the wall, it startled people. He was talking to several reporters and somebody asked him about the state's problems, and Jerry said maybe one answer was a unicameral legislature.[1] The reporters couldn't believe their ears.

"You mean, abolish one of the houses of the legislature?" one of the reporters asked him.

Yes, that was what Jerry was talking about.

But what about the members of the house that was going to be abolished? somebody wanted to know. Wouldn't they be just a little displeased?

Jerry didn't seem to care.

And wasn't the idea somewhat obsolete? Nebraska was the only state that had a unicameral legislature, and that was a product of the horse-and-buggy era.

Jerry felt the idea was worth consideration.

Some of the reporters, however, thought it was a crazy idea, and they reported it as such. For the first time since Jerry had announced his candidacy nine months before, he was sounding like an immature kid with crazy ideas. It was exactly the impression he wanted to avoid giving because we all knew Flournoy was going to make an issue of Jerry's youth and play on the notion that Jerry was an eccentric. But here Jerry was, handing Flournoy the issue with a flourish.

"Do you think Jerry knows what he's doing?" one of his assistants asked me the day after the statement was reported in the press. "I mean, is he flipping out?"

The assistant said that except for the difficulties between Tom and Jerry and Jerry and Richard and Richard and Tom, he wouldn't have thought twice about the interview. But there seemed to be a pattern, and there was the strain of the primary as well, when Jerry was running against Bob Moretti, Speaker of the assembly, and Joe Alioto, mayor of San Fran-

4

cisco. The primary was rough sledding. Moretti walked in unannounced at two of Jerry's public appearances and attacked him personally, and some members of Jerry's staff felt Alioto tried to rattle Jerry by insinuating he was a homosexual. ("Jerry Brown continues to campaign in the closet," Alioto had told startled reporters on March 26, 1974.)[2] And although Jerry stood up to Moretti and it was generally acknowledged that the Alioto innuendo was never documented in any form or fashion, perhaps Jerry was hurt more than he let on. "I mean," the assistant said, "Moretti and Alioto obviously picked up on the fact that Jerry doesn't enjoy close-in, one-to-one confrontations. Well, maybe the infighting took something out of him."

We would never know. Shortly after the unicameral legislature remark, Jerry isolated himself for several days, and when he returned, he was, in the vernacular of the day, "cooled out." He was more cooperative. He stuck to the media script. He seemed resigned to the monotony of the campaign.

The campaign staff was greatly relieved. I think the general feeling was that Jerry had stumbled in the press interview but had recovered nicely. My own view was somewhat different. I believed the press interview was part of the recovery. Jerry used a small crisis (the interview) to head off a larger problem (his own boredom). The fallout from the interview was like a slap in the face. It woke him up. It got the adrenalin flowing.

Jerry was going through a process of self-adjustment, I decided. He was really quite a remarkable person. He would move off course and seem quite lost, and then some internal navigational system would take over and he would correct his bearings. I must say, over the four months of the campaign I grew quite fond of him.

I was supposed to be Jerry's adviser on the issues and help prepare him for the TV debates, but most of the time, he was the one who did the talking. In fact, it was the opposite of what Richard had described. Jerry was pouring his water into my glass. I would bring him a position paper on welfare or land use or housing; he wouldn't even read it. He would just start talking, his mind racing ahead to the time when he would assume office. I suppose he wanted to think out loud about how he would govern. And because I was available and didn't put pressure on him and liked to listen, I was chosen as the audience. It was a fascinating experience. Some of his observations seemed — how shall I put it? — right out of Machiavelli's *The Prince* or Castiglione's *The Courtier*. And throughout the discussions ran the Renaissance ideal that politics could be a conscious process and the state, a work of art.

I gathered Jerry felt these lessons in statecraft were successful because several days before Christmas 1974, he passed the word that he wanted to appoint me head of the state's Employment Development Department. I was quite flattered. Although I had not finished the employment program, it had already produced its first fruits — a job for me.

The campaign was exhausting work. So was the transition from the Reagan to the Brown administration, which I helped Jerry to manage. And so it was agreed that when the bulk of the transition work was completed, several of us would go off for a few days to rest up for the push ahead. Jerry was going to Mexico. I decided to fly to Hawaii. "We'll issue the press release on your appointment when you return," one of Jerry's aides told me. There was plenty of time; most of Jerry's appointments would not be made until late January. Within an hour after I had stepped off the plane from Honolulu, however, Jerry's aide was on the phone. "Get over to the Governor's office immediately. The press has been asking where you are and Jerry's upset you're not here."

It turned out that two days before I returned, the state's newspapers had carried the following story:

In his enthusiasm in replying to a Los Angeles questioner, Governor Edmund G. Brown Jr. beat his press staff to the announcement that James Lorenz, founder of California Rural Legal Assistance, is the new director of the Employment Development Department.

Brown late yesterday was ticking off a list of efforts to ease unemployment. He named the founder of the controversial legal services agency as new employment director, then caught himself.

"I haven't announced that yet — it just popped out," said Brown."[3]

So I was the Governor's Freudian slip. And having popped out, I was supposed to be present and accounted for, immediately. Otherwise, Jerry's aide explained, the new administration might appear disorganized, and that impression we had to avoid at all costs. The Governor was thirty-six years old. The polls taken during the campaign indicated that many voters felt he was too inexperienced. We needed to convey a sense of competence, even if we didn't know yet what we were doing. And since the Governor's working style was unpredictable, his appointees needed to be available at all times, ready to adjust to last-minute changes in direction. "In fact," one of Jerry's aides said to me humorously, "working with Jerry can be likened to the Brownian movement in physics: 'the constant zigzag movement of particles in a gas or liquid, the position of none of which can be predicted ahead of time.' "

I looked up Brownian movement in the dictionary. That's what it was, all right.[4] For some reason, the Governor's assistant had memorized the definition.

Chapter Two

ABOUT THE PAPER SHREDDER AND OTHER REMNANTS OF
THE REAGAN ADMINISTRATION. ROBERT GNAIZDA, ESQUIRE,
INTRODUCED. THE AUTHOR EXPLORES THE BUREAUCRATIC
LABYRINTH.

THE EMPLOYMENT DEVELOPMENT DEPARTMENT occupied most of an enormous building that ran for two blocks along Sacramento's Capitol Mall. The edifice was so imposing, it extended *over* a street that ran perpendicular to the mall. How phenomenal, I thought as I drove underneath my new domain. I was quite overwhelmed. It was like... Buckingham Palace.

I was equally impressed by my new office. Windows on two sides, overlooking the mall and the capitol. Wood paneling. A walnut desk a foot longer than anyone else's in the department. An intercom with two rows of buttons. A couch. A coffee table. Four easy chairs. A row of plants in Styrofoam containers imported from the state's greenhouse. An executive washroom. A nineteen-inch color television set. There was no question the director was adequately equipped to fight the problems of unemployment.

I also noticed a metal container with lawnmowerlike blades on top and a little motor that plugged into the wall socket. ELECTRIC WASTEBASKET, the label on the top read.

"What's an electric wastebasket?" I asked my new secretary.

"It's a paper shredder," she said.

What in the world was the employment department doing with a paper shredder.

She didn't know or wouldn't say.

I soon discovered that the paper shredder wasn't the only curiosity in the department. There were also the name changes. The department had had *three* names in the preceding five years. It had gone from the State Department of Employment to Human Resources Development to the Employment Development Department. Yes. And five different individuals had served as director in the past four years. Poor, departed souls, their pictures hung in a row in the anteroom to my office. And also, I was told, the department had undergone frequent reorganizations. I finally lost track of all the different organizational charts I was given. It was bizarre, almost as if the whole operation was resting on quicksand. Policies kept changing. People kept disappearing. Something was going on. I made a mental note to sit down sometime and figure out what was so dangerous about employment.

Several mornings after I arrived at EDD, I received a telephone call from my old friend Bob Gnaizda, the new deputy secretary of the Health and Welfare Agency. Bob was one of the first attorneys I had hired at California Rural Legal Assistance when we were starting out in the spring of 1966. He was also a consummate dart thrower and gin rummy player. We had stayed in touch even after he left CRLA, exchanging anecdotes over an occasional luncheon. Now he was second-in-command of the umbrella agency that was supposed to serve as the intermediary between the Governor's office and the state employment, health, welfare, and prison departments.

"Have I got a story for you," Bob said on the phone that morning. "You know I was assigned a space in the EDD parking lot. Well, somebody was taking my spot in the evenings, so I called one of your administrators to see if there was anything he could do. He said he'd look into it. This morning I received a three-page memo. It was incredible, just like the military. He said EDD couldn't give me a portable sign and they couldn't paint a 'Reserved Evenings' notice on the blacktop, but they could post a guard." Gnaizda chortled. "And on weekends too," he added, guffawing.

The laugh was unmistakable, a staccato, machine-gun-like sound that, one of our associates once said, was capable of causing bodily harm. Bob was in fine form. As a lawyer, his greatest talent was his sense of the ridiculous. He loved to poke fun at the contradictions in his opponent's position. There was an employment discrimination case he handled against the San Francisco Police Department, for example. I remembered because he told me about it just before we came up to Sacramento. A group of women wanted to become police officers, but they couldn't pass the department's physical proficiency test. The women contended that the exam required much more physical prowess than was needed by the ordinary police officer. The department disagreed. Bob said the case boiled down to the question of whether the exam was "job related." In order to prove it wasn't, Bob persuaded the judge to issue an order requiring everyone in the department to take the test. "You should have seen the reaction," Bob told me. "It had been years since the senior officers had done anything athletic. Many held desk jobs. Some were overweight." He laughed. "Not only were the men required to take the test," he said, "they were forced to compete against the women. It was humiliating." Soon afterward the department agreed to modify the examination. It was a question of survival.

When the bureaucracy was involved, I was to discover, it was always a question of survival. Bob's story about the offer of the parking lot guard wasn't as incredible as it seemed. Many of the Reagan holdovers were falling all over themselves trying to please the new administration. "Would you like the paneling in your office refinished?" I was asked my second day at EDD. "Do you want to drive the Mercury four-door sedan that's reserved for the director?"

I knew what was happening. The holdovers were plying

me with favors in the hope they could stay on. And yet, no matter how blatant their efforts were, I found myself touched by their gestures of hospitality. It was hard to dislike someone who was trying to help you, especially when he seemed so vulnerable.

But why the desperation? The answer was: Most of the upper-level people were no longer protected by the regular civil service classification system. They were "career executive appointees." Whereas ordinary civil servants couldn't be demoted without showing good cause, the CEA's served totally at the pleasure of the director. Within certain broad limits, they could be promoted — or demoted — at will. That was the reason the Reagan administration had instituted the CEA system in the first place. They wanted to provide a series of rewards and punishments that would encourage the top bureaucrats to be more responsive to their wishes.

Several days after I talked with Bob Gnaizda on the phone, he suggested I appoint as my deputy director an experienced civil servant we could trust. He had just the right person in mind, he said. Dick Bernheimer, an up-and-coming civil servant with the state Personnel Board. Bernheimer knew the civil service and CEA systems backward and forward, Gnaizda felt. Indeed, Bernheimer was like the sorceror's apprentice. Snap your fingers and he would do anything you wanted. Your wish is my command. That sort of thing. But he was a hot commodity, Gnaizda advised. If I didn't snap up Bernheimer immediately, somebody else would.

I wasn't completely sold. We wanted someone with experience in state government, but we also needed someone with ties to the people we were serving. Maybe the answer was two deputies. I knew who I wanted for one of the positions. Catherine Day Jermany. In her early thirties. Black. A former welfare recipient. For two years head of the California Welfare Rights organization. Presently a deputy director at the National Paralegal Institute in Washington, D.C., where I had worked as a consultant. Catherine knew what it was like to be an EDD client. She had collected unemployment compensation, and while she was on welfare, she had come to one of our Employment Services offices looking for a job. The interviewer there told her she was "unemployable." She proved him wrong. Now she was earning $15,000 a year, she was a recognized expert in welfare and social security law, and she was a special consultant to the U. S. Department of Labor. If anyone knew what was wrong with EDD, it was Catherine.

I suggested to Gnaizda that we hire two deputies, Catherine and someone like Bernheimer.

"That's a terrific idea," he said.

I agreed to interview Bernheimer the next day.

I needed help, I realized. After a week on the job, I hadn't talked to a single unemployed person. Nor had I seen a local EDD office. I was turning into an oyster, encased in a shell of bureaucracy. It was clear what I needed to do. I arranged a visit to the San Francisco EDD office for January 23, 1975.

"You're the first director in four years to visit this office," a lady from the disputed claims section said during the coffee break. "I might as well tell you what the problems are. You may never be here again."

She spoke with great concern abut the department. Her attitude was in marked contrast to Sacramento, where much of the game was devoted to advancing one's own position. Other employees joined in. They felt abandoned, they said. They would write a memo to Sacramento, requesting permission to look for office space in a safer neighborhood. Nothing would happen for three months. Sacramento called only when Sacramento wanted something from them.

The bureaucracy was like a tall ladder. The executives in Sacramento who ran the department expended much of their energies trying to climb up to the next highest rung. The people in the local offices who were standing down below were forgotten, for the most part, so long as they held the ladder steady.

Two days after my visit, a short reference to it appeared in Herb Caen's column in the San Francisco *Chronicle:*

13

Meet the People: If you'd dropped in at the Employment Development Department (EDD) office at Third and Bryant [a] couple of days ago, you'd have seen a youngish man with shaggy hair, wearing an old tweed coat with torn lining and a skinny 1952 necktie, interviewing claimants throughout the day. Far as the unemployed were concerned, he was just another civil servant — perhaps more civil than some — but actually he's the new director of EDD ... Another example of the Jerry Brown administration in action. I like it, don't you?[5]

We had originally decided against publicizing the visit because we didn't want the employees to feel they were being used for a publicity stunt. But apparently someone in the organization had been unable to resist.

Gnaizda thought the column was "terrific," however. When I told him I'd never talked to Herb Caen and had nothing to do with the news item, he said, "So much the better if it appears you had nothing to do with it."

Jerry made no direct reference to the story, but one day while we were in his office he said to me, "You know, we should think about meetings state employees could stage in their neighborhoods. They could find out what people are thinking. They could explain what we're doing. We're too cut off in Sacramento."

I agreed, suggesting we start on a small scale.

"Fine," he replied.

"That article made an impression," an aide said after the meeting. "Jerry rarely compliments people, but if they're doing something that's applauded in the press, he'll appropriate it. With him, imitation is the sweetest form of flattery."

I called this particular aide "the Shadow" because he was so ubiquitous in the early days of the administration, but this time I wondered whether he knew what he was talking about. Was Jerry really referring to my San Francisco visit or was the Shadow trying to flatter me?

Chapter Three

ABOUT THE GAMES PEOPLE PLAYED IN THE GOVERNOR'S OFFICE. CRISIS AND CONFUSION. HIDE-AND-SEEK. THE AUTHOR TRIES TO CONVINCE THE GOVERNOR TO MAKE A DECISION. THE AUTHOR FAILS. THE AUTHOR MEETS THE INIMITABLE MR. BARZAGHI, WHOSE LADY FRIEND READS ABOUT RASPUTIN WHILE MR. BARZAGHI SERVES AS THE GOVERNOR'S HOUSEKEEPER.

"WHEN ARE YOU going to give me a jobs program?" Jerry asked me in late January of 1975.

"When am I going to get some help?" I replied.

The appointments bottleneck was a big problem in the new administration. Jerry was holding up on all candidates until he personally interviewed them, but much of the time he was too busy to conduct interviews. I guess it was what the psychologists call "a double bind" — a damned-if-you-do and damned-if-you-don't situation. Jerry yelled at people if they hired staff on their own — he had gotten furious at Gnaizda, for example, when he hired a black executive assistant without consulting him — but he also became upset if you didn't produce something tangible right away. Well, how, I wanted to know, were we going to get moving when practically the only executives around were the Reagan holdovers.

For once that month, Jerry was standing still, so I told him about the two people I was considering for deputy director, Catherine Jermany and Dick Bernheimer. Was it all right to fly Catherine out from Washington? I asked.

"Yes, yes," Jerry said. He was losing interest fast.

"What about next week?" I asked. He told his secretary Agnes to give me a time.

"What about interviewing Dick Bernheimer?" I continued.

He said something about Gnaizda having introduced Bernheimer already.

I had lost him. Another adviser was walking through the door with news about an emergency Jerry had to resolve immediately. Our meeting had lasted four minutes.

That was the way it was in the Governor's office and in the Brown-for-Governor campaign and in the secretary of state's office, where Jerry had served before being elected Governor. When Jerry had his way, the business of the day wasn't organized. It just evolved in fits and starts — five minutes here, two minutes there, a two-hour meeting interrupted by a one-hour digression — quantums of time that people around Jerry disputed for like schoolboys fighting for a football. If you were lucky, he would engross himself in your problem and would talk to you for several hours, picking up the phone, asking people their opinions, firing questions, laying out options, making a big fuss. If you were less fortunate and he was bored or distracted or acting hyperactive, you tried to keep it short and resolve what you could in three or four minutes. Jerry was very unpredictable. The worst thing of all was when you had a long meeting with him on some problem and returned with several solutions — only to discover he had completely lost interest.

Gray Davis, Jerry's executive assistant, contended that the Governor's office was full of "creative confusion." Marc Poche, Jerry's liaison with the state senate, said the Governor's office was an exciting place to work because it was like "a playground." Tony Kline, Jerry's legal counsel, argued that the lack of structure gave Jerry the freedom to go to the root of the issue he was studying. But I wasn't so sure. Maybe Jerry got lost along the way.

Part of the problem was Jerry's unwillingness to delegate authority. Early in his second year in office, in fact, the Sacramento *Bee* would run a political cartoon entitled "The Organizational Chart of State Government." The top line of the chart read "Governor." It ran to several boxes underneath, each of which read "Governor," and these secondary positions, in turn, branched off into tertiary positions that also read "Governor." Every line on the organizational chart read "Governor."

It wasn't too hard to figure out why some days we felt like we were chasing our tails. Because Jerry insisted on making every decision, trivial matters piled up until he was ready to deal with them. However, because he was so disorganized, he rarely found the time.

We were caught in a vicious cycle. Whenever Jerry was in town, his office was characterized by a kind of perpetual disorder that the staff came to accept as a normal part of their existence. Indeed, crisis became part of their *modus operandi*. That is to say, in an environment where there was too much experience to process and where the experience was too confused besides, and where, furthermore, a great many people found themselves on overload much of the time, the only way to get somebody else's attention was to have a crisis. It started with Jerry and then it spread.

Of course the lesson was not lost on Jerry's advisers. Some of them were quick to see the possibilities. If crises could happen, why then, they could also be manufactured. And so it was not surprising that, by the end of January 1975, a veritable cottage industry of crisis manufacture was growing up in the inner reaches of the Brown administration.

One enterprising fellow became adept at identifying and stashing away small emergencies that could be produced at a moment's notice. Another ingenious sort used the press as his instrument. He would select some problem that Jerry was unwilling to deal with; and then, like a ne'er-do-well taking the family jewels to a pawnshop for appraisal, he would confidentially reveal part of the problem to a friendly reporter. The reporter would call the press secretary at the Governor's office, the press secretary would ring the Governor, the Governor would become alarmed about the possibility of adverse publicity, all hell would break loose, and the problem would be resolved, usually before the story got out of hand.

A third acquaintance of mine played a waiting game. He would lay back until somebody else's crisis arose and then hop into the confusion and introduce his own problems. "I try to keep my problem related to the main crisis," he said. "I piggyback." His hope was, of course, that the whole kit and caboodle would be resolved at the same time.

A fourth official in the administration (it was the Shadow, in fact) used what he called "the *fait accompli* maneuver." He would look around for some problem that he knew how Jerry would resolve. And then, when Jerry was out of town, he would resolve the problem himself. "Was that okay?" he would ask Jerry later. "You see," he said to me once, "it's easier to get Jerry to concur with something that's already been done than it is to convince him that he should assume responsibility for setting the wheels in motion. I just make his natural inertia work for me, that's all."

The trick was not to push Jerry too far. That was why all the variations of the crisis game were conducted according to very strict rules.

Rule Number One was: The more significant the crisis, the less imminent it had to be. Otherwise, Jerry would start asking why the problem hadn't been flagged sooner.

Rule Number Two was: The crisis couldn't be the fault of the aide who sounded the alarm. Otherwise, he would be blamed.

Rule Number Three was: The game could be played only by insiders whom Jerry trusted. Otherwise, his anxiety level would be raised even further and nothing would be accomplished.

Rule Number Four was: The purpose of the game was not to force Jerry to do something against his better judgment. The objective was only to goad him into consenting to some action he would have taken anyway, had he been more organized or willing to take the initiative.

When the game was played properly, by persons close to Jerry who had his best interests at heart, the whole process was quite paternalistic. Jerry was the child. His advisers were the parents. The parents were just devising different ways of saying to the child, "Jerry, eat your spinach."

Of course, the child in Jerry was elusive and ever so cunning. Some days he didn't want to follow the menu. He wanted to eat hot dogs. Perhaps that was why he played "confusion," refusing to delegate authority, changing plans all the time, and operating without any set schedule. Was "confusion" an antidote to "crisis," or was "crisis" the defense against "confusion"? In some fashion, the games seemed to reinforce one another.

Catherine Jermany arrived in Sacramento on a morning when Jerry was supposed to have a light schedule — and, to my great surprise, he ushered us into his office almost as soon as we checked in with the receptionist. Jerry greeted Catherine. She said she was glad to meet him. He sat down on the couch. She sat down on the couch. And then he did something curious. He didn't ask Catherine a single question about herself. In fact, he didn't give her a chance to say anything. Picking up a copy of the legislative analyst's commentary on the state budget, he began reading a section describing the programs administered by EDD. "What does this word mean?" he would say, jabbing his finger at the page. "What's this program about?" he would ask, not waiting for an answer. "It sounds like gobbledegook to me." For seven or eight minutes he continued like that. Then, after he had asked Catherine two questions about herself, he got up to leave. "Sorry," he said, "I can't talk to you anymore. There are some people I've got to see."

"What about getting together later on?" I asked.

"Maybe," he said.

I knew enough about Jerry to realize he was doing an avoidance number. He had a number of ways of putting you off. He would start shuffling through papers. Or he would call out for Agnes to get him so-and-so on the telephone. Or he would ask why you didn't talk to someone else about this, when he knew perfectly well that no one else had the authority to make the decision.

But why was he doing this with Catherine? If he didn't want to interview her, why did he agree to the expenditure of several hundred dollars to fly her out from Washington? And if he didn't think she was suitable because she had once been a welfare recipient, why didn't he say so directly when I first told him about her?

There was a morning in Los Angeles in November of 1974, I recollected. It was the day after the election. We were standing in Jerry's inner office, just the two of us. "You see this book," he said, holding up some writing about practical politics. "I've often wondered why politicians tell so many long-winded stories. Now I know. The more they talk the less chance there is people will make demands on them." He smiled a little ruefully and turned away.

Maybe, I thought after the interview, Jerry's afraid I'm making some kind of demand on him. But if that was the case, what was I supposed to do? If I kept after him, he might feel I was putting more pressure on him; if I didn't, he might forget about Catherine. Somewhat in a quandary, I asked the Shadow what he thought the proper course of action was.

"You've got to keep after him," the Shadow said. "Jerry may be testing you to see how much you want her. Or he may be trying to see how she'll behave under pressure."

"Catherine's not under pressure," I replied. "She's in limbo."

"It's the same thing with Jerry," the Shadow pointed out. "Of course," he said, "maybe he doesn't want her at all."

"But how could he decide that when he hasn't found out anything about her?" I asked.

"He looked at her, didn't he?" the Shadow replied. "He could see she's black, couldn't he? Maybe he doesn't want a black person in that position."

"Then why didn't he say so before she flew out here?" I asked.

"Oh, come on," the Shadow said. "We're dealing with a highly defensed individual. Not only about appointments. About everything. Remember where he's coming from. He was the Governor's son. He's seen everything. Flattery. Dissimulation. Back-stabbing. Prominent men falling all over themselves hustling judicial appointments."

The Shadow paused. "His cynicism's only part of the problem," he said. "As a kid, Jerry must have felt very unsure of himself. You know what I mean. Were people being nice to him because they liked him or because they wanted to impress his father?"

The Shadow was going far afield. He loved psychology, which Jerry hated. But I was beginning to get the picture. No wonder Jerry was so cold and distant. If he cut himself off emotionally, he wouldn't have to experience either the uncertainty or the pain. He no longer cared; therefore, he was protected.

It was fascinating, talking to the Shadow. It was also sad. I realized that when the adult Jerry talked about lowering expectations, there might be a fifteen- or a thirteen- or a ten-year-old underneath who was saying, "I don't expect you to be my friend. I don't need you to like me."

"Of course," the Shadow continued, "even someone as strong and determined as Jerry couldn't wall himself off completely. After all, how stoical can a thirteen-year-old be?" On some level, the Shadow speculated, Jerry must have wanted desperately to be befriended. But given the stern demeanor he had adopted, he couldn't express the need directly, or the whole system would be undermined. So consequently, he made contact circuitously. First there was the proximity, the long hours he worked with people around him. Next there were the clues he dropped about himself, like the seemingly random comment he made to me about politicians telling anecdotes. Then there were the trials and tribulations he put people through. It was as if he was saying, "Only those who really care about me are willing to put up with this kind of grief."

He was playing hide-and-seek.

"Did you ever think about why Jerry entered the seminary?" the Shadow asked. "His father's influence didn't work there. It was a different system of rewards and punishments. Since his peers had nothing to gain by being friendly with him, he could let down his guard a little."

The Shadow hesitated. "Berkeley and Yale Law School were probably variations on the seminary," he said. "A little more secular, but still removed."

"Is that why the people in the administration who are closest to Jerry all go back that far?" I asked.

"You mean Rose and Don and Tony?" the Shadow replied. "I think so."

Rose Bird was the new secretary of agriculture and general services. She had known Jerry in the Berkeley days. Don Burns was secretary of business and transportation. Like Jerry, he had been in the seminary; they had also attended Yale Law School together. Tony Kline was legal counsel to the Governor. He had been Jerry's law school roommate. Together, the three of them made up the administration's Praetorian Guard, the inner circle that formed a protective ring around Jerry.

"Getting back to Catherine," the Shadow said, "watch out. Jerry may try to throw a curve ball."

He did. Later the same day, he sent Bill Stall and Jacques Barzaghi over to EDD to interview Catherine. Bill looked as disconcerted to be there as I was to see him. He was Jerry's press secretary. Interviewing people wasn't part of his job.

Jacques Barzaghi was a more ominous sign. About the same age as Jerry. The last name pronounced "bar-zey-gee," with the accent on the "zey." French-born, of Catholic, French-Italian parents. Raised by his grandfather. Former naval navigator, actor, assistant to a director, and philosophy student. A clerical trainee and clerical assistant in the California secretary of state's office from 1972 until 1974, when he joined the Brown-for-Governor campaign. Currently, special assistant to the Governor for the arts. Aristocratic in bearing, cold, aloof. I couldn't think of anyone less like Catherine.

Jacques was also Jerry's spoiler, the guy Jerry called on to put the kibosh on things he didn't approve of. Jacques was like the character in the "Li'l Abner" comic strip who was always followed around by a dark cloud. Bad things seemed to happen when he was in the vicinity. It wasn't necessarily anything he did. It was more his manner, the way he looked at people. Only the eyes moved, back and forth, back and forth, behind steel-rimmed spectacles. The rest of him remained perfectly still: arms folded across the chest, shaven head held erect, and mouth set in a tight, thin smile. The coldness combined with the bemusement to give people the impression that he was laughing at them rather than with them.

Jacques was like a sphinx, really, Jerry's sphinx.

Jerry, Jacques said, had taught him more in two years than he had learned in his whole life. "Teacher is not the word," Jacques said once. "Example, that is what he is. He has concern for people and he cares."[6]

The first time I met Jacques, in August of 1974, he was straightening up the furniture in Jerry's living room. Although Jacques was listed in the campaign roster as public relations adviser, he spent much of his time running errands for Jerry: taking his shirts to the laundry, making sure his kitchen was stocked with food, and picking him up at the airport at odd hours. It was clear that Jacques was more than a housekeeper, however. He picked out the furniture for

Jerry's office and for his living room. (The décor was always the same: two white sofas set perpendicular to each other, a glass coffee table, large potted palms, and abstract art on the walls.) He selected some of the avant-garde literature which was arranged underneath the coffee table. He talked with Jerry about philosophy, art, and literature. He even patronized the same French couturier.

The day I encountered Jacques, his girlfriend told me she was reading three different books about Rasputin, the Russian mystic who mesmerized the czar shortly before the Russian Revolution. I was a little unsettled by the news. Even campaign workers who knew nothing about Jacques's personal life had referred to him as a Rasputin-like person who enjoyed exercising power in indirect ways.

Jacques had been the subject of much discussion within the campaign organization, in fact.

One of Jerry's aides claimed he was glad Jacques was around. "At least somebody makes sure Jerry takes an extra shirt when he goes on an overnight trip," he commented.

Another aide felt he was a more pernicious influence. "Jacques passes himself off as a great mystic," he said right before the end of the campaign, "but actually the mysticism is a way of avoiding accountability. He's not the type of person who should be working here. He makes people nervous."

As best I could determine, the uneasiness about Jacques increased around September of 1974, the time when Jerry seemed to rely on Jacques more and more and on Richard Maulin and Tom Quinn less and less. Some of the concerns people expressed — such as the view that Jacques had hypnotic powers he might try to use on Jerry — were just plain silly. There were other interpretations, however, that seemed more plausible.

"Jacques lives vicariously off the Governor," one of the campaign veterans said in what I felt was the best analysis of the Jacques-Jerry friendship. "Jacques can't get any real power himself, so he'll settle for the symbols. Jerry is a consummate politician, but he doesn't know much about personal relationships. He doesn't choose to put out on that level, to give and take and nourish a friendship through all its trials and tribulations. You give Jerry a friendship and he takes what's useful out of it. He'll draw on your energies. So, see, Jacques is useful. He makes no demands.

"Jacques is like having a friend without having to put up with all the trouble of getting close, which would be okay, except Jacques at the same time is dealing on two levels. One, he's very political no matter what he might tell you. Not on issues, but in the manipulation of power — who gets in to see Jerry, who doesn't — things like that. Secondly, it's all that mystical bullshit. Jacques can't accept that he's an ordinary human being. He blows the simplest things into great mystical events. Sometimes Jerry gets drawn into it; sometimes he just lets Jacques talk. In the end, Jerry makes up his own mind — he's very rational.

"But the point is, Jacques can — and has — ruined relationships of Jerry's. He keeps Jerry from dealing with them himself. Jerry is afraid of deep personal commitments, and Jacques is there telling him it's okay because he's the Governor — he's the philosopher king — he has to remain pure and chaste and cold and tough, with his energies intact. That's what is scary about Jacques Barzaghi. Jerry needs someone to keep him off the mountaintop, not someone like Jacques running around flattering him all the time . . . Jerry needs to come right out and say, 'I'm scared, I need . . .' But there's Barzaghi, translating simple fear into some goddamn grandiose mysticism."[7]

The comment was touching on some of the same themes the Shadow had talked about, such as Jerry's uneasiness about personal relationships and his desire to distance himself. All in all, it made sense to me. The mysticism was another aspect of the distancing process. By seeming mysterious or by keeping Jacques around for odd jobs that were never explained, Jerry could keep people off-balance and a little uncertain about what was going on. He could prevent them from pressing in on him. He could discourage them from making demands. In a sense, the mysticism accomplished the same purpose as the politician's anecdotes that Jerry had talked about the morning after the election.

Of course, the question remained as to why Jerry had retreated when Catherine arrived. Carlotta Mellon, Jerry's appointments secretary, felt that Jerry was still miffed about the black woman Bob Gnaizda had hired. Catherine arrived at the wrong time, she said.

Derek Shearer, a friend of mine from Los Angeles, thought the problem went deeper. He told me about the day he was standing in the hallway to the Governor's office. A little boy started crying and stretching out his arms for his mother to pick him up. Jerry pointed at the little boy and said, "See, we have to protect the male species. They're too dependent on their mothers." "I remembered the comment very distinctly," Derek recalled, "because Jacques had said almost the same thing the previous week. 'Women should be kept out of politics,' Jacques said. 'They're kind of evil geniuses who have too much power over children as it is. They shouldn't be out in the world exerting more.'"

The stories just seemed to go on and on. What was one supposed to make of all of this? We were walking around in a hall of mirrors. It was incredible. A large number of appointees in the Brown administration were spending a good deal of their time speculating about the Governor's psychology. Although Jerry despised psychology, he encouraged the psychological speculation by being so mysterious and by making himself so much the center of attention.

I realized that for the first time since I had started working with Jerry I was angry at him. There was no need to bring Catherine on a six-thousand-mile round-trip wild goose chase. Nor was there any reason to stage a mock interview. If he didn't want her, he could have said no in a straightforward fashion and saved everybody a lot of time and trouble.

Catherine wasn't going to bite; she was no evil genius; and we didn't need to be protected from her, even though she was the mother of three children.

Catherine endured the interviews with great composure. Her only comment about Jerry was, "He seemed nice but a little agitated." Jacques she found strange, but after all, she pointed out, that was California. "You meet a lot of unusual people in California," she mused.

Chapter Four

THE GREAT DIALECTIC IN OPERATION. THE GOVERNOR RE-
VIVES THE HORATIO ALGER MYTH AND THE AMERICAN
DREAM. THE AUTHOR RELATES HOW COZY IT FELT BEING
ON THE INSIDE FOR A CHANGE.

"OF ALL THE ironies," Catherine exclaimed as she was
boarding the plane back to Washington. "You as head of
EDD." She was right. It was ironic in the extreme. During
the late 1960s, EDD was the base from which Governor
Reagan launched his major attacks against California Rural
Legal Assistance, the legal services program that I founded
and, for three years, directed. The state's investigation was
run out of EDD. The publicity was released from a subsidiary
of EDD's, the Office of Economic Opportunity. The state's
battle plans were supposedly reviewed in the EDD director's
office. And now I was sitting in the EDD director's chair.

Jerry was well aware of the Reagan-CRLA conflict. He
also knew something about the role EDD had played in the
struggle because his legal counsel in the secretary of state's
office, Dan Lowenstein, was an old CRLA boy who had
helped defend against the EDD attack. I think it was partly
because of this history that Jerry offered me the EDD direc-
torship. He was fascinated by the possibility of bringing
opposites together, of synthesizing what appeared to be ir-
reconcilable positions. Not only did the synthesizing demonstrate his ability to master the difficult art of compromise, it

produced a cathartic effect that was good for the body politic. Tension was released. Hostility was dispelled. New energy was generated.

During the 1974 campaign, the example Jerry gave of bringing opposites together was Janet Adams and Jimmie Lee. Janet Adams was the leader of the Coastal Alliance, an environmental group that successfully lobbied for a partial building moratorium along California's coastline. Jimmie Lee directed the statewide building trades council, a group that wanted as much construction as possible. Janet and Jimmie had been at loggerheads for years, but after Jerry was elected he kept saying he was going to sit them down in the same room and resolve their differences. That was what politics was all about: the resolution of a conflict. Without conflict, there was no need for politicians.

Jerry sometimes referred to the push-and-pull as a "dialectical process."

The "dialectical process" was hardly a phrase one was accustomed to hearing in conventional political circles. It was a philosophical term. The ancient Greeks described it as the method of disputation by question and answer that Socrates used to arrive at the truth. Hegel, the nineteenth-century German philosopher, defined it more grandly, as the opposition of great ideas throughout history. Each idea, or "thesis," in Hegel's view, brought with itself an idea that was its negation, or "antithesis." The two concepts did battle, and out of their opposition arose a new idea, or "synthesis," to be fought and conquered in its turn. The process was perpetual, Hegel believed.

The point was not that Jerry fell into one or the other philosophical school — he was very eclectic in his use of concepts — but rather that he was drawing on thinkers who had a very dynamic view of the world. Conflict was inevitable, Jerry believed. A resolution was also unavoidable, in some form or other. The only questions were: When was the process ripe for resolution, and what kind of resolution was appropriate? Jerry was always looking for the proper place and time to intervene. The proper place and time might involve a present conflict, or it might arise in connection with a past dispute that lingered on in people's minds. In some respects, the past conflicts were easier to deal with because they could often be resolved symbolically.

The Japanese-Americans were a case in point. Although there was little about their present situation that demanded a politician's attention (many of them lived in suburban affluence), there was a past experience that could be touched upon: the detention of the Japanese-Americans during World War II.

Now the conventional way for a politician to demonstrate his solidarity with the Japanese-American community was to give a speech recalling the injustices of the interment or, say, to dedicate a bronze plaque at one of the old detention centers. But Jerry was not a conventional politician. He wanted to do something more. When it came to the selection of a gesture, Jerry was as precise as a Zen flower arranger. The gesture had to be original. It had to fit in just a certain way. It had to be simple but dramatic, like a single, perfectly formed rose in an exquisitely modeled vase. It had to take people by surprise and at the same time cause them to murmur, "Of course, how appropriate."

With the Japanese-Americans, I remember, the chance presented itself in December 1974. I knew as soon as I reviewed the résumé how the Governor-elect was going to react. The man's name was Jerry Enomoto. He was the warden at the women's prison at Chino. A protégé of Ray Procunier, Reagan's prison director, he was known as a good administrator and was considered to be unflappable under pressure. He was, in addition, a Japanese-American who, along with his parents, had been interned in a detention center for eighteen months during World War II.

It was perfect, a Horatio Alger story in one sentence. A Japanese-American who had been jailed in a World War II detention center was being appointed head of California's prison system. I could see the green light go on in Tony Kline's eyes the moment I told him about Jerry Enomoto. Jerry Brown was also fascinated. He wanted Enomoto's qualifications thoroughly checked out, of course, but already he seemed to be writing the press release in his mind. The coincidence was almost too good to be true. The difference between a bronze plaque and Jerry Enomoto was the difference between a page 15 and a page 1 newspaper story. Jerry Brown would be honoring the Nisei community. He would also be demonstrating the viability of the American political system. Only in America, it seemed, could a man go from prisoner to prison director in one generation.

Mario Obledo was another example of how Jerry used the appointment power for symbolic effect. The news story that came out when Mario was selected secretary of health and welfare was that he was now in charge of the kinds of services he and his family had received when he had been a poor boy in Texas. Mario had supervisory responsibility for the health department, for example; his family had been so poor, they had had to go to the public health clinic in Texas. The welfare department was now part of his domain; his family had been on welfare. The employment director reported to him; Mario had once received unemployment compensation. As Jerry Enomoto's immediate supervisor, Mario was in overall charge of the prisons; several of his brothers, reportedly, had gone to jail. It was the rags-to-riches story all over again. Jerry Brown was reviving the American dream.

My appointment was the third in the series of turnabouts Jerry enacted in the winter of 1974–1975, although, since I came from a well-to-do family, I didn't fit into the Horatio Alger theme exactly. With me it was more an instance of a squaring of accounts, of simple justice being done. Governor Reagan had used EDD to attack CRLA and its farmworker clients, so Jerry would appoint a CRLA representative as head of EDD.

I don't think Jerry would have given me a second thought if we had lost the lawsuits we filed against Governor Reagan. But most of the time we won. In the small part of the "dialectical process" that was operating in California, our "antithesis" overcame Reagan's "thesis." And so Jerry was disposed toward incorporating me in an administration that was to be the "synthesis" of the prior conflict.

There was always purpose in what Jerry did.

One day in October 1974, for example, while we were meeting at his house, Jerry said to me, "You know, these big corporations are stupid. They'd do much better in court if they hired a public interest lawyer like you, because then the judges would be more inclined to think they were acting in the public interest."

I wasn't quite sure what he was getting at, but he dropped another clue that December. "I wonder," he mused, "if I appoint all the capable public interest lawyers in the state, will there be anyone left to sue me?"

He said it in such an offhand manner, I thought he was kidding. It seemed so outlandish, the idea of extinguishing the lawsuits by hiring the lawyers. But he returned to the same theme in January, remarking somewhat triumphantly to a group of us, "I've appointed every lawyer who could sue me."

We all laughed at the time. It seemed like a good joke, an insider's joke. Seven of the people working around Jerry — and most of those in line to receive appointments — were members of the legal services old-boy network. It was incredible, really, how cozy it was. The people Reagan had treated like untouchables were now being promoted to the Brahmin class. Or, as Jerry put it at a cabinet meeting one afternoon in early February, "The only way a person can get a job in this administration is if he's a poverty lawyer, a kook, or a priest who worked with Cesar Chavez." We all laughed again. Who ever thought of being coopted? It felt so good, being on the inside for a change.

Chapter Five

MY FRIEND ROSENBERG was fit to be tied. Working in the
assembly Office of Research, he had run across an idea that
could save the state $50 million; but no one in the Gover-
nor's office would listen to him.

"I don't get it," Rosenberg said. "The idea's so good, the
Speaker asked me to draft a memo for the Governor's immediate attention. I draft the memo. The Governor's office
loses it. I send down another copy. They can't find it. I send
down a third copy. They say the Governor's busy. What's
the matter with those people, anyway? Don't they want to
save money?"

The idea Rosenberg was talking about was the Refundable
Tax Credit, a flat payment that the federal government would
make to each taxpayer whether or not the taxpayer had paid
any taxes the preceding year. Congress was going to authorize a $20 billion tax refund anyway, Rosenberg said, for
people who had paid taxes. It was part of their anti-reces-
sionary program. So why shouldn't the tax refund be modified to benefit nontaxpayers, who were mostly welfare recipients? Since the state was entitled to 50 per cent of any
extra money welfare recipients received, the state stood to
gain a minimum of $50 million if the RTC passed. That
was the beauty of the idea, Rosenberg argued. "It's a great

35

way of generating money for a jobs program without raising state or local taxes."

The trouble was, the Refundable Tax Credit idea had been picked up at the last moment by a few senators and congressmen. More support was needed. That was why Rosenberg was so concerned about Jerry endorsing the idea. As the Governor of the nation's largest state, Jerry might make a difference.

I promised to raise the idea with him.

I got nowhere. The week the RTC's fate was hanging in the balance, Jerry was preoccupied with the issue of the briefcases. The state was spending $20,000 a year on the briefcases it was giving to its employees. Jerry was exploring the pros and cons of ending the practice. Department of Finance officials were being cross-examined. The head purchasing agent was called in. A good deal of time was consumed preparing the press release. Jerry wasn't interested in anything else.

"My God," Rosenberg exclaimed when I told him what was going on. "He saves $20,000 while $50 million goes down the drain?"

Yes, I agreed, it was pretty strange, but that was the way Jerry was. If a picture was worth a thousand words, then, in Jerry's view, the right symbol was worth a thousand pictures. The briefcase issue was one of a series of symbols Jerry was developing in the winter of 1975 to dramatize his frugality. First, there was his criticism of the lavish Governor's mansion Reagan had built, which Jerry termed "the Taj Mahal." Next, there was Jerry's widely publicized decision to live in a modest apartment within walking distance of the capitol. Then Jerry made a great to-do about riding around in a Plymouth sedan rather than in a Cadillac limousine. During the three months since his election, Jerry had expended an enormous amount of energy in crafting and disseminating these images. Along with a balanced budget, Jerry said, the first priority was "winning the hearts and minds of the people."

Rosenberg wasn't convinced. Jerry could have made a few phone calls, he said. Besides, the Refundable Tax Credit was only one of the things that was bothering him. Jerry was holding up on the cost-of-living increase for welfare recipients who were aged, blind, and disabled, even though an automatic increase was mandated by the legislature. Then, too, there was a recent Evans and Novak column in which Jerry was quoted as saying that welfare mothers were just going to have "to tighten their belts." "It sounds like Reagan all over again," Rosenberg said.

Rosenberg was a veteran of Reagan's welfare wars. For two and a half years he had advised Democratic legislators on ways to resist the most Draconian of Reagan's welfare reforms. "And now," Rosenberg exclaimed, "when a Democrat is elected governor and we throw down our weapons and climb out of our foxholes, our own troops start shooting at us."

It wasn't necessarily so, I contended. Probably Jerry was sounding off. "You know," I said, "sound and fury signifying nothing." I tried to explain Jerry's media world.

There was an incident that had occurred in October 1974, for example. Jerry was scheduled to give a talk to a group of housing developers and savings and loan executives who were having lunch at Perrino's, one of Los Angeles's most expensive restaurants. Since we knew he was going to be asked what his housing program was, I was supposed to give him a briefing on housing. I would drive while he would read the memo I had written. Or so I thought. But he wasn't interested in discussing housing, either with me or with the businessmen. He wanted to talk about a television ad he had filmed that morning. He was quite excited about it, he said. It was his law and order ad. He was shown sitting with a group of older people, telling how his grandmother had taken a walk in the park every day of her adult life until she had become too afraid of being mugged. Jerry ran through the ad verbatim, and every five words or so he would chop

37

the air with his right hand and say "Buzz word." "Buzz word, buzz word, buzz word, buzz word, buzz word," he said gleefully. "That ad has five buzz words in it. I sound tougher than Flournoy, and I haven't proposed anything the liberals can criticize me for. In fact," he crowed, "I haven't committed myself to do anything at all."

I had never heard the term "buzz word" before, but the sound was so descriptive, I knew what Jerry meant as soon as he ran through his little pedagogical exercise. "Buzz word" was a word or phrase which, when spoken in front of a particular audience, would summon up in their minds a series of associations that were never directly stated by the speaker. The beauty of the buzz word was that, by depending on implication rather than explication, it could evoke a powerful response without pinning down the politician to anything specific he could be held accountable for.

One of the buzz phrases Jerry was fond of during the 1974 campaign was: criminal punishment that was "swift, sure, and just." It was short, direct, and punchy, yet it conveyed different meanings to different audiences. "Swift" sounded like the guillotine. It was for people who were afraid of criminals roaming around on bail while their trials were delayed interminably. "Sure" was for those who were outraged by criminals getting off on technicalities. And "just" was for those who were concerned about due process. The phrase had something for everybody, opening up with an appeal to the conservatives and concluding with reassurance for the liberals.

What distinguished Jerry from other politicians, I think, was not that he used buzz words but that he was more adept at making them up. He had a real gift as a wordsmith. He also worked at it, constantly. Hours were spent concocting the right theme or phrase for a five-minute talk. And then when the presentation had been plotted out, paragraph by paragraph and even including the lead in the story he wanted the reporters to write, Jerry would take additional time to consider how to make it all look extemporaneous.

He was a media master!

One day during the middle of the 1974 fall campaign, I remember, several of us were meeting with Jerry at his house to discuss how he was going to handle the next television debate with Houston Flournoy. The debate was to deal exclusively with the subject of education. Since Flournoy was an expert on education, I assumed that Jerry would want to study the lengthy position paper we had prepared. I was mistaken, of course. There was no way he could "outexpertise" Flournoy, Jerry said, so rather than wading through forty pages of material, he would look for one issue that could capture the first thirty seconds on the evening news. "We're looking for a newsworthy issue," Jerry's campaign manager, Tom Quinn, explained, "something quick and dirty."

But what was newsworthy? Newsworthy, I learned that afternoon, was disagreement, conflict, contrast. (The newspaper reporters stuffed their notebooks in their pockets when Jerry and Flournoy agreed with each other.) Newsworthy was new news, something television viewers hadn't seen before. Newsworthy was a hero and a villain. Newsworthy was being specific, concrete, and unequivocal. Newsworthy was making the point in fifteen words or less. Newsworthy was the correlation between what the speaker talked about and the environment in which he was speaking. (The Brown-Flournoy debate was going to be held at the University of California campus at Irvine.) Newsworthy was what the speaker started out talking about. Newsworthy was what the audience responded to. Newsworthy was emotional intensity. Newsworthy was a well-turned phrase, a quotable remark. Newsworthy was putting it all together.

It seemed like a big order, coming up with a statement to satisfy all these criteria. But Tom and Jerry did it in half an hour. They were like two good short-order cooks. Tom remembered that when Flournoy was state treasurer, he had headed the state Lands Commission, which negotiated leases with the oil companies for offshore drilling sites owned by the State of California. Part of the revenues from the oil leases, Tom thought, were deposited in a special construction fund for the University of California. If we could plausibly argue that the leases had been negotiated for too low a price, then Jerry could appear in front of a student audience and charge Flournoy with shortchanging the university.

It was a good issue, we all agreed. Students hated oil companies. They liked the university, presumably. Flournoy was tied in. The only trouble with the Flournoy–oil company–university connection was that it was difficult to state simply and succinctly. But once the wording was ironed out, it was all downhill. Jerry spent the remainder of the afternoon reviewing the areas where Flournoy might try to put him on the defensive. "If I were Flournoy," he said, "I would pick busing." And so we worked on ways he could come down on both sides of the issue without sounding wishy-washy. One of the few contributions I made that afternoon was to tell Jerry about the "magnet school" concept, which used enriched curricula and reduced student-teacher ratios to attract black and white students on a voluntary basis. Jerry approved of the voluntary approach to integration. He also liked the ring of the words. "Magnet school," he kept saying. "It sounds positive. It sounds like I know what I'm talking about."

The debate went off like a charm. Jerry opened up on the offensive. The audience responded enthusiastically. Flournoy spent several minutes explaining himself in somewhat muddled fashion. He didn't even raise the busing issue. The evening television news featured Jerry's attack, along with a picture of an oil company headquarters and a university building. Jerry had not only fashioned the right theme for the right place, he had presented the TV cameramen with the opportunity for a "visual," a picture story that could be shown on the screen. The result was even more prominent coverage on the evening news.[8]

The picture was the thing because television was king. The electronic media reached more people than the print media. Moreover, it touched people more intimately, beaming an image into their living rooms and bedrooms that they could see and hear and even touch, if they wanted to. Nothing compared with the influence TV exerted on a day-to-day basis. A politician who appeared frequently on TV was like a next-door neighbor who dropped in every few days for a cup of coffee. If the politician acted right, he could be accepted like a member of the family.

Jerry and Tom recognized the power of TV, of course. In fact, they were so aware of the superiority of the electronic media that while Jerry was secretary of state, he set up his main office in Los Angeles in order to reach the gigantic Southern California TV market. The same bias obtained during the 1974 campaign. Almost no time was spent building a grassroots organization. Very few campaign posters and bumper stickers were printed. Position papers were scarce. Jerry said the same thing over and over again to the print media reporters, who became increasingly restive. Most of the campaign budget was reserved for TV advertising, and a good portion of Jerry's itinerary was devoted to appearances that would show well on television.

It was a strange place, this electronic media world. Audience reactions were important, I learned, not so much because of how the people in the audience might vote, but because of how they look on television. The great issues of the day could only be dealt with in two or three sentences because that was all there was space for on the evening news. It was better for the candidate to give the wrong answer and look confident than for him to give the right response and seem ill at ease. The print medium was still important, but more and more as a device for reaching small elites who would determine the financing and programming for the larger struggle on TV. In a sense, the newspapers were becoming the handmaidens of the new television empire, developing stories for television to disseminate. Watergate was a case in point. Without the assiduous work of two newspaper reporters, the story would never have broken. But without the enormous exposure that television subsequently gave the issue, the President would never have been driven from office.

The 1974 Brown-for-Governor campaign was right out of Marshall McLuhan's *Understanding Media,* the revolutionary work on television that appeared in the early 1960s.[9] In fact, the similarity between what McLuhan preached and what Jerry did was startling.

McLuhan's central thesis was that, throughout history, the means by which man communicated was the single most important factor in determining his perception of the world.

Jerry's preoccupation was with how to communicate with the public.

McLuhan argued that the medium used was more significant than what was said in or on it. ("The medium is the message" was his memorable phrase.)

Jerry agreed totally.

McLuhan observed that, by the second half of the twentieth century, electronic media was supplanting print media.

Jerry was in accord.

McLuhan contended that in order to use a medium like television properly, one had to understand the peculiar properties of that medium.

Jerry did so to a T.

McLuhan pointed out that because television was capable of communicating less data than a newspaper or a magazine, one had to be careful not to overload the television with too much information.

Jerry was very aware of the overload problem, usually restricting himself to one point when he appeared before the cameras.

McLuhan maintained that while television appealed less intensely to one particular sense (the eye) than print media did, it involved more of the senses and was more capable of communicating a total impression of the performer appearing before the cameras and, consequently, was more personality oriented than the print media.

Jerry was, of course, terribly good at projecting his personality when he appeared before the electronic media.

McLuhan said that because television was a close-up medium, the effective performer needed to talk spontaneously and intimately.

Jerry did so more effectively than any other California politician.

McLuhan taught that since television magnified the emotions expressed on camera, a performer had to be wary about coming on too strong.

Jerry avoided this trap, too, being by nature cool and detached.

It was eerie, considering how Jerry's diffident, slightly withdrawn style fitted the new "cool" electronic medium. In the 1964 edition of his book, McLuhan likened the television mode of communicating to the art and poetry of Zen, which, he said, used the "interval," rather than the explicit "connection," to heighten audience involvement. Now, ten years later, we were seeing the emergence of the first so-called Zen politician.[10] Employing metaphor, symbols, abstractions, and rhetorical questioning, Jerry created an ambiance of possibility that gave the viewer space: space to project his fondest wishes onto Jerry, space to identify with Jerry. The interval was the key to Jerry's method. Jerry gave voters the feeling he was creating an opening for them to fit into. He asked questions rather than provided answers. He refused to fill up the screen with information. He made fun of experts who relied on complicated knowledge. He spoke of a process of getting from here to there rather than about firm positions. He was like a Rorschach test. People saw in him what they wanted to see. Or, as Jerry once bragged to me, "In politics, beauty is in the eyes of the beholder."

It was true! It also worked. In the last analysis, the new, cool method was not only suited to television, it also involved a correct reading of the body politic. And what was this reading? In the fall of 1974, it went something like this:

The average California voter was driving home on the Santa Monica Freeway at five-thirty at night, feeling a little on edge. A yellowish cloud of air pollutants hung over the Los Angeles basin. The radio was full of noise: the top forty blaring away, three to four commercials strung together at a time, and news bulletins that jangled the nerves. The basic problem was overload. There was too much data coming in for the human system to process properly. Noise. Pollution. Bills to pay during a recession. The energy crisis. A new residence every eighteen months. Constant change. Divorces. Inflation. Problems in the schools. Watergate. The overload problem was especially severe in California, where more things seemed possible and, therefore, more had to be considered. Many California voters had emigrated from Middle America because they wanted to escape from inclement weather, small-town mores, and cloying family ties, but now, living in the new Eden, they found themselves with no roots, no restrictions and a seeming infinity of choice. The openness was exhilarating. It was also frightening at times, the lack of permanence. Everything seemed negotiable in the end, easy come, easy go, a throwaway, Dixie cup culture.

The trouble with most politicians, Jerry believed, was that they added to the overload problem when they communicated with the public. Joe Alioto talked too much, for example; Bob Moretti was too emotional; Houston Flournoy provided too much information. Jerry was resolved not to make the same mistake. He started out the 1974 fall campaign by pledging opposition to any general tax increase his first year in office, his idea being that once the voters realized he wasn't going to add to their financial burdens, they might relax enough to listen to what else he had to say. Then, when the election was over, he started simplifying, reducing complicated problems to simple symbols, inveighing against bureaucratic gobbledegook, complaining about the proliferation of paperwork, making fun of experts, and emphasizing the virtues of inaction. Jerry even made a point of lampooning the $7 million computer-operated electronic sign that the state had erected over the Santa Monica Freeway in order to tell commuters what the traffic and weather conditions were like. "We don't need a $7 million sign to tell us whether it's raining," he would tell delighted campaign audiences.

In the new politics of less-is-more Jerry was developing, personality replaced program. A great deal was made over Jerry's personal life. Jerry expounded at length about his philosophy while conveying the clear sense that the words wouldn't lead to any action that could infringe on other people's space. "They're just words," he said to me once after an interview with a newspaper reporter.

Jerry had discovered the way to use the media to get his message through in the way he wanted when he wanted. Be truthful. Be trivial and nonthreatening. Be entertaining. The rationale behind his approach was simplicity itself. If he never said anything that threatened interest groups that could fight back (he would try to defer the heavy-duty work to his appointees and to the legislature, he told me once), his public statements would go unchallenged, and he would appear to be right more often than not, in charge, the master of the situation. And if he was amusing and made good copy, he would help to sell more newspapers and television time, and the media would love him.

I don't think the media people realized how constantly they figured in Jerry's plans. Most days he had read through eight or nine newspapers by midmorning, checking to see what the press was saying about him. One Monday morning early on in the administration, I received an "urgent call" from the Governor's office. It seemed our state OEO office had hired a San Jose woman who, greatly exaggerating the importance of her position, had told her local newspaper that the Governor had asked her to come to Sacramento. Although the story was small potatoes, taking up two column inches on page 17 of the San Jose *Mercury,* the Governor wanted to know "who in God's name" this woman was. The surveillance network operated that quickly.

In reality, Jerry was his own press person. He had a press secretary to help him, but, especially after Tom Quinn became chairman of the Air Resources Board, Jerry took charge, working at it an average of three to four hours a day, selecting appropriate stories for the media, outlining and editing the press releases, holding interviews, and making surprise appearances. (A sense of spontaneity was encouraged to build media interest.) I think he was relieved to be away from Tom and out from under the rumor that Tom, a former radio news executive, was the brains behind the media operation. Tom had taught Jerry a great deal — he had kept after Jerry to focus his statements, to concentrate on one point at a time, and to look for the eyecatching paradox — but by the time Jerry was elected Governor, he knew the techniques.

"Jerry has a real genius for the media," Richard Maulin told me one morning during the campaign. We were standing outside the Los Angeles Airport. It was 7:30 A.M. Richard had been up a good deal of the night. I had just flown down from San Francisco for a breakfast meeting. But despite his fatigue and my schedule, we talked intensely for ten minutes as if nothing else in the world were going on. It was a memorable interlude. Richard was trying to explain to me why he stuck with Jerry even though Jerry was hard to work with on a day-to-day basis. Jerry was disorganized. He changed his plans with maddening regularity. He was sometimes bitchy with subordinates, and when he made a mistake, he expected them to clean up after him. He rarely expressed gratitude or warmth. Twenty per cent of the time Jerry acted like a "spoiled brat," Richard said. Nevertheless, Richard contended, Jerry had this special quality that enabled him to communicate with masses of people.

"Jerry's a marginal personality," Richard said coldly. "It's his strength as well as his weakness. Jerry doesn't have the

46

same attachments other people do. He doesn't care about friends or possessions or sports. He's totally into power." And because of this single-minded devotion, and because, as Richard put it, "Jerry lives on the fringe," he possessed a direct line into the collective unconscious. Jerry was in touch with people's anger, their resentments, their hopes — often before they were themselves — and he was able to express these feelings in terms people understood. The resentment was particularly important to touch upon, Richard felt. Any politician who wished to establish deep contact with the voters had to be "a little bit mean." The day was over when decent people like Flournoy could do well, Richard said. "Flournoy acts as if the world was as nice a place as the pretty suburb where he lives," but it wasn't. Ordinary people were subjected to all sorts of pressure. They felt irritated a lot of the time. Jerry was going to express their irritation for them. George Wallace was the first to play on the anger, Richard said, but Jerry would be more effective because he would be more respectable. Jerry would be the thinking man's George Wallace.

It was as if there was a deep, deep well that most of the citizens of the town never ventured near. But Jerry would. He would let his bucket down, down to the bottom, and swish it around and pull up . . . a symbol, and archetype from the collective experience. No wonder my friend Rosenberg had a hard time understanding what was going on. Jerry was a kind of alchemist, inhabiting a netherworld of images, symbols, buzz words, and appearances. It wasn't simply a technique he was implementing. It was a very special view of life.

We were working in the Governor's office in early February 1975, I remember. The loggers and the environmentalists were engaged in a very bitter dispute. The environmentalists had succeeded in obtaining a court order compelling the loggers to file environmental impact statements before they proceeded with their logging in Northern California. The loggers were outraged, contending with some justification that hundreds of men would be thrown out of work before the necessary paperwork was completed. A group of them drove their giant trucks down to Sacramento to protest. One afternoon, the capitol grounds were surrounded with loggers' rigs. Violence was in the air. The environmentalists' lawyers were even afraid to travel into the little town where the order had been issued. And in the midst of it all, Jerry walked out of his office and said to me, "It's all symbols. All they're arguing about is symbols." He seemed perplexed that the interest groups couldn't see this as clearly as he could. They were simply arguing about pieces of paper. The forms they had to fill out could be changed, or they could be completed in less time than the loggers thought. It was "all symbols," and on a certain level, in Jerry's view, everything was a symbol, *everyone* was a symbol. It was all in our minds, and what was in our minds could be modified. So what were people so bothered about anyway?

Chapter Six

RUMORS CIRCULATE ABOUT A SCANDAL IN THE HEALTH
DEPARTMENT. THE GOVERNOR PLAYS HOOKY. ROSENBERG
HAS PREMONITIONS OF DISASTER.

FEBRUARY 19, 1975. Rumors, rumors, the rumor mill was
working overtime. A scandal involving the prepaid health
programs was supposed to be brewing. Both Democrats and
Republicans were said to be involved, the recipients of hundreds of thousands of dollars in payoffs that a handful of
hastily organized nonprofit corporations conferred in return
for lucrative state contracts. There was even a report that
the Mafia had infiltrated the data processing division of the
state welfare department. I had given Bob Gnaizda a list
of thirty-two names of health department employees who
were considered incompetent or corrupt, but despite the
reliability of our source, one of the most trusted aides in the
legislature, nothing happened. Bob said later that he threw
the list in the wastebasket.

It was peculiar. Since early December, the word was out
that prepaid health was going to be the big scandal. Yet, by
the time Bob was sent in to take over the health department,
twenty days after Jerry's inauguration, the wrongdoers had
had plenty of time to cover their tracks. Bob made a big
to-do about locking all the files within three hours after he
moved into the health director's office, but most of the
incriminating stuff, I suspected, had already been removed.
Bob didn't seem to care. He intimated that Jerry wasn't

interested in criminal prosecutions. I gathered Jerry felt too much trouble would be stirred up.

The day before my chief deputy, Dick Bernheimer, had told me that Bob had told him that Jerry was turning thumbs down on Catherine Jermany for the other chief deputy's job. It seemed to me like a roundabout way to communicate the news, so I went over to see Bob in his new office.

Bob didn't say a word about Catherine. Instead, he started talking about Jerry's recent visit to the health department. "You know how much Brown hates to make decisions," Bob said, chuckling. Well, Bob had convinced Jerry to take a two-day sojourn in the health department. "He would be the health director and everything," Bob said. "It was a circus." Jerry didn't have to do anything. He and Bob just sat around on the tenth floor of the health department and talked philosophy and counted the number of memos that came in every day. Every so often, Bob said, they would send out a memo in order to see how long it took to receive a reply. They decided that since they couldn't do anything constructive with the bureaucracy, they might as well play with it. The health department was like a new toy they'd just discovered under the Christmas tree. Bob felt he and Jerry had a lot in common. They both recognized the absurdity of it all.

"It's all a game," Bob said on another occasion. He related to me what Michael Phillips, a friend of his, had told him before he left for Sacramento. "Don't expect to accomplish anything," Phillips said, "because you won't. So you might as well have a good time." Bob said he was following Phillips's advice. He was having a terrific time and so was the Governor. "The thing I like about Brown," Bob said, "is he doesn't take it too seriously." Deep down, Jerry didn't care. He just wanted to avoid boredom. The first week he worked with Jerry, Bob told me, he realized Jerry had a low boredom threshold. So, he determined, the first step in winning Jerry's affection was to keep him amused.

50

"What about Catherine?" I asked.

"She's out," Bob replied. "Brown doesn't want her. He's afraid she'll be a rabble-rouser."

"Rabble-rouser?" I said, not sure I had heard him right.

"Rabble-rouser," Gnaizda said.

This was the first I'd heard of Catherine's loyalty being called into question.

Bob shifted in his chair. He crossed his legs. Then he uncrossed his legs. He was uneasy.

"Brown also feels she doesn't have enough administrative experience," he added. He shrugged with his hands.

Few of Jerry's appointees *did* have much administrative experience, I pointed out. Besides, there was Bernheimer to do administration.

Bob said there was no point in arguing. Jerry had made up his mind.

I wondered whether part of the problem was Catherine's being black. In December 1974, Jerry told me he was going "to tilt toward the Mexican-Americans," which meant tilting away from the blacks. Maybe his plan extended to lower-level appointments like Catherine's. I gathered he felt easier, more relaxed, with Mexican-Americans, as well as regarding them as virgin territory, politically. But he also communicated the feeling that blacks were a liability. It wasn't prejudice on Jerry's part, because he was not biased. He was simply realistic. "Blacks are the wrong symbol in the 1970s," he said to me at one point during the gubernatorial campaign. They summoned up in the average white voter's mind too many memories of riots, welfare, and crime-in-the-streets, all the issues that crippled the Democrats in the late 1960s. Jerry wanted to get away from all that. He was willing, even eager, to be photographed with Los Angeles's Mayor Tom Bradley, who was black, and he appointed Leonard Grimes, a black businessman, head of the state's General Services Administration, but both Bradley and Grimes had sanitized images. Bradley was a former police officer and

Grimes was the vice-president of an insurance company. Mervyn Dymally, the newly elected black Lieutenant-Governor, was something else again. Dymally was reputed to have made a lot of money through his political connections, which made Jerry uneasy. Jerry avoided Mervyn like the plague. One October afternoon during the campaign, in fact, when Jerry saw Mervyn walking toward him in the Burbank airport, he ducked into the men's room in order to avoid being photographed with him.

Bob crossed his legs again. He looked a little sheepish, as if he wanted to make amends. "I did persuade Jerry to consider Catherine for another position," he said, "that is, if you want to nominate her for one." He brightened. "Of course," he added, "I can't guarantee anything." I should be thankful for small favors. The door was still ajar.

When I told Bob Rosenberg about the meeting, he scratched his head and asked, "But wasn't Catherine part of a package deal? You know, you would take Bernheimer if they took Catherine?"

I said it wasn't quite that explicit. In any case, though, I was left with Bernheimer, whom Gnaizda was pushing.

"Do you think Gnaizda argued for or against Catherine when he talked to the Governor?" Rosenberg asked.

I realized I had forgotten to ask.

Rosenberg was still feeling low. At times he seemed to me like a medium-sized black bear ruminating around the house. He was a big man with dark hair and a bushy black beard, approximately two hundred pounds of weight distributed on a five-foot nine-inch frame, and when he paced back and forth across the living room, talking about some problem that was not being tended to by the powers that were, he swayed slightly from side to side, his shoulders hunched, his arms swinging a bit in front of his body.

I asked him why he didn't work in the administration, either as director of the state's welfare department or as head of EDD's research division. He was well versed in welfare and employment matters, he had been a loyal Brown campaign worker, and he was an excellent writer, the best I had run across since coming to Sacramento. Why wasn't he interested?

He was, he said. He just didn't want to be pushy. He promised he would talk with Mario Obledo about the welfare job.

The meeting with Mario didn't clarify matters very much, however. Although Bob Rosenberg was well suited for the director's job, Mario said, Bob Gnaizda wanted a black in the position. On the other hand, Mario added, they would be interested in having Rosenberg serve as the deputy director, except that they couldn't make a decision for two weeks. "And so saying," Rosenberg reported to me, "Mario held up four fingers." He shook his head. "Either Mario is very subtle," he said, "or he can't count."

Bob determined to wait for further clarification. In the meantime, there was the question of the house to deal with. Bob didn't own it. He was taking care of it for Mignon Fogarty, a retired social worker who was traveling in Spain. Having heard from friends that her home was being converted into a boarding house for the Brown administration, Mignon wrote to ask if everything was all right. In particular, she wanted to know, was Critter, her cat, in good health? Bob composed the following reply to reassure her:

Dear Mignon,
Got the check for the roofer and I'm sure relieved. The guy says getting paid in full for the first job will make it easier for him to talk his partner into a pretty good break for you on the new job.

As soon as I sent off the letter to you about the little trouble we had here, I got to thinking that you might worry more than you should. Really, it's not all that bad, and I feel this progress report will calm you down.

We've already got temporary electricity, and the plumbing should be working again in a week or two. They say the smell will persist for a couple of months, but it's amazing how people can adjust to such things when they have to.

The biggest piece of luck was the way the septic tank backed up and put out the fire before too much damage was done.

I know it had you a little upset when I told you about the people that had moved in here with me. Well, you'll be relieved to know that the population has been reduced, which is really much better, seeing as how there's only one usable bedroom. What happened was that all the single people decided to move out because they felt — rightly — that a family with five little kids really needed the shelter more.

Scientists have just been overrunning the place. They say when the meteorite hit it couldn't have been much bigger than your fist, and they're just mystified how such a little object could wreak such devastation. Anyway, you'll be famous.

Because of the loss of the papers, I can't figure out who to contact on the insurance. I sure hope you're covered.

Critter, remarkably enough, is fine. The vet says his fur will grow back — here and there, at least — although it may be a funny color. It's a good thing there are still some rafters left, because that's the only place he'll sleep. Poor little guy really freaked.

The neighbors have been just great. They took turns guarding against looters, and they've been picking through the rubble looking for any of your valuables that might have survived.

One of the things that was particularly ironic was the way I had just gotten your car back and put it in the garage just before it happened. But I guess your insurance will cover that, too, won't it? That one did have me a little depressed, I must admit.

It's just incredible the way prices have gone up. You won't believe some of the estimates. Take glass, for example. In the first place, do you have any idea how much glass there is in a little place like this? Fantastic amounts.

And appliances. I hope your policy is based on replacement costs.

Oops! Gotta sign off now. Looks like the shoring on that wall isn't going to hold after all.

Just relax and have a great time over there, Mignon. Actually, you wouldn't want to be here just now anyway.

Love,

Bob and the gang

Mignon responded by return mail. She was pleased, she wrote. It sounded as if we were making good use of the house. Still, she said, she was glad she was in Spain if what she was hearing from her friends in the welfare department was any indication.

Rosenberg opted for the EDD job. Four fingers, he decided, was too long a time to wait.

Chapter Seven

THE GOVERNOR TAKES TWO HUNDRED AND FIFTY PEOPLE
ON A WILD GOOSE CHASE.

PATIENCE. TENACITY. Endurance. Those were the qualities
one needed to cultivate in the Brown administration if one
were to keep from going batty. I tried to remind myself
that everything comes to him who waits. I also tried to
look on the bright side of things — and there was, in fact, a
bright side. The Governor had given me a commission.

"Spend $100,000 on consultants if you have to," Jerry
said in the middle of February, "but get me a jobs program."

I was pleasantly surprised. One hundred thousand dollars?
He must be serious about jobs. He had just spent several
days worrying about $20,000 being spent on briefcases.

I told him a little bit about the measures Congress was
considering to fight the recession: a $22 billion tax cut; a
multibillion-dollar public works appropriation for the be-
leaguered construction industry; and public service jobs for
the hard-core unemployed. It wasn't perfect, I said, but what
else was there? If we wanted to do something about unemployment in 1975, we had to work within the existing system.

Jerry asked me how much job money California would
get under the new legislation.

I estimated $300 million in public service money alone.

"Good," he replied. "Let's get the money." He told me to

work on ways in which the money could be spent without creating a lot of "leaf raking" and "paper shuffling." Jerry said he wasn't sure what the public service jobs did, but he was convinced they were "the wrong image." "People are convinced they're make-work," he added. "We have to change that image."

I promised to try. We would compile a list of all the useful work that needed doing in state agencies, I told Jerry. He seemed enthusiastic about the idea. He also consented to give the luncheon speech at a jobs conference EDD was sponsoring on February 27, 1975. Two hundred and fifty local government officials would be coming in from all over the state. It seemed like a good opportunity to open up discussions on how we could fight unemployment.

The morning of February 27 broke hot and humid, the kind of summer day that sometimes happens in Sacramento in the middle of the winter. I arrived at the luncheon a few minutes before Jerry did. Two or three reporters were already standing outside the dining room. "What do you think of the jobs legislation before Congress?" one of them asked me. I said I was in favor of it and thought the Governor was too. A few more questions were asked. We chatted a bit. And then Jerry walked through the door.

"What position are you taking on the federal jobs legislation?" they asked him. I think they caught him unawares. He looked like he was thinking about something else.

"Just hitching up your saddles and going back to Washington to get more federal dollars won't do it," Jerry replied. "Money is money, that's all, just paper."

Uh-oh. Jerry was zigging where I was zagging. He was playing Mr. Conservative today, apparently, and support for the jobs bill might go down the drain in the process. I sensed it was a spur-of-the-moment thing on Jerry's part. He wanted a foil to demonstrate his fiscal responsibility, and so he lashed out at the nearest thing in sight, the jobs bill.

The reporters looked surprised. "How can jobs be created

without money?" one of them asked him. But Jerry wasn't going to play the reporters' game. He was going to make the point he wanted to make. The question was partly ignored.

"There's not a lot of money on the money tree," Jerry said. "Money's not the answer to your problems." He wanted to make sure the fiscal conservative line was the lead paragraph in the reporters' stories.

The reporters kept pressing, however. "Does that mean California will turn back its share of the pending $7.5 billion federal jobs program?" one of them asked.

Jerry sensed a trap. During the campaign, he had criticized Reagan for spurning millions of dollars in federal funds. Now he was opening himself up to the same charge.

Jerry retreated to the conditional "if." "If I thought it would be spent well I would obviously make use of it, if I thought the federal government had the money and could afford it." He had left himself three outs.

But the reporters were still perplexed. In his inaugural address, hadn't he talked about sponsoring the same sort of public service jobs that Congress was financing in the $7.5 billion appropriation?

Jerry moved toward the dining room. He didn't want to answer and he didn't want any more questions. Usually the reporters wrote down whatever he said and let it go at that, but today they were confronting him with prior inconsistent statements.[11]

Jerry walked into the dining room, where he was greeted with applause. The conference participants were waiting expectantly for him. Jerry sat down, listened to a brief introduction, and rose to speak. The microphone had been set up next to the door so he could make a fast getaway.

"Does anyone have any questions?" he began.

The audience was taken aback. They expected him to say something first. But he wasn't going to give them anything to shoot at. He was shifting the burden of responsibility back to them. They were going to have to do the work.

Except for a few coughs and the clinking of silverware, there was silence in the room for ten or fifteen seconds.

"Well," Jerry said, "if there are no questions, I might as well leave." He turned away from the microphone and began walking toward the door. A few people gasped in surprise. There were scattered murmurs. The audience couldn't believe what it was seeing. The Governor was walking out on them! But Jerry was only bluffing. It would be too great an insult, walking out like this. The newspapers would report that he was acting eccentrically, arrogantly. He ambled slowly back to the microphone, drawing out the drama of the moment. He had succeeded in his purpose. He had intimidated them, and now that they were off-balance, he would run the meeting his way.

"State Manpower Planning Council," he proclaimed with mock bravado, reading from the conference program. "What does that mean, anyway?"

The audience rustled uneasily. Did the Governor really expect them to answer? Then a few people began waving their arms in the air, like schoolchildren trying to get the teacher's attention. They didn't want to run the risk of his walking out again. They would say something, anything, to keep the meeting going.

Jerry pointed to one man. The man said something about coordination of the various manpower efforts that local prime sponsors were undertaking throughout the state.

" 'Coordination,' 'manpower,' 'local prime sponsors,' " Jerry replied. "What do those words mean?"

The man tried to explain, but his explanation included some of the same words he was attempting to define.

Jerry shook his head. He was not satisfied with the bureaucratic jargon that was being tossed around. The audience was out of its element. About half were black or Mexican-American; many of them were junior college graduates who had worked their way up the hard way. They hadn't studied logic and semantics for four years in the seminary the way

Jerry had, and they hadn't gone to Yale Law School. He was running circles around them. It wasn't simply his educational background he was demonstrating, it was also a class difference. He was pulling rank.

At least one member of the audience refused to be intimidated, however. He was Al Pinon, the director of the Santa Clara Valley manpower program. I had known him since the CRLA days, when he served on our board. Pinon engaged Jerry in a colloquy about how local and state agencies could work closer together. "That's your personal opinion," Pinon said to Jerry at one point.

"What other kind can you have?" Jerry replied aggressively. The audience laughed, sensing that Jerry was moving in for the kill.

"Those that I read and those I get off of toilet walls," Pinon shot back.

There was more laughter, only this time it was directed at Jerry. They were waiting to see what he would do next.

Jerry backed off. He could only get into trouble with bathroom humor. He jumped to another point. He reminded the audience that there was only so much money to go around. Classroom teachers wanted money, vocational teachers wanted money. There wasn't enough to satisfy both. Jerry was trying to set the two groups of teachers in opposition. He would make the audience choose. Presumably the audience would be divided, confused.

"Where are the priorities?" he asked.

That was what the audience wanted to know. They wished to find out what he was going to do. They weren't even expecting details. They were just looking for a general direction and a sense that he cared.

Jerry refused to give them satisfaction. "Everybody comes to Sacramento with his pot of gold in mind at the end of the rainbow," Jerry said. "The problem is, there's not much gold in the pot. In fact, there's not even a rainbow."

The metaphor was beginning to get him off the hook.

People weren't thinking about jobs or vocational education anymore. They were trying to visualize this rainbow that didn't exist.

"The expectation all through the 1960s," Jerry continued, "was that if you get enough geniuses and enough Ph.D.'s and enough Harvard scholars that you can put it all into a grand scheme and you can just load it onto people's backs, and all of a sudden the problem is solved."

A few heads were nodding in agreement now. They didn't like geniuses and Ph.D.'s and Harvard scholars any better than Jerry did. Jerry had done a 180-degree turn on them. He had started out using the scholastic method in order to rattle the audience and now he was attacking the scholastics themselves. He was covering himself.

"That was the theory behind Vietnam," Jerry said, his voice rising a little. "You get your technology and your kill ratios and your cost-effective analyses and your consultants and you send them over and tell these people that this is the way it's going to be, and you just bomb 'em right into enlightenment."

He was finishing up now, and a lot of anger was coming out in his voice. But it wasn't clear who had tripped off the anger. Was it the government officials sitting in the room? Was Jerry suggesting that fighting unemployment was as futile as fighting the war in Vietnam? Was Jerry holding his audience responsible for the horrors of the past decade? I didn't see the connection. Many of the people in the audience were from the black and Mexican-American communities, which had suffered the highest casualty rates in Vietnam. I also didn't understand the timing of Jerry's remarks. I had seen him meet with aerospace executives and Rand Institute intellectuals, and he had never once raised Vietnam with them. Perhaps, I decided, Jerry feels safer with this audience; he feels more able to . . . let go.

We would never know for sure. Later on, after the conference, I was talking to Alice Daniel, Jerry's deputy legal counsel, about Jerry's change of direction on the federal jobs legislation, and Alice said, "It's so typical. Jerry has a whim of iron."

"A will of iron?" I replied, not sure I had heard her correctly.

"No, no," she said, "a whim, a whim of iron. He changes his mind all the time, but he does it so resolutely."

Chapter Eight

THE AUTHOR LEARNS ABOUT THE COST OF UNEMPLOY-
MENT: THEFT, HOMICIDE, AND SCHIZOPHRENIA. THE
AUTHOR CONSIDERS HOW TO PERSUADE THE GOVERNOR
TO MOVE AHEAD.

JERRY WAS EVADING. He was ducking the unemployment
issue. But why? It didn't make sense to me. Unemployment
was a vicious problem. Something had to be done about it.
We could cite books, scholarly monographs, and government
studies that showed a direct connection between unemployment, on the one hand, and burglary, robbery, homicide,
petty theft, infant mortality, child abuse, alcoholism, schizophrenia, and manic-depression psychosis, on the other hand.[12]

There didn't seem to be much dispute about the data.
Unemployment was a disrupter, a destroyer, a killer. Even
the *Wall Street Journal* was acknowledging a connection.
CRIME RATE IS RISING AS JOBLESSNESS SPREADS ... a
Journal headline stated on February 25, 1975. The federal
Bureau of Prisons had just completed a study, the *Journal*
said. The study showed "a very strong correlation" between
increases in national unemployment levels and the federal
prison population twelve to fifteen months later. "The message is very clear," a prison bureau spokesman was quoted as
saying. "Come 1976, watch out, brother."

He was right. In Buffalo, Pittsburgh, Davenport, and
Sacramento, police officials were explaining significant increases in property crimes in terms of the 1974–1975 re-

cession. In Detroit, police commander James Bannon was noting that people had more leisure to interact with one another, "and that results in homicide." In Southern California, criminologist Daniel Glaser was making the same observation. "Assault and murder seem to be functions of the prevalence of guns," he stated, "and they have always been associated with unemployment."

The accounts went on and on. There was a 1963 article in the *Journal of Political Economy* which found that over a thirty-six-year period in Boston, Cincinnati, and Buffalo, "a 100 per cent increase in the unemployment rate would be associated with a 25 per cent rise in the delinquency rate."[13]

There was also a book, *Mental Illness and the Economy*, that reported that over a 126-year period in New York State, mental hospital admissions rose precipitously during hard times.[14] The admissions increased with predictable regularity, the author, a Johns Hopkins professor, said, despite the development of the psychiatric profession, improvements in psychiatric treatment, and increases in mental health appropriations. It didn't make any difference whether the economic downturn was long or short. All that needed to happen was for people to lose their jobs, and some would start cracking up.

It seemed so simple. Jobs were the answer and everything else was peripheral. Once jobs were generated, the government could lay off some of the psychiatrists and social workers and the welfare state could be reduced and we could all save money. It seemed like jobs was the perfect political program. Jerry could appeal to liberals and conservatives alike. He could say he was fighting mental illness and crime. He could talk about reaffirming the work ethic and strengthening family ties. He could oppose welfare with a clear conscience because he would know he was replacing it (partially, at least) with something better. He could even inveigh against the welfare state.

The only problem was, he was balking, and I didn't know why.

Chapter Nine

THE LOS ANGELES *Times* CRITICIZES THE GOVERNOR FOR
NOT DOING ANYTHING. THE GOVERNOR RESPONDS BY
PULLING A FAST ONE.

THE MORNING OF February 28, I walked over to Jerry's
office to see whether he wanted to talk about a fifteen-point
jobs program I had given him three days before. He was
agitated.

"The Los Angeles *Times* says I'm not doing anything," he
exclaimed, referring to an article on the coffee table.

He shook his head, as if he wasn't going to contest the ac-
curacy of the criticism.

"I'll show them," he said. "I'll do something. What is
today, the last day of the month? All right, we'll have a
flurry of activity."

It was as if we had to do our business before the clock
struck twelve and the coach turned into a pumpkin. The last
day of February was a benchmark. The honeymoon was ending. The press was beginning to scrutinize the record of the
new administration. So far, there was no record, just buzz
words and symbols.

"What am I going to do?" Jerry said. It seemed like a
rhetorical question. "Maybe I'll make some appointments."

He laughed. He was improvising. Appointments were
safer than programs, he once said to me. The appointees
didn't need to do anything. They just had to symbolize something.

"What about Industrial Relations?" Jerry asked no one in particular. Several of us were standing in the room. "Labor's been criticizing me for not appointing anyone."

The labor unions considered the Department of Industrial Relations, which made safety inspections at job sites, their special preserve. Jerry had interviewed a candidate with good labor credentials, Don Vial. Affiliated with the Institute of Industrial Relations at the University of California. Former research director for the California AFL-CIO. Don was a cut above anyone else who had been proposed, but Jerry had left him hanging for a month after the interview. Don was miffed. He felt he had been toyed with — and in a way, he was right. Jerry liked to rev people up and then keep them on Hold. Would they come back when he called? It was another way he had of demonstrating his power.

"We can announce Vial's appointment today," Jerry said.

I said there might be a problem. He hadn't called Vial to see if he was still interested.

"Well, somebody check it out," Jerry replied.

I telephoned Rose Bird, who headed the agency DIR was part of. Rose was one of Don's strongest backers.

I returned to Jerry's office. He was talking about an appointment to the Water Resources Board. He was really flying now.

I mentioned the job memo. Tom Quinn cut in. He had something ready for a Saturday press release, he said. A billion dollars' worth of sewer projects. Thirty-seven thousand construction jobs. Tom had been working on expediting the projects, cutting red tape, moving up the starting dates.

Jerry looked interested. He scanned the paper Tom handed him. Thirty-seven thousand jobs? The building trades unions would love it. Sewers? He could tell the Sierra Club he was cleaning up the environment. Cutting red tape? The conservatives would think we were making the government more efficient.

"I could do a press conference in Los Angeles," Jerry said.

68

"Jimmie Lee on one side, the Sierra Club on the other. Me in the middle. It would be great."

Yes. I could see it clearly. Jerry would demonstrate that environmental protection need not wipe out jobs, as the building trades had been arguing. He would bring the warring groups together. Mr. Synthesis.

I admired Tom's facility. Better than any of the rest of us, he knew how to nudge Jerry into a decision. He would wait until Jerry hit one of his we've-got-to-make-a-decision days and then he would present Jerry with a program that was prepackaged for the press. Tom had it down so he could make his pitch in a minute or less. The cover memo was never more than three pages long, double spaced.

Tom began fiddling with the press release. Jerry was talking about something else. "I never was elected head of anything when I was in school," Jerry said. "Not even nominated. Other kids were the popular ones." He grinned a little self-consciously. "I had to run for statewide office to be chosen."

It was another one of those revelations, like the morning after the election when he was talking about politicians' anecdotes. Jerry was showing us something of himself. "Underneath," he seemed to be saying, "I feel like the ugly duckling." The image he crafted was a compensation for the natural attractiveness he felt he lacked. But it worked. The other, more conventional politicians overlooked the image sometimes, measuring Jerry up close, and when they found he exuded less sheer animal magnetism than they did, they assumed they could dominate him everywhere, and they let down their guard. They were mistaken. They underestimated him. Jerry projected his energy elsewhere, past the one-on-one encounter, past the room in which he was standing, past Sacramento even. He happened on the screen, in television land.

I think some of us were drawn to Jerry because of the combination of the image, which seemed so magical, and the vulnerability, which made people care for him. If there had been only the image, he would have seemed too remote; and if there had been only the vulnerability . . . well, we might not have bothered.

There was also the magnetism of the situation, of course. We were on top. We could see the whole. The exhilaration of working in the Governor's office was like the feeling one got standing on a mountaintop, gazing down on all below. Look, this is where the river meets the town; look, those are the two interest groups that are really putting pressure on the government. Look, that road isn't straight after all; look, this is the issue people are up in arms about right now. Look, a thunderstorm is coming in from the west; look, this is how the ecology issue fits together with the jobs issue. Look, this is where the old quarter of town leaves off and the new section begins; look, this is how the old politics ends and the new, Jerry Brown politics begins.

All I can say is, it was like that working in the Governor's office. We had put specialized knowledge behind us. We saw the whole because we were responsible for the whole. We were on top of the world.

The press conference went according to plan. Jimmie Lee agreed to a last-minute appearance. The president of the Sierra Club was there too. On the morning of March 2, 1975, their pictures were prominently displayed in California's newspapers. Jerry was sitting between them, of course. The accompanying dispatch went like this:

> A dual purpose program to clean up the State's water and ease unemployment was announced yesterday by Governor Brown.
> Brown said by speeding up planned projects bogged down in bureaucracy, $1 billion can be pumped into the economy and 37,000 jobs created starting next month . . .
> Brown said it was the first time the Sierra Club president and the leaders of the building and construction trades had sat down together.[15]

"Bogged down in bureaucracy," "planned projects . . . pumped into the economy" — the alternative language was designed to stir the hearts of the staunchest conservatives and liberals alike. The only difficulty I had with the performance was that it seemed too easy. A billion dollars' worth of projects! Expedited by several months! It must have taken a lot of work. But until Tom Quinn sprang it in Jerry's office on the morning of the twenty-eighth, I hadn't heard a single thing about it. It was as if a gigantic pyramid had been moved one night by thousands of slaves who didn't make the slightest sound. How did Tom Quinn do it, anyway?

Several days after the press conference, I ran across two news articles dated February 18. They read as follows:

> Former President Nixon exceeded his authority in withholding $9 billion authorized by Congress for pollution control, the Supreme Court declared unanimously today.
>
> It was the first time the court has ruled on a presidential impoundment of funds . . .
>
> In 1972, Congress authorized the appropriations . . . for sewage treatment grants . . .
>
> California stands to gain nearly $1 billion with release of the impounded funds intended for municipal sewage projects.[16]

So that was how the red tape was cut. Tom didn't do it. The Supreme Court did. Tom and Jerry just took credit for it. They pulled a fast one, so to speak. Jerry needed something he could do immediately, so Tom gave it to him. They were running true to form. It was like the Shadow said. Seventy-five per cent of the concern in politics was how the box was wrapped, not what went into the box. This was especially true of the quickies, the wondrous projects that were assembled on a moment's notice. You couldn't do a quickie unless you restricted yourself to cosmetics.

I should have realized. Rome wasn't built in a day — unless it was a set on the back lot at Paramount.

Chapter Ten

THE LABOR UNIONS PLAN A MARCH ON SACRAMENTO TO DEMAND MORE JOBS. THE AUTHOR DESCRIBES HOW CESAR CHAVEZ PUT PRESSURE ON THE GOVERNOR AND WONDERS WHETHER THE JOBS MARCHERS WILL BE ABLE TO DO THE SAME. THE GOVERNOR SPEAKS TO THE MARCHERS BUT IS HECKLED. THE GOVERNOR GETS OUT OF THE JAM. THE AUTHOR RECOUNTS THE SAGA OF THE PORTABLE TOILETS.

THE JOBS MARCH was scheduled for Saturday, March 8, 1975. The demonstrators were supposed to gather at the Sacramento River bridge at noon and proceed down Capitol Mall, reaching the capitol around one o'clock. Jack Henning, secretary-treasurer of the California AFL-CIO, would be speaking, as would representatives of the building trades, the teachers, and the auto workers. The rank and file were being bused in from as far away as Los Angeles, Bakersfield, and San Bernardino.

I was following the preparations for the rally with some interest. The demonstration was the first indication of how hard organized labor was going to press for a jobs program. It was like a barometer that would tell us whether a high- or low-pressure area was moving in. If 5000 to 10,000 people showed up and the speeches were hard-hitting and the labor leaders followed up afterward with grassroots committees and public meetings all over the state and press interviews and legislative proposals and more demonstrations in May and June, then the monkey would be on our backs. We would be forced to leave the Alice in Wonderland world of image politics and — who knows? — we might even be compelled to do something. But if, on the other hand, the turnout was light and the speakers went through the motions and the whole subject was dropped afterward, then Jerry would view the rally as a gesture and he would put the jobs issue on the back burner.

The thing people didn't realize about demonstrations was, they could show weakness as well as strength.

The Shadow, my friend in the Governor's office, was betting the march would fizzle. "Three thousand people will show up," he said, "but there won't be any follow-through. The labor leaders have too much else to worry about."

He had a point. A large backlog of issues had accumulated during the Reagan years, including collective bargaining for farm workers and public employees, housing subsidies to boost the number of construction jobs, and an increase in unemployment compensation benefits.

"But what about three months from now?" I asked.

The Shadow conceded it was a possibility. Once collective bargaining for farmworkers was resolved, there might be an opening the jobs issue could slip into. "In which case," the Shadow said, "the labor guys will have to start building it now. It takes three months to activate the locals."

The Shadow wasn't talking about a quickie campaign run by three to five lobbyists. He was thinking of a major effort involving thousands of members ringing doorbells, calling their legislators day and night, besieging Sacramento. The bottom line, the Shadow explained, was that on June 15, Jimmie Lee had to be able to walk into Jerry's office and say he was going to be in big trouble with *his* rank and file unless Jerry passed some jobs legislation pronto. That was the kind of talk Jerry understood, the Shadow said. Jerry would know that Jimmie was ready to go to the mat on the jobs issue because Jimmie's job depended on it.

I speculated whether Jimmie Lee was going to organize pressure against himself in order to prevail upon Jerry. But of course there were other ways of delivering the message. Jimmie Lee could set up a series of meetings that Jerry's people were barred from attending. (Avoidance and secrecy were sure to pique Jerry's curiosity.) Or he could drop a few critical comments in the press. (Jerry wasn't good about returning phone calls, but he always read the newspapers.)

The important thing to remember about Jerry was that you had to rattle his cage a bit if you wanted to capture his attention. The Shadow said it was a little sadomasochistic. Perhaps it was the seminary experience. "In fact," the Shadow said, "it's like a seminary around here. We have to flagellate ourselves before we can say grace, and if the pressure groups don't do it to us, Jerry will with the questions, the indecisiveness, the all-night meetings."

I recollected a conversation I had had with Jerry about a week before. We were talking about a labor leader who had opposed Jerry during the primary but who was extremely friendly and helpful after the election. "I've got him eating out of the palm of my hand," Jerry said, somewhat contemptuously. All the labor leader wanted, apparently, was one or two friends appointed to regulatory commissions, a half-hour meeting, and a photograph of himself standing next to the Governor. He hadn't hung tough, he hadn't demanded anything for his members, and so Jerry had written him off as a cookie pusher. "Now you take Ed Koupal," Jerry added with some enthusiasm. (Koupal was the leader of the People's Lobby who had campaigned for Jerry's political reform initiative and then turned against him, attacking him for selling out to the special interests.))"Koupal's crazy," Jerry said, "but he doesn't sell out. If I deviate one inch from the straight and narrow, he's on me like a hawk." Jerry laughed. He seemed to get a kick out of Koupal. Koupal made life interesting.

Cesar Chavez, the leader of the farmworkers' union, was

another one who livened up Jerry's days. It was incredible how much Cesar did with so little. His union had 7000 to 9000 dues-paying members, or less than one-half of 1 per cent of the State Federation of Labor's total membership, and yet here was collective bargaining for farmworkers occupying the number one position on Jerry's legislative priorities list.

Outsiders tended to explain Jerry's support for Cesar in terms of idealism or sentimental attachment, but there was precious little of either in Jerry. "The fact is," Jerry told me one day in October 1974, as we were driving back from a meeting with the Teamsters at the Beverly Hills Hotel, "the Teamsters may be a better union. They're more businesslike. They may be able to represent the farmworkers better. But how do you fight this racial thing? It's inevitable." Cesar was Mexican-American. Most of the farmworkers were Mexican-American. Cesar had spent ten hard years of his life organizing Mexican-American farmworkers. They would walk over hot coals for him, Jerry believed.

The month before the Beverly Hills Hotel meeting, Cesar had sent Jerry a little calling card. Jerry was fiddling around with the farmworker collective bargaining bill that Cesar had introduced in the legislature, not exactly opposing the bill but not coming down foursquare in favor of it, either. And so Cesar threw a sit-in at him. The sit-ins appeared one morning, unannounced, at the Brown-for-Governor headquarters in Hollywood, college kids and farmworkers carrying the distinctive red and black flag with the thunderbird emblazoned on the front. Although the sit-ins were polite, they succeeded in throwing Jerry's campaign staff into a tizzy. Those of us who liked to think we were working on the side of the angels didn't enjoy having the angels tell us we were in league with the devil. But there it was, and Jerry acted immediately for a change, hopping on the phone, calling around the state, talking to Leo McCarthy, the Speaker of the assembly, and Jim Mills, the president pro tem of the state senate, working out his position. The next day Jerry announced full-fledged support for Cesar's bill. It was quite extraordinary, really, the extent to which Jerry was going down the line for Cesar. He was even supporting the section in the bill that provided for the invalidation of the old contracts the Teamsters had signed with the growers.

Cesar's sense of timing was superb. He had delivered his rabbit punch at just the instant in the campaign when Jerry was most vulnerable. Jerry was still ahead in the polls, but Flournoy was beginning to make up lost ground. If Cesar had undertaken an extended, well-publicized sit-in or picket line, he could have cost Jerry 25,000 votes in the Mexican-American community, enough perhaps to swing the election the other way. The images of the pickets on the TV screen would also have turned off white middle-class voters, who, recalling the disturbances of the 1960s, would have started wondering whether Jerry was ushering in a new era of disorder. Jerry was particularly vulnerable on the civil disobedience issue, his aides felt, first, because of his youth; second, because of his identification with the peace movement and civil rights struggle in the 1960s; and third because of the bumbling way his father had handled the Watts riots in 1965. And so Jerry bailed out quickly, before the newspapers could learn about the disturbance at campaign headquarters.

"Cesar jammed him," a black friend of mine said when she heard about the picket. "He jammed Jerry real good."

"Jammed?" I inquired.

"Interfering with the other guy's signals," she said, "like on the radio. Sticking it to him. Running down the other guy's game and calling him on it. Breaking his rhythm. Moving in close when he backs away. You know, pressure."

I gathered the word came from street talk.

"It does," my friend said. "Black folks have a need for the word 'cause we get horsed around all the time."

My friend thought Jerry was a jive artist par excellence. "He moves the shells around so fast, you can't tell where the pea is," she said. "He's going to be President someday."

Jamming, I came to realize, was the opposite of jiving.

The jiver danced around a lot. He tried to distance himself. The jammer burrowed in. He sought to make contact. The jiver hid behind generalities. The jammer insisted on specifics. The jiver was an image maker. The jammer was an image breaker. The jiver tried to avoid accountability. The jammer attempted to nail it down.

In some respects, I think, Cesar Chavez and the farmworkers were the perfect antidotes to Jerry. The men of the soil were, literally as well as figuratively, bringing the man of words down to earth. They were forcing him to take a stand. It was another example of the dialectic in operation.

Jerry wasn't overjoyed about the pressure. He didn't like being pushed around. Once during the campaign he blurted out to me, "Cesar's too radical," meaning, I think, that Cesar was too independent. But what could Jerry do during the campaign? Cesar had nailed him at a critical time.

I wondered whether the Jobs March people would be as persistent as Cesar was. Would they justify their cause as persuasively on the media? Would they be able to broaden their support base to include the universities and the suburban middle class the way Cesar had? I guessed that if the unions that were putting together the march could sustain a good effort for three months, they could persuade Jerry to lobby in Washington for them, they could induce him to set aside half of the state's projected $500 million surplus for a jobs program, and they could secure another $100 million to $150 million in increased unemployment compensation benefits. It sounded like a tall order, but it wasn't impossible. The unions that were sponsoring the rally had well over a million members, and each of these members, in turn, had two to three dependents. The unemployment rate was at record levels and Jerry had already stated that jobs were a major concern. There was, potentially, a far broader base of support for jobs than there was for farmworker legislation. The only problem was putting it all together.

The morning of March 8 broke overcast and cool, good

weather for a demonstration if it didn't rain. By noon, some 2000 members were assembled at the far end of Capitol Mall, about eight blocks from the front steps of the capitol. All the major unions were represented as well as some of the minority groups. At the last moment, Jerry agreed to speak to the marchers. (I think he was wary of seeming callous and unfeeling, the way his father had appeared nine years before when he failed to meet with the farmworkers on Easter Sunday.) It looked like a propitious beginning for what might be an extensive campaign.

Around twelve-thirty the marchers began to move down Capitol Mall. There were 100 to 150 signs, reading: JOBS NOW and WORK, NOT WELFARE. The farmworkers were carrying the red and black flag. Although they weren't particularly hard-hit by the recession, they were demonstrating their solidarity with the rest of the labor movement, in the hope, perhaps, that the other unions would support them when their turn came on collective bargaining.

By one-thirty the speeches were under way. The Brown administration was urged "to show compassion," "to take the lead," and "to do something about the unemployment problem," but few specifics were mentioned, and some of the speakers seemed to direct their remarks to the President and the Congress in faraway Washington, D.C. There was — how shall I put it? — a certain lack of focus. Listening to the speeches, we were hard-pressed to determine what, specifically, we were expected to do.

And then Jerry stepped in front of the microphone. I had heard him give his standard talk on at least twenty occasions, the one where he said we were going to have to "lower our expectations" and "tighten our belts." But he wasn't starting out in that vein today, not in front of this crowd. There were too many people standing in front of him who had already been forced to tighten their belts, and so Jerry opened with a few conciliatory remarks. But the loudspeaker system wasn't operating properly, and his voice wasn't carrying over the noise of the crowd. He tried another beginning. It was drowned out as well. His voice cracked. Some 100 to 150 people were on the capitol steps now. Some of them were pushing and shoving. Although Jerry was flanked on his right and his left by legislators and union leaders, there was no one in front to shield him. He was surrounded, and the people in front of him were pressing in closer. A heckler standing about six feet away from him called out an unkind remark, and the man standing next to him chimed in, "Don't give us that horseshit. We want specifics." The two men didn't seem to be part of the regular labor contingent. They were dressed in old army fatigue jackets. Jerry didn't respond to them. He continued to try to speak. The crowd was growing restless, impatient, distracted. Out on the fringes, a few people were eating picnic lunches. Women and children were lined up in front of the portable toilets that had been installed on the capitol lawn. Directly in front of us, three older men were engaged in conversation. Jerry wasn't reaching them. Standing about five feet behind Jerry, I could sense a ripple of resentment running through the crowd. It hadn't fixed on Jerry yet, but in thirty seconds or so it was going to. It was a critical moment. I looked down. Jerry's right trouser leg was quivering, shaking, just behind the knee. He was obviously feeling rattled, afraid. But who wouldn't be? The crowd. The situation. It was intimidating.

And then Jerry seemed to pull himself together. He collected his energy, and his voice rose, and the microphone was working, and he launched out on a diatribe. He said he was trying to pass a housing bill to allow the state to sell bonds that would finance the construction of housing. More jobs would be created, he promised. But the savings and loan industry was raising objections. They didn't want the state to get into the housing business and so they were opposing the bill. "Lobbyists are walking the halls of the capitol trying to torpedo the bill," Jerry yelled. "They have an inordinate appetite for profits. They want the profits but not the risk." The noise level of the crowd subsided a little bit. A few people clapped and shouted approval. Jerry spoke for a little longer, but the crisis was over. He had succeeded in deflecting their hostility.

Jerry had reached safety by reverting to form. He went on the attack, finally, as was his style. Speaking in front of a blue-collar audience, he selected a scapegoat they were bound to dislike. He also did something else that was typical. Even when he was cornered, he committed himself to nothing. The housing finance bill was going through whether or not the demonstration was held. Both Jerry and his opponent, Houston Flournoy, had come out in favor of the bill early on in the gubernatorial campaign. There was no major difficulty with the savings and loans, which supported the legislation. The only question raised during the hearings on the bill was how much of a cut they were going to receive when they extended the loans guaranteed by the state bonds.

It was a close call. There had been a critical moment. If only the people in the crowd could see the pant leg, I thought to myself at the time, they will realize how strong they are. They will be encouraged to push harder over the months ahead. But they didn't see it. The labor leaders were facing outward, away from the shaking pant leg, and the rest of the demonstrators seemed too caught up in their roles as protesters or supplicants to observe what was going on. And so the moment was lost.

After the demonstration was over, John Kidder, the research director for the State Federation of Labor, came up to me and said: "This year, you guys are on the hot seat. Next year, it's our turn. If this jobs issue isn't resolved by then, our business agents are going to start losing elections."

John seemed to feel that the labor people had no choice but to pressure us on the jobs issue. But if that was so, I wondered, where was the pressure? For a week after the demonstration, I checked the newspapers, the legislature, and the Sacramento grapevine for signs of agitation. There was none. No newspaper stories. No new legislation introduced. No grass-roots organizing committees. No emergency meetings. Nothing.

"You see," said the Shadow. "Business as usual."

About the only noticeable impact of the Jobs March was that it forced a resolution of the portable toilets issue. Several days before the march, I was talking to Harry Finks, the head of the AFL-CIO in Sacramento. I asked him if it would be a good idea for the state to provide some portable toilets for the marchers. He was very enthusiastic about the idea. The demonstration was going to take several hours, and there was no place to go to the bathroom unless people walked inside the capitol. The toilets were a way of showing that the administration was sympathetic to people's basic needs.

I checked into the possibility of leasing six portable toilets for the afternoon and found they cost $45 apiece. Well $270 was well within EDD's budgetary capability, but I called Mario Obledo anyway to discuss the matter, and he thought it was sufficiently important to bring before the cabinet. So we did. I explained the problem, laying it out for the secretaries of business and transportation and natural resources and agriculture and general services, as well as for the Governor's finance director and the Governor's legal counsel and five or six other people, and Mario Obledo added a few words of support and a few questions were asked, such as what the portable toilets looked like and whether each unit had one hole or two; and after ten minutes or so, everyone was in general agreement that it was a good idea. A consensus had been reached, so to speak, except that Jerry walked in toward the tail end of the discussion and he wasn't convinced. He was concerned about the amount of money involved and he also felt we might be setting a dangerous precedent. If we supplied toilets for the jobs marchers, then the farmworkers would want them too when they came to Sacramento, and the abortionists and antiabortionists would demand them as well, and if we didn't supply toilets to one of these groups, they would accuse us of discrimination. So Mario proposed a compromise. He said that if it was inappropriate for the state to pay, the Obledo family would be happy to pledge one portable toilet personally. And I said the Lorenz family would do the same. And one or two of the other cabinet members looked like they were about to follow suit. But Jerry cut in. "All right, all right," he said. He gave in.

Mario had shamed him into it. Mario was an expert at looking mournful when he didn't like the way things were going, and he had a good sense of timing. He seemed so sad and anguished, people would consent sometimes just to make him feel better.

The Shadow laughed when he heard about the interchange. "Who says the Jobs March wasn't successful?" he asked. They pressured the Governor into leasing six portable toilets, didn't they?"

Chapter Eleven

ROSENBERG IS THE BEARER OF BAD TIDINGS. THE ECONOMY HAS COME A CROPPER. THE PRESIDENT OF GENERAL MOTORS APPEARS AND TOUCHES THE GOVERNOR REPEATEDLY WITH HIS FINGER. THE GOVERNOR LOOKS AS IF HE HAS SEEN A VAMPIRE.

ROSENBERG WALKED INTO my office around the middle of March. "Want to hear something interesting?" he asked, looking like Jack Horner dipping into the Christmas pie. "Do you know how unemployment during the 1970s compares with unemployment during the 1950s and 1960s?"

I indicated I didn't know.

"Well," he said, drawing the word out in order to increase the dramatic effect of what he was going to tell me, "the lowest unemployment rate we had in the United States during the 1950s was 2.9 per cent. In the 1960s, it was 3.5 per cent. But for the first five years of the 1970s, the low hasn't fallen below 4.9 per cent."[17]

What was it going to be next month? I inquired.

"Oh, 8.5 per cent at least," he replied.

Did that mean there was a long-range trend? I wondered.

"Something strange is going on," he said. "In the 1961 recession, the national unemployment rate reached 6.7 per cent, but the Consumer Price Index increased only 1 per cent during the year. The advantage of a relatively high unemployment rate was a very low rate of inflation, in other words.

"During the next major economic downturn, the 1971 recession, the unemployment rate rose to 6.7 per cent while the CPI increased 4.3 per cent. Not so good.

"In 1974, unemployment was 5.9 per cent while the CPI jumped 11 per cent, an even worse state of affairs.[18]

"This year, the national unemployment rate is expected to hit 8.8 per cent, the highest since 1940, and the CPI will still increase 8.1 per cent."

It was as though the throttle got stuck while the motor was running out of gas. Prices remained high as employment opportunities were diminishing.

The situation we were looking at was completely contrary to the rule of economic behavior, officially entitled the Phillips Curve, which economists had been preaching as gospel for twenty years. According to the doctrine of the Phillips Curve, the more unemployment there was, the less inflation there would be. Or, the less unemployment there was, the more prices would rise. You couldn't have your cake and eat it too, in other words, but, to mix a metaphor, you would always be assured of ending up with half a loaf.[19] Now, however, we were receiving less than half a loaf. In fact, we were experiencing the worst of both worlds, high unemployment *and* high inflation.

"There's another set of statistics that are interesting," Rosenberg said. "The real disposable income of working people has declined for thirty-three consecutive months. Wages are going up, but the cost of living and taxes are rising even faster, leaving people with 8.8 per cent less money in 1975 than they had in 1973."

Rosenberg was saying in numbers what several of us had been sensing for months. The unprecedented prosperity we had experienced since World War II might be petering out. During the next thirty years, the gross national product would be hard-pressed to grow by five times, as it did from 1945 to 1975. The days of cheap raw materials seemed to be gone for good. U.S. manufacturers were facing increasing competition in world markets. Inflation appeared inevitable. Unemployment was also a fact of life. With the economic pie expanding less, the public would be more concerned with the question of how the slices were divided up. Income redistribution would become an issue. Class conflicts might increase.

No wonder there was a renewed interest in gangster movies, double-breasted suits, Art Deco, Studs Terkel's book *Hard Times,* knee-length dresses, and Busby Berkeley.[20] The Depression was being revisited in our culture if not in our economy. It was as if we were using the fashions, movies, and books of the 1930s to prepare ourselves psychologically for harder times ahead.

Perhaps the most significant changes involved our presumptions about the future. During the salad days of the postwar era, Americans came to expect more of everything: more growth, more jobs, more income, more credit, and more government spending to take up the slack; a second car and then a second home. Now, abruptly, the talk was of less: less consumption of energy and less highway construction, less work, less money; wage-and-price controls and car pools, vocational training instead of a college education, bankruptcy in New York City and zero population growth. Jerry spoke of "lowering expectations" and quoted from E. F. Schumacher's *Small Is Beautiful,* while New York's Governor Carey put the matter more bluntly: "The days of wine and roses are over," he said.[21]

The new, more pessimistic viewpoint was not simply the result of worsening economic conditions. Once commenced, it took on a life of its own, not only sustaining itself but also reinforcing the economic downturn. The plain fact was: Prosperity depended on consumer confidence. Business conditions were influenced by psychological ups and downs.

The economy's vulnerability to psychological forces was graphically illustrated to me one day when the president of General Motors was talking to a group of us in Sacramento about the problems his company was running into. "The average American holds on to his car 2.3 years," Mr. Estes, the GM president, said, "but the cars are built to run seven years without major repairs. If we can't persuade him to buy a new car 4.7 years before he needs to, we're in trouble."

In other words, General Motors was up against it in 1975, not only because the average wage earner was less able to spend money for what he needed, but also because he was less willing to spend money for what he didn't need.

Mr. Estes was up against it too, it turned out. Later in the morning, after he had met with me and Tom Quinn, he went into Jerry's office for a private séance. According to one of the persons who were present at this encounter, it was a disaster. Apparently Mr. Estes had taken some sort of Dale Carnegie how-to-make-friends-and-influence-people course, and now he proceeded to touch Jerry with his hand whenever he tried to make a point. Pat, pat, pat, nudge, nudge, nudge. Seven physical contacts were recorded. And Jerry, the man who hated to be touched, was in excruciating pain. But Jerry didn't complain. The president of General Motors was too important to be told to buzz off. After the meeting, though, when Mr. Estes had been departed for some minutes, Jerry still looked as if he had seen a vampire.

Chapter Twelve

THE MORE THINGS CHANGE, THE MORE THEY STAY THE SAME. THE AUTHOR DISCOVERS THE WELFARE STATE IS MORE IMPREGNABLE THAN IT LOOKS. THE GOVERNOR SPEAKS OUT AGAINST FOREIGN IMPORTS BUT PROMISES MORE THAN HE CAN DELIVER.

THE TELEPHONE rang. Agnes, Jerry's receptionist, was on the line. Would I come over immediately? Jerry had seen a newspaper article about some people in Orange County who were going to the beach while they were receiving unemployment compensation. One man was quoted as saying that he was having too good a time swimming to look for a job. Jerry was upset.

"I know plenty of actors in Hollywood who feel the same way," Jerry said after I walked into his office. "It's crazy. They make fifty grand a year, own big Cadillacs, and twice a month drive down from the hills to pick up their unemployment checks."

Bob Gnaizda was sitting next to Jerry on the sofa, partly sheltered by a large potted palm. Paul Halvonik and I were sitting on the other side of the glass coffee table. Paul was Jerry's liaison with the state assembly.

"There's a woman working in the back room right now," Jerry continued. "While she was on unemployment, she spent most of her time trying to persuade the government to fund some arts projects she was working on." He shook his head in disgust over the prospect of the lady using government money to raise more government money.

The witness was produced for our inspection. A medium-sized, dark-haired woman of approximately twenty-six years of age, she had dated Jerry at one time, I gathered. Standing next to the potted palm, she attempted to respond calmly to Jerry's questions.

Yes, she had been on unemployment.

No, she didn't expend much energy looking for a job while she worked on the arts proposal.

Yes, she was living in her mother's house at the time.

Yes, it was a big house with several bathrooms.

"You see?" Jerry declared as he pointed his forefinger at the woman.

Still unnamed, the woman remained standing next to the potted palm for perhaps twenty seconds; then, hearing no further questions, she walked out of the room.

Jerry wanted to know why we couldn't force unemployment insurance recipients to work. Maybe we could set up jobs programs in the community, he said. The UI recipients could work twenty to thirty hours a week, doing odd jobs, while they received UI. It would help solve the unemployment problem.

I inquired how many UI recipients he was thinking about including in the experiment. As of March 1975, there were over 450,000 Californians drawing UI.

Jerry didn't respond.

"It can really be an attractive program if we do it on a voluntary basis," Gnaizda interjected, moving quickly to intercept the Governor before he commissioned a political disaster. A mandatory work program that required unemployed carpenters to empty bedpans in the hospitals? The building trades unions would scream bloody murder.

Jerry nodded, appearing to assent to Gnaizda's restatement.

I threw in my two cents' worth. People would be more willing to participate in the experiment if they were paid a small bonus, I pointed out.

Paul Halvonik tried to reinforce the point Gnaizda and I were making without directly challenging the Governor. "My father wouldn't have appreciated a forced-work program while he was unemployed," Halvonik said. "After all, I'm probably the only person in the room whose father was working class." He laughed. By placing an exaggerated emphasis on the words "working class," he seemed to be making fun of the term. At the same time, however, he was gently chastizing Jerry for being unrealistic.

Halvonik was very skillful at employing a slightly self-deprecatory sense of humor in order to cajole Jerry into dropping the tough-guy pose he assumed from time to time. Gnaizda used flattery for much the same effect, often expressing exaggerated approval of Jerry's opinions while he was recasting them in safer forms.

We talked about the work program a little more. Jerry seemed to lose interest in the discussion. I promised to return in ten days with a draft proposal. The meeting was adjourned.

Rosenberg laughed when I told him about the meeting. "It sounds like a jerry-built proposal to me," he punned.

The EDD staff people who worked on the idea were equally unenthusiastic. It was contradictory, they said. On the one hand, we expected UI recipients to search for jobs so they would stop drawing UI. On the other hand, we were talking about community service work, which would probably keep them on UI longer because they wouldn't have time to look for regular, full-time jobs. The employers who were financing the UI fund would raise holy hell with us; they would see their costs going up. The labor unions would also raise objections; they would view the voluntary work as the first step toward a forced-work program. If we didn't watch out, we were liable to find ourselves in no man's land.

I sent off a memo to Jerry explaining the contradiction. I never heard another word about the experiment. That wasn't the end of the inquiry, however, for the fact was, Jerry had a valid concern. It *was* a crazy situation. The United States was going to spend $19 billion on unemployment insurance in 1975. Another $14 billion, approximately, was going to be shelled out for welfare and food stamps. There seemed to be no valid reason why we couldn't turn the situation around and use the money to create jobs for the unemployed.

But there was a problem, I discovered. The problem was economics. Each year the state of California paid out an average of $950 to sustain one UI claimant and approximately $2550 to support the average welfare family. A year-long public service job, by contrast, cost a minimum of $5500 per person — or two times as much as the average welfare grant and five and a half times the average UI claim. If the state provided subsidized child care as well, the cost of the public service job would rise to $8000, minimum. The state was providing welfare and unemployment compensation because it was cheaper to do it that way!

I realized I had stumbled across one of those little-known but very real facts of political life. Although all politicians loved to castigate the welfare program, when push came to shove, they voted for welfare year in and year out because they preferred it to the alternatives. They were secret supporters of the welfare state, it turned out, and anything they said to the contrary was pure rhetoric.

It was becoming an old story, the preaching not conforming with the practice. One afternoon in the early spring, Jerry appeared before the California Conference of the International Association of Machinists and said he would place on his "state-owned American-made 1974 Plymouth" a union bumper sticker reading: IMPORTS CAUSE UNEMPLOYMENT. BUY AMERICAN. Jerry also said he would look into complaints that California tax dollars were being used to purchase imported goods.[22] The following day I made an informal check. At least 40 per cent of Jerry's top appointees were driving foreign cars.

Chapter Thirteen

THE AUTHOR'S BIRTHDAY; THE GOVERNOR'S BIRTHDAY.
THE AUTHOR CONSULTS AN ASTROLOGY BOOK AND WON-
DERS WHETHER IT MAKES ANY SENSE.

"WHAT DO YOU WANT for your birthday?" my mother asked
me over the phone. "A check or some shaving lotion? I never
know what to get you."

I was going to be thirty-seven on March 23. Not only that,
Jerry's birthday was on April 7, fifteen days later. He was
also going to be thirty-seven. We were born in the same
year, 1938. "Astrologically speaking," a friend of mine from
San Francisco said, "you're both Aries, Aries 1938." Jerry
and I were practically twins.

Nineteen thirty-eight wasn't exactly a vintage year for
starting out, what with Hitler, Munich, Czechoslovakia, and
the Great Depression, but there were compensations. Our
mothers were home a lot; there were fewer divorces and not
as many diversions. Families had to content themselves more
with each other. In a certain sense, I think, our generation
of late-depression, prewar babies would always be a curious
amalgam of expectations. On the one hand, within the family,
we would regard love and security as our due. On the other
hand, outside the home, we would look for some disaster or
other lurking just around the corner, the natural order of the
universe.

Two days before my birthday, my astrology friend gave me
a book on horoscopes. "It's a birthday present," she said.

"What am I supposed to do with it?" I asked.

"Sensitize yourself," she replied. "You're an Aries, Jerry's an Aries. You may learn to work more effectively with him."

I granted that the rational processes sometimes broke down in Sacramento, but what next? Tea leaves? A Ouija board?

"You could throw the *I Ching*," she suggested. The *I Ching* was a Chinese book of fortunes, which were selected by throwing coins.[23]

I leafed through the astrology book, which was titled *The Pulse of Life*.[24] There was no indication of what the author, a man named Dane Rudhyar, did for a living, but his observations were provocative, to say the least.

Aries was the sign of spring, Rudhyar wrote, the sprouting seed bursting through the soil. It was also the time of adolescence. Emotional instability combined with a fate-compelled desire; acute sensitivity masqueraded under a devil-may-care attitude; the Aries person cared so much, he couldn't let on he cared at all. The Aries person did not know quite who he was, and so he was constantly in the process of forming himself. His first priority was the assertion of his self, the establishment of his own personality. He cared less about finishing what he attempted than about involving himself in the process of becoming. He was always in the process of becoming and he sought to demonstrate himself to himself.

It sounded all too familiar, although what was one to suppose? Astrology was superstition, it had no scientific validity; and yet here was Rudhyar, striking close to home, emphasizing the importance of the process, which Jerry kept talking about, and the concern with uniqueness which Jerry seemed obsessed with. Rudhyar even seemed to refer to the dialectic when he observed that "the Aries person is always in a state of unstable equilibrium, pulled internally by opposites."

I thought about the morning Richard Maulin spoke of Jerry's incredible power to tap the collective unconscious. Now here was Rudhyar writing about the same phenomenon.

"Aries power," Rudhyar observed,

is the power of the lightning which descends from above, which strikes out of the darkness of the collective unconscious. It is the power of revelation...Such a power... gives to the action of an Aries fateful strength... As such a person senses the meaning of the destiny...pride may roar through his ego. He may become arrogant. He may make demands upon society, as if all kinds of privileges were his by divine right! Yet, more often than not, his pride is rather adolescent, mixed with humility and a peculiar form of insecurity; for he knows inwardly that he does not own the source of the pride-giving power.[25]

Rudhyar was a real find. I read the Shadow the key passages.

"Unbelieveable," he commented.

I asked him whether he thought we should give Jerry *The Pulse of Life* for a birthday present.

"Don't breathe a word of this to anybody," he said.

"Why?" I aked.

"It scares people," he said, "this talk about the manifest destiny of the great leader. That's why Jerry always underplays his power drive. You watch the next time the reporters ask him if he has any political plans. He'll say something like he's just living from day to day. It's complete hooey, of course. He's always planning ahead where his political career is concerned. But he knows he has to keep the calculating, ambitious part of himself under wraps, especially because he wants to go all the way."

"You mean the presidency?" I asked.

"I mean the presidency," he replied.

"Do you think he's thinking about it now?" I wondered.

"Thinking about it?" the Shadow exclaimed. "Everything he's doing has that purpose in mind."

"You're joking," I said. "He's been in office two and a half months."

"I'm serious," the Shadow said. "There're people in the

Governor's office talking about it right now. They can smell the bacon."

"You mean 1976?" I asked. I was skeptical.

"I mean sometime in the future," the Shadow said. "Jerry takes the long view."

"By the way," I said, "what do you think of the Rudhyar passage?"

"Astrology is bunkum," the Shadow said.

"Okay," I said, "conceding that but assuming the passage was just written about Jerry with no reference to Aries."

"Oh," he replied. "Well, on that basis, accurate, remarkably accurate."

Chapter Fourteen

FATHERS AND SONS. THE AUTHOR TALKS ABOUT A SUB-
STITUTE FATHER AND A REAL FATHER AND SPECULATES
ABOUT THE KIND OF RELATIONSHIP BROWN THE ELDER
AND BROWN THE YOUNGER HAVE WITH EACH OTHER.

SHORTLY AFTER my thirty-seventh birthday, I made a stupid,
unnecessary mistake. I was testifying before a U.S. Senate
Labor Committee hearing chaired by Senator Alan Cranston
of California. Jack Henning, secretary-treasurer of the California AFL-CIO, was present. Quite out of the blue, I said
that one of the reasons we had high unemployment in the
construction industry was that the federal government was
fixing prices under the Davis-Bacon Act. (Davis-Bacon required prevailing, top-level wages to be paid on any construction project paid for with federal money.) If the federal
government had more flexibility, I contended, particularly on
housing rehabilitation projects in the inner city, more jobs
would be available for the money, more workmen would
work more of the time, and they would end up making more
money even though they were paid a slightly lower hourly
wage.

Henning hit the roof. My cock-eyed suggestion, he said,
was another example of the Brown administration's forgetting its true friends, the working people of California. Wages
were too low already; I was talking about making the problem worse. He was insulted.

Although Henning didn't list the other instances where the Brown administration was remiss, I had heard via the grapevine that he was unhappy about Jerry's criticism of the federal jobs legislation on February 27, and most certainly he was displeased with Jerry for pushing the Political Reform Initiative the previous spring. (Since the Political Reform Initiative prohibited labor leaders from dispensing political contributions while they acted as lobbyists, it was perceived as a direct attempt to clip Henning's wings.) My comment proved to be the last straw.[26] It would have been one thing if I had been presenting a carefully thought out position that the Governor regarded as important, but my remark was totally gratuitous.

Several days after the hearing, I received a telephone call from David Commons, a good friend who had worked in the Brown-for-Governor campaign. "I hear you're having problems with Henning," he said. "Maybe I can straighten it out. I'll arrange a luncheon with the building trade guys."

David was as good as his word. A noon powwow was set for Sacramento. Jimmie Lee was there, as was John Cinquemani, head of the Los Angeles Building Trades. They were very patient with me, explaining how, before Davis-Bacon was passed, construction workers were subjected to ruthless wage-cutting. Workers were hired from out-of-state with promises of higher wages, but when they arrived in California, the wages were cut in half. They had no choice but to accept; they couldn't afford the bus fare back home. When the projects were finished, they were left stranded. Jimmie said they never again wanted to return to that dog-eat-dog situation. I agreed with him, I apologized for my remarks, we shook hands, Lee passed the word to Henning that I was okay, and that was that.

David was pleased. "It may be a blessing in disguise," he remarked. "Now that you know one another, there's no reason why you can't work closely together."

Events were to prove him right. The following month,

Jimmie Lee and John Cinquemani of the Building Trades and Jerry Whipple of the United Automobile Workers spent a morning in my office talking about an employment program.

We were moving on other fronts as well. David was setting up more meetings with union leaders. We were talking about a coalition of groups that would get behind a jobs program. David Commons became an informal member of my executive staff. He had a good sense of the labor leaders (he was the same generation as they were), and he was emotionally committed to developing a jobs program. He was even reassuring to look at. A rotund, grandfatherly man about sixty years of age, his waist a perfect circle, a pipe clamped perpetually in his teeth, and a mischievous wink in his eye, he was a kind of Jewish Santa Claus who passed out advice like stocking presents.

David's counsel was usually good. He had a very strong reality principle. He didn't bother much with what *should* be. He talked about what *could* be. "Don't fall in love with the problem," he would say over and over again. "Work on the solution. Appeal to people's self-interests." That was the way we could sell Jerry on a jobs program, he felt. "You get good press on a few projects, he'll want to climb on board."

David impressed upon me the importance of giving Jerry the credit. Jerry wouldn't support anything, David said, unless he was cast in the leading role. David seemed to understand what made Jerry tick, the same way the Shadow did. He wasn't taken in by Jerry's play-acting. "Most of it is a request for reassurance," David told me one morning in the Governor's office, "but if I say anything, I get drawn into the word games. I try to respond nonverbally. I smile. I nod my head. He usually calms down."

David was very fond of Jerry. He also felt that Jerry had the potential to be a great leader. David told me how he and Tom Quinn had coached Jerry when Jerry was starting out in politics. Jerry was very green, David said. He had been stuck in the seminary too long; he knew very little about the real world. But David had been in radio advertising; he knew how you reached people, and he had kicked around on the fringes of California politics. He pushed books on Jerry. He told him to be tough and calculating. (Jerry did not require much encouragement in this regard.) David believed Jerry could be like Franklin Roosevelt: pragmatic, flexible, possessed of a great intuitive sense, capable of doing contradictory things without feeling remorse.

There was a book about Roosevelt that David read and reread, *Roosevelt: The Lion and the Fox.*[27] His copy was underlined and marked with asterisks and exclamation points. David said Jerry had read the book too. He was convinced Jerry was following Roosevelt's strategies like a road map. "Look," David said once as he pointed out one passage, "it's all explained here. Roosevelt delivered a jobs program. Jerry will too."

I said I wasn't so sure anymore; the Jesuits didn't teach much economics in the seminary.

David told me not to be a doubting Thomas. Jerry was moving right because he had to secure his conservative flank, but he would turn left again. "Don't be misled by the rhetoric," he explained. "It's only a cover."

David was expressing the prevailing view of the Brown administration's liberal wing. Jerry was supposedly building a Trojan horse out of conservative rhetoric, but all along, the liberal shock troops were hiding inside, waiting for the moment of reckoning, and one night they would descend by ropes and ladders: on the farmworkers issue, on the jobs issue, and on God knows what else.

One summer, I gathered, Jerry and Don Burns had lived with David at his house off Hollywood Boulevard. Apparently, it was while they were still in law school. I was never very clear on why Jerry stayed with David, but one of the secretaries in the campaign said she thought David served as a substitute father for a while. Jerry was having trouble with Pat, he wanted to get out from under his father's shadow, and so he turned to David, who was very fatherly and having trouble with his own sons.

The interpretation sounded a little like five-and-dime-store Freudian analysis to me, but still, who could say for sure one way or the other?

Certainly there *were* frictions between Pat and Jerry. That I had to acknowledge. Even as recently as the winter of 1976, Jerry was going out of his way to put Pat down. He refused to return his father's phone calls, he ignored his father when they appeared publicly, he talked about Pat's political cronies as if they were the last people on earth he would appoint to regulatory boards and commissions, he even seemed adverse to appointing people from his father's generation; and although some of Jerry's slights were obvious attempts to establish a separate political identity, others were not so easily explained.

If the facts be known, there were ways Pat got under Jerry's skin. Pat was so warm and friendly with everyone, he didn't appear to reserve anything special, emotionally, for his son. Then, too, there were the remarks Pat made from time to time that drove Jerry up the wall. There was the interview Pat gave several days before Jerry's inauguration, for example. Although Jerry was going to be a fine governor, Pat said, he was worried about Jerry's unwillingness to delegate authority. Also, Pat revealed (in yet another interview), there was an incident in 1963 that he had never discussed publicly before. While Pat was Governor, Jerry had persuaded him to delay Caryl Chessman's execution! It was a thousand-to-one shot, Pat indicated, Chessman's request for a new trial having already been denied by the higher courts, but Jerry had talked him into it. Jerry was only a student at the time.[28]

Well, of course, the press made a big thing of Pat's revelation; and while, in one respect, the story was very complimentary to Jerry, showing his concern for human life and his precocious ability to influence his father, in another respect the story cast Jerry in a terrible light. Caryl Chessman was a notorious rapist. The Chessman case was the first big mistake Pat made in his political career. If Jerry was behind Pat's fateful decision, then Jerry was not only soft on convicted felons, he was also responsible for the decline in his father's political fortunes. It was the last freewheeling interview Pat would give for some time.

The Chessman interview wasn't the end of the story, however, for if Jerry pushed his father away in the public arena, he continued to rely on Pat in private, asking his advice, comparing notes with him on a large number of important and not-so-important issues. The relationship Jerry established may have been a very complicated, ambivalent sort of don't-call-me-I'll-call-you relationship, but Jerry *did* call Pat, and the antagonism he and his father expressed toward one another *was* leavened by a good deal of natural respect and need. Indeed, the negative and positive feelings they expressed toward one another almost seemed to be complementary, in a curious kind of way. After all, one *did* have to have continual, close contact with somebody else in order to have friction with him; the repulsion could occur over and over again only when there was an attraction that preceded it. And so it was with Pat and Jerry, I think. They each needed the other far more than they let on to outsiders.

In Pat's case, the need was quite easy to understand. Pat was noticed more after Jerry was elected Governor, he was an important personage once again. Now, not only was he the former Governor of California, he was the father of the present Governor, the pater familias of a state of 20 million people. It was no mean accomplishment. How many people in American history could say they had founded a political dynasty? Very few. Because of what Jerry had done, and of what Pat had done for Jerry, the Brown family was right up there with the Adamses and the Kennedys. Pat had good reason to feel warmly toward Jerry.

And Jerry, of course, had good reason to feel grateful as well. Not only did Pat provide Jerry with political contacts

102

and financial backing and a name that millions of people recognized, he gave him a wisdom and confidence and certainty that Jerry never would have felt had he started out on his own. Pat had been there before. He knew what it felt like to sit in the chief executive's chair. He had a sense of perspective that he could pass on to his son. He also had a certain friendly way with people that was very effective. He joked, he made small talk, he asked how the family was, he showed a little humanity. The manner was not easy for Jerry to assume — it was the side of his father that he had the least natural sympathy for, I think — but he forced himself to do it at times, gritting his teeth while he smiled and exchanged pleasantries he couldn't have cared less about. This manner was the true indication of how much the father influenced the son, I decided. Particularly on days when Jerry had to deal with the political types, he would turn on the charm and play the hale-fellow-well-met in very much the same way his father did. He would kid around a little, he would ask after the person's health, he would ask the person why he didn't drop around more. His voice would even take on the resonance and warmth characteristic of his father's voice. In the final analysis, Jerry was his father's son.

One evening, I remember, while I was having dinner at David Commons's house, he showed me a large, glossy color photograph he had taken of Pat and Jerry shortly after Jerry was elected Governor. It was a real father-son picture, the kind families take on Christmas morning after the presents are unwrapped. Pat and Jerry, dressed in identical coat sweaters, were standing side by side in Pat's living room: Brown the elder and Brown the younger. The father looked very proud of the son; the son looked very proud of the father. "You see this photograph?" David Commons asked, puffing himself up like a Bantam rooster. "Pat has one, Jerry has the second, and I have the third. There are no other copies."

The picture showed a side of Jerry that wasn't often revealed in public. But it was there. It was there.

Chapter Fifteen

THE AUTHOR DISCOVERS SEVERAL WAYS IN WHICH WORK-
ING WOMEN ARE DISCRIMINATED AGAINST. HE ATTEMPTS
TO TAKE CORRECTIVE ACTION. THE GOVERNOR IS UN-
SYMPATHETIC. THE GOVERNOR AND THE AUTHOR CON-
SIDER AN IMPORTANT QUESTION.

"CONGRATULATIONS," Gnaizda enthused. "I didn't think
you could do it." Bob was referring to the fact that, over the
space of seven days, the EDD legal staff had written ten bills
for introduction in the legislature. They had also identified
five other pieces of legislation they hoped the Governor's office would support.

Bob told me he and Mario Obledo were "100 per cent behind" the EDD proposals and would do everything possible
to secure the Governor's concurrence. Although it wasn't
clear when Jerry would set forth his position — there were
over 1500 bills he hadn't reviewed yet — we had the green
light to begin lobbying. The only proviso was, we had to tell
the legislators that the Governor hadn't made a final decision.

I was more than happy to agree to the condition. Although most of our bills involved little more than technical
changes in the Unemployment Insurance Code, two had
greater significance. One was the so-called domestic quits
bill. The second provided pregnancy benefits for working
women.

The domestic quits bill repealed an old section in the Unemployment Insurance Code; it provided that if a person quit work to accompany his spouse to a place from which it was impractical to commute to work, he was ineligible to receive UI benefits unless he could show he provided the sole or major support for the family.[29] While, theoretically, the disqualification applied to both sexes, in practice it was enforced only against women, who were presumed to be the secondary means of support in their families, and indeed, it was added in the 1940s only after the telephone companies complained about the amount of unemployment compensation they were paying to telephone operators who followed their servicemen-husbands around the country. The disqualification was discriminatory in purpose as well as in effect.

The pregnancy benefits bill we introduced dealt with a similar problem. Under the old law, women were barred from receiving disability payments for normal pregnancies and childbirth, even though every other kind of hospital treatment was covered, and even though the stated purpose of California's Disability Insurance Act was "to compensate . . . for the wage loss sustained by individuals unemployed because of sickness or injury."[30] The traditional justification for the exclusion was that pregnancies were voluntarily conceived, but plastic surgery was voluntary too, and plastic surgery was covered. We decided to provide pregnancy benefits for three weeks before childbirth and six weeks after. It seemed only logical. "After all," Rosenberg said, "if a woman can be reimbursed for having a nose job or a face lift, why shouldn't she be reimbursed for having a baby?"

In a sense, I think, it was altogether fitting and proper that our two major legislative initiatives should deal with working women. Working women were the unsung heroines of the 1960s and early 1970s. From 1968 to 1974, almost 9 million of them entered the labor market for the first time, and the female labor force rose by a remarkable 34 per cent. (The male labor force, by contrast, increased only 12 per cent.)[31] Women helped support their families while their husbands were fighting in Vietnam; they supplied a needed second income in many instances. Indeed, the primary way many low-income families climbed out of poverty was to send their wives to work. It wasn't very spectacular and it didn't receive as much publicity as the War on Poverty, but in the end, the second-income strategy was far more effective in lifting families out of destitution. It was the quiet revolution, and we were only acknowledging that fact when we introduced our bills.

For several days, the lobbying went without a hitch. Bipartisan support developed for the no quits bill, and George Moscone, one of the state senate's most respected Democrats, agreed to carry the pregnancy benefits legislation. And then one afternoon I talked to Jerry. "What are you doing, giving this bill to Moscone?" Jerry asked. Moscone had been one of Jerry's early rivals in the Democratic gubernatorial primary and had received considerable labor support. I gathered that Jerry didn't want to make Moscone any more popular than he already was. "I don't like this bill," Jerry said. He conceded we could find the money to pay for it, but he was still adamant. "I campaigned for Governor for four years. Not a single women's group ever talked to me about this problem."

It was an interesting admission. During much of the four years Jerry served as secretary of state, his public posture was that he wasn't worrying about higher office; he was only concerned with doing a good job as secretary of state. Now he was saying, in effect, that the public posture had been a sham.

Jerry continued his explanation. He was obviously irritated with me. Why should he do something for nothing? There was no pressure. He didn't *have* to back the bill. Probably he wouldn't receive much credit if he did. It was a nice idea, but so what? If the women wanted it, let them lobby for it.

I suggested letting the bill go ahead and see if support developed, but he would have none of it. "I don't want to be put in that position," he replied. The bill would be too popular with the women's groups, once it saw the light of day. All the knee-jerk liberals would support it. He didn't want to be forced into a corner, where he would have no choice but to sign the bill. "You're supposed to protect me, not put pressure on me," he exclaimed. "I want the bill killed immediately."

I agreed to do it. What else was there to do? We talked about other matters. Jerry was irritated with somebody else in the administration who was supporting a school lunch bill for low-income children. "Are poor kids really hungry," he asked rhetorically, "or is that another liberal myth? I don't know why we should subsidize school lunches. Nobody ever gave me a school lunch when I was a kid."

I couldn't believe what I was hearing. *His* father had been Governor of California. All the time he had been growing up, he had received the red carpet treatment. There had never been a day in his life when he had to worry where the next meal was coming from. He would inherit at least a million dollars when his mother and father died. And yet here he was, dressed in a three-hundred-dollar tailor-made suit, a hundred-dollar pair of alligator shoes, and a special monogrammed shirt, telling me how rough it had been.

I sensed he was feeling vulnerable about something. Maybe it was the issues we were talking about. Pregnancies, babies, working wives, children — these were all issues that involved experiences he had had very little contact with in his adult life. If the women's groups wanted to play hardball the way Jerry Brown would have if the situations had been reversed, they would say something like: "Of course Jerry Brown doesn't understand, he's never been married, he's never been a father." And they would hit on a sensitive nerve, they would raise a consideration Flournoy had touched upon in the campaign: that Jerry Brown was a little different, a little eccentric, a little cut off from the mainstream of American experience.

"Read E. F. Schumacher," Jerry said. "He's got the right idea. More women should be in the home, taking care of their children. Then we'd have fewer social problems."

I didn't remember E. F. Schumacher talking about consigning women to the home, but maybe there was a part of *Small Is Beautiful* I'd missed. In any case, I caught Jerry's drift. If more women stayed home, there would be less demand for government-subsidized child-care programs, fewer women would be competing for jobs, the unemployment rate would go down, and Jerry's job would be made a lot easier. If only...

If only women would do the patriotic thing...

If only they would assume more of a traditional role...

If only ... if only ...

Yes, that was it, that was what Jerry was saying in a funny, roundabout way: If only the women of today could be more like our mothers were.

Why can't the women of today be more like our mothers? That was the question Jerry was really asking.

Why can't they behave toward their children the way our mothers behaved toward us?

Why does the government have to assume more and more of the parental role?

These were good questions — some of them, anyway.

I wasn't even sure Jerry was placing the whole responsibility on the shoulders of American women. He would have been perfectly willing to have men stay home and women work, if that was, in fact, feasible and so long as he, Jerry Brown, didn't have to do it. He was merely suggesting that someone should remain in the home on a full-time basis, and if that meant the end of the second income and the second car and rapid upward mobility, well, people should lower their expectations, as he kept saying; the American Dream didn't have to be defined solely in economic terms.

There was even a precedent for what he was talking about, that is, about women pulling the disappearing act at a propitious time. It was after World War II. The female labor force had expanded by 33 per cent from 1940 to 1944, the women having taken up the slack while the men were in the armed services; but when the men returned home, 2 million women dropped out of the labor force.[32] It was either that, the economists said, or restructure the economy, and most of them didn't want to do that. And so the women left. They were the path of least resistance. They came when they were called and then left when their usefulness was ended, and if there were questions about what they were going to do when they retired behind the four walls of their bungalows, the answer was simple in the 1940s.[33] They were supposed to have babies, they were expected to make their children their life's work. There was even Dr. Benjamin Spock saying it was all right, preaching the new child-centered psychology. Dr. Spock came riding to the rescue at just the right time, in fact. He helped to bail out the economy by legitimating child-bearing as a full-time occupation.[34]

There was only one problem with the historical analogy. In the 1940s it was perfectly all right to have babies. In the 1970s, it was no longer as socially acceptable, what with the talk about food shortages and environmental pollution and zero population growth. So what were the women supposed to do with their time when they retired from the labor force? Do macramé? Rake leaves? Take Seconal? Watch daytime TV? Jerry and I didn't talk about those questions the day we considered the problems of working women.

Chapter Sixteen

THE AUTHOR DESCRIBES WAYS IN WHICH SOME OF THE
GOVERNOR'S ASSOCIATES PROSTRATE THEMSELVES IN
ORDER TO WIN THE GOVERNOR'S FAVOR. A RITE OF INITIA-
TION IS SCHEDULED FOR THE AUTHOR. THE AUTHOR
SUSPECTS HE HAS FLUNKED THE TEST.

"YOU BETTER GET over here immediately," Gnaizda said on
the telephone. "The Governor's really angry with you." Bob
was calling from the Governor's office. A cabinet meeting
was in progress.

I rushed over. Gnaizda was standing outside the main conference room, waiting to intercept me. "What's going on?"
I asked. I couldn't for the life of me figure out what I'd done
wrong.

"You know that domestic quits bill?" Gnaizda said. "Well,
the Governor's been having a fit over it. He's been talking
about practically nothing else. But I said to him, I persuaded
him, 'Governor,' I said, 'before you do anything drastic, let
Lorenz explain his position.'" Gnaizda glared at me fero-
ciously. "You've got some explaining to do. You could lose
your job over this!"

At first I thought he was joking. *I* had some explaining to
do, *I* could lose my job. Bob and Mario Obledo had signed
off on the bill, as had Paul Halvonik, Jerry's legislation liaison man. Domestic quits was one of the bills Gnaizda and
Obledo were "100 per cent behind," supposedly. If I was in

trouble, they should be too. Yet here was Gnaizda, scrambling wildly for the fire exits.

I realized Bob was terrified, terrified and angry. I had never before seen him this frightened. He was terrified because he was afraid the Governor's wrath would descend on him, and he was angry because I had put him in that position, and so he had called me in to shoulder the blame. The only reason he was talking to me, in fact, was that he wanted to dissociate himself from me before I talked to the Governor.

I walked into the conference room and sat down next to Jerry. One or two of the cabinet members looked at me apprehensively. Jerry was talking about another agenda item, but he broke off the discussion to return to the domestic quits bill. "I have trouble with this legislation you're supporting," he said. He sounded perfectly calm, perfectly reasonable, as he went on to explain his objection. There was too much mobility in the country, he said; it was one of the reasons for divorces and family troubles. If we continued to deny unemployment compensation to women whose husbands wanted to move, maybe they would be more likely to pressure their husbands to stay put, and perhaps, then, family solidarity would be strengthened.

It was a specious argument — families weren't going to stop moving just because the wife was ineligible to draw unemployment benefits — but I was so relieved to hear Jerry speaking to me in an even, good-natured tone of voice! After my encounter with Gnaizda, I half-expected him to yell and pound the table.

I tried to explain the reasons why we should support the bill. Among other things, I said, it was discriminatory against women.

"It's *not* discriminatory against women," Tony Kline, the Governor's legal counsel, interjected. Six months before, when he was a public interest lawyer representing women's groups, he would have made the opposite argument and contended that the domestic quits disqualification was a gross violation of the Equal Protection Clause of the Fourteenth Amendment to the U.S. Constitution, but now he was representing Jerry's interests. It was that simple.

I looked around the room. Nobody else said anything. Bob Gnaizda grinned and cleared his throat. Mario Obledo had already bailed out; I knew I couldn't count on him. The day after Jerry berated me for the pregnancy benefits bill, Mario and Bob and Jerry and I were talking, and Mario denied any knowledge of the bill's existence. "Don't you remember?" Bob had said to him at the time. "You approved it, we talked about it." But Mario had only sunk lower in his chair and said nothing. He looked like he wanted to hide under the table.

I was quite isolated. Jerry gave the order to kill the bill; I complied. After the cabinet meeting was over, I said to him, somewhat jokingly, "I'll be more than happy to kill the domestic bill if you'll agree to a jobs program," but he only stared at me. I had the feeling I'd pushed too far and had slipped over a boundary that hadn't been there four months before.

What was happening to all of us? Bob was so afraid of antagonizing the Governor, he was trembling like a leaf when he talked to me; Tony Kline was making legal arguments he would have laughed at six months before; Gray Davis, the executive secretary, was copying Jerry's clothes and speech patterns the way little boys aped O. J. Simpson; and Mario Obledo seemed the most intimidated of all. Perhaps it was the poor boy's need to make good, I don't know, but Mario would humble himself in order to please Jerry. Jerry would begin to take a hard line on welfare; Mario would anticipate where he was going and take an even harder line. Jerry would back off; Mario would too and say, "You're right, Governor." Jerry would allude to an inconsistent position Mario had taken in the past; Mario would conveniently forget he had ever made such a statement. Sometimes, it seemed to me, Jerry would weave back and forth in a series of contrary positions just to see whether Mario would follow. Once it got so bad that Mario sat mute, almost comatose, for two days while Jerry blue-penciled the welfare department's budget. "I couldn't believe it," the acting director of the welfare department told me afterward. "Here was a noted Mexican-American public interest lawyer, letting the welfare recipients take it in the ear, while I, a former member of the Reagan administration, was arguing on their behalf."

It was like an initiation rite, a male initiation rite. Mario wasn't the only one going through it, although his was the most extreme case. Bob, Tony, Gray, and now myself — all of us were being asked to jettison our prior allegiances in order to demonstrate fealty to the new leader. We were like feudal knights kneeling at the throne, waiting for the tests of submission that we would be charged to undertake. Would we be willing to avert our faces when the serfs cried out for food if that was what our lord instructed us to do? Would we be willing to forget about the damsels in distress if he told us he needed our assistance more? Would we be willing to leave our wives and children behind when he embarked upon his search for the Holy Grail?

I sensed I had flunked the first test. I had failed to anticipate the Governor's wishes on the legislation, I had argued too long at the cabinet meeting, I had refused to beg forgiveness — and so now there was something unresolved between Jerry and me.

Chapter Seventeen

THE AUTHOR LEARNS ABOUT THE DARK SIDE OF POLITICS, INCLUDING BLACKMAIL AND SCAPEGOATING. THE AUTHOR WONDERS WHY THE GOVERNOR IS RUNNING SCARED AND THINKS HE HAS DISCOVERED THE REASON. THE BLUE MEANIES ARE DRIVEN AWAY, ONLY TO REAPPEAR WITH A VENGEANCE.

"YOU'RE SUCH A BABE in the woods," the Shadow said to me in early April. "What do you think California politics is, anyway, a Sunday school picnic?"

We were talking about an article the Los Angeles *Times* ran on April 3, 1975, which reported that during the 1974 campaign, Tom Quinn, Jerry's campaign manager, had resorted to "political blackmail."[35] I had expressed surprise that the Brown campaign felt compelled to engage in this sort of thing, and the Shadow had laughed at me. He had laughed and laughed. "I keep forgetting you're a corn-fed Midwesterner," he said at one point. He made me feel like a hick, but nonetheless the Los Angeles *Times* article had given me pause.

According to several people who attended a March 19–20 conference on practical politics at San Francisco's Clift Hotel, Tom Quinn described how the Brown campaign gathered embarrassing information on Jerry's principal Democratic opponents in order to dissuade them from attempting any last-minute smear jobs on Jerry. The file on Joe Alioto supposedly covered Alioto's private business dealings while he was mayor of San Francisco, and the dossier on Bob Moretti allegedly focused on his less savory political contributors. Alioto and Moretti were reportedly informed of the findings and warned that if they tried anything dirty, the information would be made public. Although the Los Angeles *Times* story quoted Tom as denying he had engaged in "political blackmail," the article also indicated he had refused to make public the taped recording of his remarks at the Clift Hotel meeting.

The Shadow contended that political blackmail happened all the time. "Look at Lyndon Johnson's career, look at the CIA, look at what the FBI tried to do to Martin Luther King. The public sees only the tip of the iceberg, the scandals that pop out because the blackmail doesn't work, but for every exposé you read about, there're ten that never see the light of day. The parties make a deal. A won't expose B if B won't expose A. C will run down D unless D drops out of the race. E will reveal some fact about F unless F votes for E's bill. The only sure way to protect yourself is to have the goods on all the other key players, and practically everyone has something to hide. Jerry and Tom just wanted to run a clean campaign, that's all. They didn't hurt anybody with the information. Why, there are much worse stories around. There's one politician in the state who runs a newspaper. If you think he publishes all the news that's fit to print, you're crazy. He runs a blackmail operation. There's another guy who was a very attractive candidate a few years back. He was forced out of the race because of some compromising snapshots of him and a woman who wasn't his wife. I could go on and on, but, God forbid, I don't want to disillusion you."

The Shadow shook his head, as if to mock me. I asked him questions. He talked some more. The Shadow believed that "defensive" or "preventive blackmail," as he called it, became part and parcel of California politics after Richard Nixon succeeded in his last-minute smear job to defeat Jerry

Voorhis and Helen Gahagan Douglas in the 1946 and 1950 campaigns. Although there were no figures that indicated whether the quick character assassination happened more in California than in other places (political scientists didn't keep statistics on this sort of thing), a case could be made that it did and that Nixon was in some ways a product of his surroundings. There were so many newcomers in post–World War II California, people had little real familiarity with one another. They were forced to rely on very superficial impressions or images, and the images were very fragile things indeed, they could be altered (for better or worse) very rapidly. If Nixon and Jerry Voorhis had been running against each other in Iowa and Nixon had tried a last-minute character assassination, the voters might have said, "Why, we've known Jerry Voorhis for twenty years, his office is just down the street and he attends our local church; his views may be a little funny but he's no Communist." They might have been guided by a real sense of the man, in other words. But who ever heard of reality in Southern California, the home of Hollywood, the dream factory of the world? Reality in Southern California was whatever people said it was; it was the fresh start, the self-fulfilling prophecy, the victory of mind over matter. In a land without roots, reality was image, image replaced roots, and if the image could be constructed quickly, like a prefabricated house, it could also be torn down quickly.[36] Image making and image assassination went hand in hand, in other words, and preventive blackmail naturally followed from the first two. Preventive blackmail was the best insurance policy a politician had that his opponent would walk the straight and narrow. Or, as the Shadow so graphically put it, "You don't have to be a mean, dirty son of a bitch to succeed in California politics, but you do have to let people know you're capable of becoming one if and when the need arises. Turning the other cheek is for dumb schmucks and saints who were martyred four hundred years ago."

I could hardly argue with him there, but what about the

implications of what we were talking about? Who was to say that political blackmail could be kept within the strict limits the Shadow described? I knew Jerry would never use it offensively and zap someone who wasn't about to get him — he was one of the most scrupulously honest politicians I had ever met — but what about one or two of his aides? Did the practice continue after we arrived in Sacramento and had the full powers of the state government at our disposal? What if the opposition wasn't, in fact, developing a dossier on our man but we thought they were and acted accordingly? Was our "reaction" any less acceptable when it turned out to be an initiation of hostilities? How, in the hall of mirrors that was politics, could we ever know for sure who was initiating the hostilities, and if this was the case, didn't we have to engage in blackmail whenever the stakes were high? What if the farmworkers legislation wasn't going to pass unless a particular state senator changed his vote and we knew he was mixed up in the prepaid health mess? If it was all right to use blackmail to protect Jerry's reputation, why wasn't it okay to use it to "protect" the farmworkers legislation?

I felt as though I was looking at a pet boa constrictor in the bathtub. It was growing bigger and bigger. Someday, perhaps, we might not be able to control it.

There were so many questions. Why weren't the facts on the prepaid health scandal being released? According to the grapevine, Democrats as well as Republicans were involved. Was Jerry protecting his own party members or didn't he know about the rumors? Perhaps the rumors had no substance, but at the very least the prepaid health plans involved considerable mismanagement by the Reagan administration. Why did Jerry seem so uninterested in publicizing Reagan's mismanagement? Reagan was going to be running for President in 1976. His image was that of the hardworking citizen candidate who had cleaned up the welfare mess and run a no-nonsense, low-cost administration in Sacramento.

The reality, which Jerry could show from state files, was quite different. Reagan tired easily, worked a nine-to-five day, and delegated much of his authority to subordinates, whom the public never saw and never voted on. The welfare savings Reagan bragged about were greatly exaggerated, and the prepaid health boondoggle cost more money than it saved. Jerry had the power to blow Reagan out of the water, but he wasn't. Why not? He was even complimenting Reagan from time to time. Why? It didn't make sense, unless... unless...

We were in the hall of mirrors once again. One hypothesis that explained Jerry's reticence was that he was buying peace with Reagan in order to improve his own political chances. Jerry wouldn't attack Reagan if Reagan wouldn't attack him. The Democrats would retain their Mr. Clean image, which was extremely valuable after Watergate; Reagan would too. No blood would be shed, and everybody would make out in the end. It wasn't blackmail per se; it was more a recognition of mutual interest. But the result was much the same. The scandalous information was more useful when it remained locked in the state's file drawers.

I was beginning to see why Jerry was running scared a lot of the time. Politics was a dangerous business. The electorate was in an angry mood. People were looking for somebody to blame, and after Watergate, politicians were a logical target. Quite understandably, Jerry didn't want to be shot at, and although the untutored political observer might have contended that he had nothing to worry about because the voters were out to punish Republicans, Jerry knew better, he understood that the discontent we were feeling around us knew no party or ideology, it was blind and could be manipulated by a skillful demagogue.

A witchhunt was a distinct possibility in 1975, in fact. The Watergate affair had ended without the central figure being punished. The war in Vietnam was lost, finally and irrevocably, and 46,000 Americans were dead for no apparent reason. The energy crisis was causing an upheaval in the economy. There were even some unsettling parallels between 1975 and the post–World War I and post–World War II periods, when witchhunts had occurred. In both of the previous postwar periods, the country was experiencing difficulties converting from a wartime to a peacetime economy. The unemployment rate was rising, there were recriminations about whether the war had been lost in the peace settlements, and the tremendous aggressive energies released during the war had no officially sanctioned place to go. The witchhunt was one way out. It not only supplied an easy explanation of why people were feeling troubled, it provided an outlet for their aggressive energies. In 1919 and 1920, the witchhunt commenced with the Red Scare; in 1948, 1949, and 1950, it was led by Richard Nixon, Joe McCarthy, and the House Un-American Activities Committee.[37] In both previous eras, complicated social and economic issues were overlooked in favor of simplistic crusades against subversion, loyalty was the primary prerequisite for public service, schoolbooks and movies were monitored for heretical ideas, restrictive immigration quotas were used to exclude foreign influences, blacks and Jews were scapegoated, anything left of center was suspect — and if it had happened twice before, it could happen again. The year 1975 could be a repeat of 1919 and 1948.

I'm not saying Jerry Brown and his young administration would have been at the top of the right wing's little list, but we were an interesting possibility, were we not? Bob Gnaizda had fraternized with the Black Panthers. Tony Kline worked with radical prison groups before he began processing extraditions and pardons in the Governor's office. My wife was a socialist for eighteen months before we separated. A high percentage of the Governor's appointees must have smoked marijuana at some point in their previous incarnations. Jerry was young, eccentric, a lapsed Catholic who dabbled in Oriental religions. The Sufis, a Middle Eastern religious group that was vaguely affiliated with the whirling dervishes, entertained at Jerry's political gatherings. Jerry spent weekends with people from the counterculture who were not unfamiliar with the drug scene. He numbered among his close acquaintances Jane Fonda, whose antiwar speeches had been broadcast over Radio Hanoi, and Tom Hayden, a co-defendant in the Chicago conspiracy trial who traveled to North Vietnam while the war was still in progress. Jerry himself had never served in the military. It didn't require too much imagination to conceive of the kind of half-baked, guilt-by-association campaign that could be waged against us. GOVERNOR LINKED TO HANOI FELLOW TRAVELERS, the headline in the right-of-center Oakland *Tribune* might say, or GOVERNOR A DRAFT EVADER? There were many possibilities: WIFE OF JOBS DIRECTOR A COMMUNIST? BLACK PANTHERS INFILTRATE BROWN ADMINISTRATION. GOVERNOR DROPS OUT WITH HIPPIES ON WEEKENDS. DRUG USE COMMON AMONG BROWN APPOINTEES. GOVERNOR AN INITIATE IN WHIRLING DERVISH CULT? It made little difference whether the charges were true or fair. A skilled propagandist could have a field day.

I suppose if we had been ancient Hebrews, the solution would have been quite simple. A high priest would have come in on the Day of Atonement, a live goat would have been chosen by lot (thus the origin of the word "scapegoat"), the priest, robed in linen garments, would have laid both his hands on the animal's head and transferred to the animal the sins and sufferings of the people, the goat would have been banished to the wilderness, and the people would have experienced a sense of relief.

But we were not so fortunate. The voters would have laughed uproariously if, after Vietnam and Watergate, we had sacrificed a live chicken on the steps of the state capitol. Animal sacrifices had gone out of style. There was no regularly scheduled Day of Atonement to serve as a safety valve for the negative feelings of the community. Organized re-

ligion didn't even address the problem, for the most part; it
deferred to the politicians, who had too much power already.
It was a very unsatisfactory state of affairs. The devils should
have been confronted in the church, where they could have
been disposed of without anybody getting hurt — but what
was Jerry supposed to do? The devils were in the political
arena now, and if he didn't direct them elsewhere, they might
start devouring him. The working principle in modern
American politics was clear: eat or be eaten, attack or be
attacked. And so Jerry began looking around.

It wasn't an easy task. Welfare recipients, who were
Ronald Reagan's favorite scapegoats, were out of the question; most of them voted Democratic. The oil companies
were a popular villain with liberal politicians after the oil
crisis, but Jerry decided to hold off on them for the time
being, not wishing to develop an antibusiness reputation. He
did criticize the Rohr Corporation for exporting jobs abroad,
but after the newspapers reported that Rohr was one of
Flournoy's major financial supporters, he backed off, not
wishing to appear as if he were playing politics. Richard
Nixon was an oldie but goodie — while Jerry was the secretary of state, he had pulled out all the stops trying to revoke
the notary public license of the Los Angeles accountant who
had allegedly falsified a date on Nixon's tax return; and after
he became Governor, he blocked a federal grant that would
have financed extra police protection for Nixon in San
Clemente — but how much could you kick a man when he
was down? The Mafia was too dangerous. The Teamsters
were too tough. The Arabs were too far away. The job of
finding a scapegoat proved to be more difficult than it first
appeared. But finally, in early February 1975, Jerry hit upon
a solution. He would scapegoat the government!

As usual, Jerry was picking up on the beat of the times.
Conservatives had blamed the government for years, and
after Vietnam and Watergate, liberals were in an antigovernment mood too. It was a time-honored American tradi-

tion, bad-mouthing the government, and with the Bicentennial coming up, the campaign would tie in nicely with the Spirit of 1776. There was no need to single out particular individuals. (Jerry didn't want to hurt anybody.) "Red tape" could be the villain, or "bureaucratic gobbledegook," or "boondoggle programs that cost the taxpayers money." The antigovernment strategy permitted great flexibility. On days when Jerry felt his popularity slipping with conservatives, he could do a number on a program they didn't like, and when he was in trouble with liberals, he could pick on one of their bêtes noires; so long as he operated on a purely symbolic level and refrained from trying to reorganize the programs he was criticizing (reorganizations took too much time, they made too many enemies), he could shuttle back and forth along the political spectrum with all the agility of a crab.

"You watch," he told me in October 1974, "I'm going to move right and left at the same time." I didn't think it was possible, but after I watched him in February and March and early April of 1975, I began to understand. He meant symbolically. It was possible to act flexibly, even contradictorily, when you restricted yourself to the symbolic level.

On February 14, 1975, Jerry made his first move. He told reporters he was "amazed" that three hundred and fifty University of California administrators earned more than $30,000 a year. "The state superintendent of instruction makes only $35,000 a year, and I make $49,100 myself," he said piously, engaging in a little ostentatious humility. The reporters didn't ask him what, if any, action he was planning to take to remedy the situation and he didn't say. As usual, they just disseminated the story he handed out.[38]

On March 1, 1975, the San Francisco *Chronicle* reported that Jerry was halting the distribution of free briefcases to state employees. Although Jerry's directive saved very little money, a fact the *Chronicle* didn't mention, it was received with enthusiasm. Voters seemed to have the feeling that the coddled, privileged bureaucrats were finally receiving their comeuppance.[39]

On March 12, 1975, Jerry and Bob Gnaizda staged a media extravaganza in front of the California Welfare Directors Association. Jerry stacked thirty-four volumes of federal and state welfare laws on a table (Bob had scurried around the night before collecting the necessary props) and announced contemptuously that the books contained about five million words. Waving a copy of the Old Testament in front of the welfare directors, he declaimed, "If I have to take my pick, I take this thing against that mishmash any day." The welfare directors shifted uneasily in their chairs, not being sure whether Jerry was commiserating with them or ridiculing them for being part of an absurd system — but in any case, what could they do? They couldn't administer the welfare system with the Old Testament. (An eye for an eye? A tooth for a tooth?) The Los Angeles *Times* carried the story on page 1, along with a picture of Jerry, Bob, and the welfare regulations.[40] There was almost no discussion about what could be done to simplify the "mishmash," no memo went out from the Governor's office requesting a study of the problem, and business continued as usual at the state's Welfare Department, which had overall responsibility for the welfare system. Jerry had staged the media event for one reason and one reason only: He wanted to dissociate himself from the bad karma of the welfare mess and sick the Blue Meanies on the welfare directors. The thirty-four volumes were *their* responsibility. *He* was opting for the Old Testament.

I decided Jerry's performance was reminiscent of the Happenings that were put on in New York and Los Angeles in the 1960s. Like the avant-garde artists, actors, and musicians who staged the Happenings, Jerry was springing a surprise on his audience in order to wake them up, he was assaulting their conventional view of the world in order to force them to realize that they too were implicated, he was juxtaposing images in a bizarre way (the welfare laws versus the Bible) in order to produce a new sense of the absurd. Jerry's audience may not have been dealt with as aggressively as some of the Happening audiences were (in one Happening in New York in March 1961, the spectators were confined inside a boxlike structure resembling a cattle car, and when the Happening was over, the walls collapsed and the spectators were driven out by someone operating a power lawn mower), but the intent was the same. As Susan Sontag, the noted critic and author, observed in reference to the New York Happenings: "Comedy is not any less comic because it is punitive. As in tragedy, every comedy needs a scapegoat, someone who will be punished . . . In the Happenings this scapegoat is the audience."[41]

On March 13, 1975, Jerry struck again. This time his contempt shifted to an affirmative action plan that the University of California had negotiated with the federal Department of Health, Education and Welfare. Pointing to a stack of documents the university had prepared, Jerry said the plan was nothing more than "a bureaucratic shuffle between HEW and Berkeley. If you were doing all you can and people believed it," he told Chancellor Bowker and the reporters who were present, "you wouldn't need all that."[42] Once again, no changes in policy were ordered, even though, as Governor, Jerry had the power to influence the university's hiring policies. Jerry was simply venting a little negative energy and shifting it to the University of California. The Blue Meanies were sitting under Chancellor Bowker's chair now.

On March 14, Jerry traveled to San Francisco to attend a meeting of the University of California's Board of Regents. Even before he walked into the conference room, which was filled with reporters and members of the public, he made a point of asking why the other regents were driving big cars while he, the Governor, was using a little compact. (He was playing his favorite game of conspicuous austerity.) Then, when he had settled into his chair, he started firing criticisms at a university vice president who was attempting to explain the 1977–78 academic plan. "I find the plan difficult to read and too abstract," Jerry declared, glaring down at notes he had made on a yellow legal pad. "I would like to focus on something more concrete and come down from the clouds." Why was a medical school needed at Irvine? Why was it better to have a small number of students in a class? Why did the university need more money from the state? Jerry wasn't saying he was going to disapprove parts of the budget. He was just asking questions.

The questions went on and on. Usually, the Board of Regents meetings ended by midafternoon, but this one ran late. Jerry criticized the $59,500 salary the university's president was earning. He observed with great pride that he, Jerry Brown, was making only $49,100. He ridiculed the number of reports the regents were receiving. "I think we are serving...the preservation of records rather than the needs of people," he said.

He was playing to the audience now, jumping from subject to subject, never alighting long enough to resolve any problem. A few of the other regents looked perplexed. They didn't realize that Jerry was using them as foils in a little guerrilla theater he was putting on. They thought it was for real. At one point, when an agenda item was tabled for further study, Jerry exclaimed, "I don't understand why it takes so much study...I really want to simplify things. I've been looking at the various forms one has to fill out to get in the [international studies] program; they go to a number of pages. I understand there are seventeen people to handle a program for three hundred [students]...I have trouble with the cost level." He gestured impatiently. A Los Angeles *Times* reporter who was covering the meeting wrote later that the Governor mixed "rudeness (plus traces of pomposity and sanctimony) with charm in his self-appointed role as academic iconoclast," but the audience loved it.[43] By the end of the meeting, Jerry had them eating out of the palm of his hand.

126

It was a new art he was creating, the Political Happening. Jerry was the director, the choreographer, and the leading man; the other regents were bit players, mere straight men. It appeared obvious enough, but few people seemed to understand. During a January meeting of the state college trustees (the California state college system is different from the University of California system), Jerry had made a big point of saying that he would meet any time, at any place, to discuss changes in the state college budget, but on three or four occasions when the trustees tried to set up a meeting, Jerry was always "unavailable." Of course he was. The purpose of the exercise was theater, not the resolution of budgetary matters. The problem Jerry was concerned with had nothing to do with the budget, it was never on the printed agenda, and it was never referred to by the press. The problem had to do with the Blue Meanies that were loose in the land.

A certain pattern was developing. Jerry avoided attacking particular people. (He was criticizing the university president's salary, not the president himself.) He jumped around a lot, never letting the negative feelings accumulate too much at any single point. He refrained from using the considerable power of the government once he had made a hit. He didn't punish, he asked questions. He was a· gadfly, and he was engaging in a benign form of scapegoating.

On April 2, 1975, Jerry announced that he was "putting on trial" a $105 million crime fighting program that, he said, was "riddled with gibberish and mishmash" and apparently only provided "leaf raking projects for white collar workers." He doubted that the program was having much effect in California, and he added that if local police officials couldn't persuade him of the program's value, he would propose the funds be returned to the federal government. "This is basically a coverup ... to fool the American people into thinking their tax dollars are being used to combat crime ... If these programs can't cut the mustard before local and State government bodies, the Federal government has no business promoting them."[44]

127

His language was far more aggressive than his intent, however. Once again, Jerry was grandstanding. Even if he decided to return all $105 million, the money would still be spent. Washington would simply by-pass the state decision-making process and fund local police forces directly. There wasn't a snowball's chance in hell that Jerry would fly to Washington and attempt to cut off federal grants to the Los Angeles Police Department. Jerry was very sensitive about his law-and-order image. He had been courting Ed Davis, the crusty, outspoken chief of the LAPD, for months. Davis would scream bloody murder if Jerry interfered with his pet projects — and so would a hundred other police chiefs in California. The April 2 announcement was a publicity puff, nothing more. It was Jerry's April Fool's joke. And because the press didn't call him on it, it was a doubly good joke. It was "too much," it was "simply outrageous," and the insiders in the Brown administration could titter appreciatively to themselves and admire Jerry's intricately constructed artifice. Jerry was fading back to pass, the receivers were streaking out, the fullback and the halfback were running a double reverse, and the ball wasn't even on the field, for God's sake. Jerry was "camping it up," he was becoming a Camp politician.

I hadn't thought of the concept of Camp for years, but it seemed like an apt description of what Jerry was doing. Camp was a certain kind of stylized behavior that produced an ironic effect; it was artifice disguised as reality; it was outrageous ambiguity. When people displayed a 1940s, steel-legged kitchen table as the centerpiece in their living room or wore 1930s thrift store clothes to the opera opening, they were being Camp. When they put a Campbell's soup can on a pedestal and passed it off as a work of art, they were being Camp. Camp involved a mixture of styles to produce an incongruous, somewhat exaggerated effect; it was love of the "off," of things-being-what-they-are-not. Camp delighted in artifice and innocent subterfuge, a private language. Camp was not only an assault on conventional meanings, it was the glorification of no meaning, the triumph of style over substance, of aesthetics over morality, of irony over tragedy, of form over feeling. Camp refused to play it straight: Camp was playful, it engaged in the hide-and-seek of double and triple entendres, it was duplicitous in a charming, inconsequential sort of way. The whole purpose of Camp was to dethrone seriousness and strong feelings. (Seriousness and strong feelings were too dangerous, too rigid . . . too boring.) Camp sought to lighten up, to skip and prance over the surface of a dangerous world; it tried to decorate the environment rather than change it.[45]

I think it was pretty obvious why Jerry was gravitating to a campy way of doing things. He was searching for a cool, nonthreatening way of communicating with the public. In the winter and spring of 1975, the electorate felt too strongly; there was too much rage, too much anxiety. People needed to lighten up. Involving them in the dance of life was one way of dealing with the Blue Meanies. If Jerry could get the Blue Meanies running around fast enough, they might exhaust themselves. He would involve, even submerge, the press and the public in a little drama. Would the police chiefs be able to justify the use of federal funds or wouldn't they? Would Jerry cut off the funds or wouldn't he? In the final analysis, the public didn't care as long as the drama was entertaining. It was the old Roman principle of bread and circuses. Jerry felt he couldn't do anything about the bread ($105 million was an infinitesimally small part of the total federal budget), so he concentrated on the circuses.

On April 21, 1975, the U.S. State Department announced that, with the sudden and unexpected capture of South Vietnam by North Vietnam, thousands of South Vietnamese refugees would be expatriated to the United States. They would land in California and would be temporarily housed there and in Arkansas and Florida, and although many would be resettled in other parts of the country, some would remain in the state of their initial residency.

Immediately, the alarm bells sounded in the Governor's

office. Welfare costs would rise, the unemployment rate would go up; the refugees posed real problems. They also represented a fantastic opportunity. Jerry had been lashing out at faceless, anonymous scapegoats for two months, but now he had real, live, flesh-and-blood ones landing in his own back yard. The refugees were adversaries everyone could rally against. The right wing would worry about rising welfare costs; union members would fear job competition; the left would view the refugees as the flotsam of a decadent society, the war profiteers and generals who were able to buy their way out in the final days. There was nothing Jerry could do to diminish the animosity, so he might as well ride it for all it was worth, voicing the resentments and fears the voters felt. And if he restricted his remarks to criticisms of the federal government and appointed a member of a minority group to lead the charge, the newspapers would have a hard time accusing him of racism. It was perfect. Within hours after Washington's announcement came over the wire services, the Governor's office had developed a strategy.

On April 23, Jerry told reporters he didn't see how California could take in a large number of refugees when the state had a million unemployed citizens and countless others who were hard-pressed financially with taxes and family responsibilities. "There is something a little strange about saying, 'Let's bring in 500,000 more people' when we can't take care of the 1 million we have who are out of work," he remarked. The Speaker of the state assembly, Leo McCarthy, sounded a different, more humanitarian note. ("We don't have the luxury of characterizing this as untimely," he told reporters the same morning that Jerry was firing his verbal mortars at the invading refugees. "The tragedy of Vietnam is deeply felt by most Americans. It would be a strange attitude, indeed, if we were not willing to do our best. We have to do the best we can.")[46] But Jerry paid no heed. The hounds of hell were charging out of the kennel now, and he was determined to ride to the hunt. Mario Obledo was authorized to set up a special task force that would pull together all the agencies of state government that might have any contact with the refugees. Bob Gnaizda would be the brains behind the operation. Together, they would do a media blitz.

Shortly after Jerry's remarks to the press, a meeting was convened in Mario's conference room. A representative of the state health department was there. (Were the refugees syphilitic? Would they spread the Asian flu among the American population?) An officer of the California National Guard was present as well. (Were the refugees going to be repulsed on the beaches of Santa Monica?) The full and wondrous panoply of government was assembled to meet the problem. Looking over the fifty to sixty people who were sitting solemnly in Mario's conference room that morning, I realized how the Vietnam War had dragged on as long as it had. Grown men loved to play soldier. A parade was such a welcome relief from the humdrum of everyday life. People didn't ask questions; they just marched. The newfound power was intoxicating.

On April 23, Mario Obledo wired Secretary of State Kissinger with a request for a meeting within forty-eight hours to discuss the refugee problem. There was virtually no chance that Kissinger would accede to the request, the critical decisions having already been made, but Gnaizda, who concocted the idea of the telegram, wanted to add a little credibility to Mario's venture. It was the chance of a lifetime. If Mario could ride the media coattails of Henry Kissinger, the most famous man in the world, Mario could make his mark in the national press.

Kissinger was too mediawise to rise to the bait, of course, and so, on April 24, Mario fired off a telegram to the commanding officer of the air force base where the refugees were being landed. The commanding officer — whose name, appropriately enough, was Colonel James T. Rock — was requested "to take no action of any kind with regard to Vietnamese refugees in California . . . until you personally clear with Secretary of State Kissinger. For your information," Mario continued, "I have sent a telegram to Secretary of State Kissinger regarding a personal meeting with him to clarify the role of the State and federal government."[47] The request was absurd on its face. Colonel Rock was responsible to his superiors in the United States Air Force, not to an unknown state official. If Rock had shut the refugees up in the aircraft and prevented the planes from returning to the Far East for more refugees, as Obledo was apparently suggesting, he would have been court-martialed.

On the afternoon of April 24, the refugee task force was given a name: Project VIC, or the Project Vietnam Interagency Commission. It sounded like one of the creations of the Department of Defense in Washington. The state of California was developing its own defense department. Obledo told reporters he was thinking about suing the federal government. He also announced he was preparing to send a representative to Guam, where planeloads of refugees were arriving almost hourly. The special state emissary would "insure that no refugees are brought into the State until some definite relocation plans are announced by the Federal government." It was an incredible statement. Pursuant to Articles I and II of the U.S. Constitution, the federal government had exclusive control over matters dealing with foreign policy, defense, and immigration. Officials of a state government had absolutely no right to travel to a foreign possession and interfere with the shipment of foreign aliens. But Mario was intoxicated by dreams of glory. He was the poor boy from Texas made good, and he wanted to make better. Bob had told him the sky was the limit, Mario could be the first Mexican-American in the President's cabinet.

Obviously Mario was in over his head. The special resentment he felt for the refugees was beginning to show. Many of Mario's boyhood acquaintances had had to sneak across the border as wetbacks; they were hunted by the border patrol.

The Vietnam refugees, in contrast, were apparently being given the red carpet treatment. In his statements to the reporters, Mario kept referring to the refugees with such distaste that a reporter from the Los Angeles *Times* finally asked him whether a "yellow peril" hysteria was creeping into the Brown administration's reaction to the situation. Mario mumbled a reply, but at the end of his dispatch the Los Angeles *Times* reporter wrote: "Some of the reasons given by Obledo for the State's opposition to the refugees recalled those put forth in the last century by leaders of the 'Chinese Must Go' movement . . ."

Bob Gnaizda tried to save Mario by shifting the press's attention back to the federal government. Bob and Mario had spoken to President Ford's special representative on Southeast Asian refugees, Bob told reporters. They were "shocked." "He [President Ford's representative] indicated the Federal government's concern was only for the next few weeks, that he would be leaving his job and there would be no interagency coordination, once he leaves the department." This meant, Gnaizda said, "that the Federal government saw its obligation solely in terms of getting people out of Vietnam and in effect dumping them in California."[48]

There was no basis for Gnaizda's remarks. In fact, the State Department wasn't planning on a two-week effort, and it wasn't talking about "dumping" the refugees anywhere. Bob and Mario — and by extension the Governor's office — were resorting to scare tactics to cover up their own media excesses. It was a good example of how scapegoating could get out of hand. Jerry and his representatives were not only playing with fire, they were feeding it now.

On April 30, 1975, the Los Angeles *Times* ran a front-page article about initial reactions to the Vietnam refugees. "Fears fed largely by rumors and misinformation with occasional overtones of racism, have sparked strong protests to Congress over the reception of Vietnamese refugees in the U.S.," the article began. " . . . 'Disease, disease, disease, that's

all I've heard,' said Representative Thomas M. Rees of
Beverly Hills. 'I've had some of the dumbest phone calls I've
ever received. They think of the Vietnamese as nothing but
diseased job seekers. If Americans had thought that way in
1912 I wouldn't be here today. That's the year my father
came over from Wales.' "[49] The article didn't mention the
role that the Brown administration had played in building
the hysteria, but several days later the Sacramento *Bee* made
the connection.[50] What had started out as "benign" scapegoating was turning into an ugly little witchhunt.

And so it was that in the latter part of April 1975, we, the
members of the Brown administration, finally caught up with
the Blue Meanies and discovered . . . that they were us.

Chapter Eighteen

CESAR CHAVEZ PUTS THE SCREWS ON. THE GOVERNOR SUBMITS BUT IN A CURIOUS WAY. THE AUTHOR DESCRIBES A FATEFUL DAY IN THE FALL OF 1974 WHEN THE GOVERNOR TALKED ABOUT THE PERILOUS STATE OF DEMOCRACY. THE MAN ON THE WHITE HORSE EMERGES.

CESAR was coming.

Cesar Chavez was coming.

He wasn't going to cross the Rubicon. He was going to cross the Sacramento River and encircle the state capitol if Jerry didn't pass a collective bargaining bill for farmworkers.

Cesar was an organizer, a very experienced, determined organizer.

Cesar was also a symbol.

Cesar was a bigger symbol than Jerry was.

Jerry had won one election, two elections, three elections. Cesar had won the hearts and minds of the young, the poor, the oppressed.

Jerry was the successor to his father. He was the son figure.

Cesar was the successor to Martin Luther King and Mahatma Gandhi. He was the father figure.

Some people felt Cesar was a saint.

Some people felt Jerry was a politician.

Cesar represented everything alienated middle-class America was not.

In suburbanized middle-class America, the critical sociological fact was that the father was absent. He drove away in the morning, he drove home at night; the kids didn't have the slightest idea what he did in the meantime. The mother was the parent who assumed most of the responsibility for providing the nurture and laying down the rules.

Cesar, on the other hand, was a throwback to an earlier, simpler America. He was always present, watching over his children in the fields, leading them in battle, showing them how to live.

Cesar was representative of a better time, when parents and children worked together and the family was whole.

He was emotion in a computer age.

He was unwavering commitment and untiring consistency in the face of perpetual change and future shock.

He was orientation in the midst of disorientation.

He symbolized the part of the human spirit industrial society was destroying.

He represented the side of the human personality the youth were afraid of losing.

The youth did not want to give up their emotion.

They did not want to lose their sense of community.

They reached out to Cesar without knowing why.

They reached out to Cesar as if he were a life preserver.

Cesar was coming.

He would climb the capitol steps.

He would walk the halls of the legislature.

He would appear before the television cameras.

The farmworkers would too.

A thousand farmworkers would come to Sacramento.

Five thousand.

Ten thousand.

Dressed in their straw hats and carrying the red and black flag and marching behind the sign of the Virgin of Guadalupe, they would make a nice "visual" on the evening news.

The farmworkers would be on the television screen while people in Orange County were eating their dinners.

The farmworkers would stay for a month.

Two months.

Five months, if necessary.

They would stay on the television screens as long as it took.

The farmworkers would assemble humbly, contritely. There would be no violence. Cesar followed Mahatma Gandhi. The farmworkers did too.

The farmworkers would hold night-long vigils.

Cesar would fast.

The farmworkers would pray for Cesar.

The Catholic priests would too.

The farmworkers would pray for Jerry.

Cesar would pray for Jerry.

Women would be kneeling on the capitol steps.

Children would be there too.

On the nights when it was cold, the children would cry, the children would cry on the television screen.

The children would be crying because it was cold, because Jerry was shutting them out in the cold.

Jerry would be making the children cry on the television screen.

The people in Orange County who were eating their dinners while they were watching television would get indigestion, heartburn. They would not enjoy their indigestion. They would reach for their Pepto-Bismol, and in their minds they would associate the indigestion with farmworkers and Jerry Brown. At the next election, they would vote against indigestion.

Jerry was cornered. He couldn't resort to symbolic politics the way he liked to do with the other groups. Cesar wouldn't take a symbol for an answer.

Jerry couldn't indulge in ostentatious austerity the way he did with the university bureaucrats. Cesar would point out that Jerry earned more in a year than six farmworker families did.

Jerry couldn't buy Cesar out by appointing him to a regulatory commission. Cesar was only interested in higher wages and better working conditions for his farmworkers.

Jerry couldn't mystify Cesar with late-night séances. Cesar would send a representative in his place.

There was no exit for Jerry, no way out.

Better than anybody else, Cesar could expose Jerry as a hype artist. Jerry talked about "lowering expectations." The farmworkers *had* lowered their expectations, they had practically nothing. Jerry spoke of austerity. Cesar practiced it. Jerry yearned for a sense of community. Cesar already had it. Jerry dropped references to Gandhi. Cesar had fasted for forty days. Jerry used the nervous system of the media as a substitute for the corporeal presence he felt he lacked, he wrapped himself in other people's identities in order to give himself meaning. Cesar was grounded in a movement of real people to whom he was accountable, he had a real presence and real convictions — and when the authenticity of Cesar's world was set up against the artificiality of Jerry's, it would become apparent how up in the air Jerry really was.

Jerry knew it. Cesar knew it. Jerry knew Cesar knew.

Jerry caved in, at least on the merits. He decided to give what Cesar wanted. Any collective bargaining bill was going to antagonize the growers anyway. Jerry might as well do what was necessary to win Cesar's support. And who knew? There might be other dividends as well. Ever the practical politician, Jerry would follow the advice of Falstaff in *King Henry IV, Part 2:* "A good wit makes use of anything. I will turn diseases into commodity."[51]

There was, first of all, Cesar's boycott network of several hundred persons spread throughout the country. If Jerry was planning on running for President in 1976, as the grapevine in the Governor's office was saying, the boycott network would be very useful in building a grassroots campaign for Jerry.

There was, next, Cesar's symbolic power. Cesar was the

last remaining charismatic leader from the 1960s; he was a touchstone for liberals and young voters and poor people. If Cesar supported Jerry, these voters would jump into Jerry's pocket.

The farmworkers were also the perfect rebuttal to the criticisms about Jerry one heard around Sacramento. When Jerry's opponents contended that Jerry didn't do anything but manipulate symbols, Jerry's friends could respond, "Yes, but the farmworkers..." When Jerry's enemies said, "Jerry doesn't have any compassion for people," Jerry's allies could say, "Yes, but the farmworkers..." Jerry was like the tin woodman in *The Wizard of Oz,* who had no heart. Cesar would give him a heart. Cesar's alliance with Jerry would supply the warmth, the compassion, the feeling, that the Jerry Brown image lacked.

It was a classic example of the dialectic in operation. The problem was pregnant with the solution. Cesar the threat could become Cesar the salvation.

There was only one problem with this analysis. At the same time Jerry was capitulating on the substance of what Cesar wanted, he was preparing to go to battle with Cesar.

It didn't make sense to me.

Cesar had a bill, Assembly Bill 1, that a young assemblyman from East Los Angeles, Richard Alatorre, had introduced for him the previous two years. The bill was far from perfect technically, and Jerry had some improvements in mind that would tighten it up and better help Cesar achieve his objectives, but there was absolutely no reason why AB 1 couldn't be amended. It was Cesar's issue. He had been organizing farmworkers for more than ten years. It seemed only fitting that when the launching ceremonies were held, the champagne bottle would be smashed on the prow of Cesar's ship. However, Jerry was preparing his own bill. The Brown initiative was to be introduced in the assembly by Howard Berman, a liberal assemblyman from Los Angeles, and in the state senate by John Dunlop, who was from Napa

County. In its basic goals and provisions, the Brown bill was identical to the Chavez bill.

At first I thought Jerry's bill was simply a negotiating ploy to force Cesar to agree to the technical modifications. But Jerry was pushing further, much further. He was planning a media blitzkrieg. The Governor's office was going to mail ten thousand letters to opinion-makers throughout the state. The United Auto Workers, the Catholic Conference of Bishops, the AFL-CIO — the core of Cesar's support base — were to be courted and won over to Jerry's position. Mario Obledo was to be used to split the Mexican-American community. ("I'm going to build him up to be the number two Mexican-American in California," Jerry had told me the previous December. "I'll use Obledo against Chavez.") In addition, Leroy Chatfield was to use his knowledge of Cesar's boycott network to round up other organizations as well. It sounded like all-out war. Leroy, who had been Cesar's trusted lieutenant during the difficult years of the 1960s, was now on Jerry's side. It was a sign to the UAW and the Catholic bishops that the political winds were changing. Cesar didn't have it anymore. Jerry did. Jerry had Leroy. If Leroy was shifting allegiances, the UAW and the Catholic bishops had damned well better think twice about sticking with Cesar.

I remember one late Friday afternoon in the early spring. Bob Gnaizda and Mario Obledo and I were in Jerry's office, pleading with him to call off the hostilities. There was no need for a hot war. The technical changes could be negotiated out ahead of time. Mario had just returned from a testimonial dinner, where the farmworkers had given him the cold shoulder. He was miserable. Bob and I knew how tenacious Cesar could be. We thought Jerry's invasion of Cesar's turf could well end up like the German invasion of Russia. Jerry would get bogged down in a land war at a time when he had other fronts to fight on.

Jerry, however, was like a man possessed. Sitting there on the couch with his legs and arms crossed, he listened to all our arguments — and we approached the problem from six different directions — but he wouldn't budge. He wanted this fight. He needed it. He had been laying back for months while the know-it-alls criticized him for not doing anything. The big kids were kicking sand in his face, and he was going to show them he wasn't a ninety-five-pound weakling! It was now or never. He had to act! It had to be this show!

At one point in our discussion, I recall, Jerry exclaimed with great intensity, "I can beat Chavez, I'll outfast him. He's too weak from the previous fasts to do one again."

It was a remarkable moment. Jerry Brown was determined to outfast Cesar Chavez! It came down to that. A primal struggle was going on. The real father, the former Governor of California, had been subdued. The symbolic father, the leader of the farmworkers' union, remained. Who would have believed it? Although we were purporting to talk about matters of state, we were actually dealing with feelings that were appropriate in a primal therapy group.

I still didn't understand, though. Why the big battle? Jerry was too smart a politician to let his unconscious aggressions run away with him. And then I remembered. A day in October 1974. Several of us were meeting Jerry at his house. I arrived a few minutes early. The front door was locked. I walked around to the back of the house and climbed over a wall. The back door was open. Two months later this would be impossible, state police would be guarding the house, but I was cold, impatient. I walked in. Jerry arrived. The others did too. We held our business meeting, and afterward Jerry started talking about nothing in particular. He was rambling, casting himself into the stream of consciousness, and the more he talked, the more I realized what a dark, pessimistic view of the world he had. It jibed with an anecdote Tom Hayden had once told me about Jerry. What did he think about when he meditated? Jerry was asked. "I think about the shortness of life and the inevitability of death," he supposedly replied. The quoted response sounded a little false, a little melodramatic, but Jerry's conversation that late fall afternoon was much in the same vein. We were making a tour of his house. He was showing me the shotgun he kept by his bed. He looked up and flung his arm out in front of him. We had been talking about whether democracy was in its terminal stages.

"People will tear each other apart if given half a chance," he exclaimed. "Politics is a jungle, and it's getting worse. People want a dictator these days, a man on a white horse. They're looking for a man on a white horse to ride in and tell them what to do. A politician can do anything he wants so long as he manipulates the right symbols."

Of course.

The Man on the White Horse.

When I heard Jerry talk about the Man on the White Horse in the fall of 1974, I assumed he was opposed to him and would do whatever was necessary to block his entry into the political arena, but now, watching him lay the battle plans for Cesar, I realized that Jerry had wanted to become the Man on the White Horse all along. Nature abhorred a vaccum, in politics as well as in anything else. If Jerry didn't fill the vacuum, somebody else would. That would be the rationalization.

I was beginning to understand. Jerry had to subdue Cesar in order to be the Man on the White Horse. Cesar was the last charismatic man in California. If Jerry was to gain charisma too, he couldn't tag along with Cesar's bill. Cesar had to submit to Jerry's bill. The father figure had to bow before the new sun in the firmament. The battle over the farm labor bill had little to do with substance, the important substantive questions having already been decided. The battle had to do with symbols, with the creation of the new symbolic hero.

It figured. In the McLuhan age of TV politics, the major conflicts were over image. In December of 1972, the Nixon administration dropped tons of high explosives on Hanoi, not to win the war but to save face, to maintain America's credibility abroad. The big political figures all tried to take on a mythic dimension. De Gaulle succeeded. So did JFK and Martin Luther King and Bobby Kennedy. Nixon and LBJ faltered in their presidencies because they failed to project a heroic sense. In the fractured, troubled world of the 1970s, the trick was to become a myth without being assassinated.

We were moving beyond the normal purview of political scientists now. Even McLuhan couldn't help us here. We were traveling in the land of myth and of the primitive mind. Myth-making. Mythology. The hero cycle. Osiris. Apollo. The young sun god. The hero archetype.

I turned to the books on the hero cycle. (Where else was there to turn to?) According to Joseph Campbell, who wrote *The Hero with a Thousand Faces,* and Erich Neumann, a brilliant psychologist who described the hero archetype in *The Origins and History of Consciousness,* there were definite stages a hero-to-be passed through in order to achieve his heroness.[52]

To begin with: He was born of a noble family. Sometimes his father was a king.

From the very beginning, he was not like other children. He felt different, he displayed precocious powers: cleverness, strength, wisdom far beyond his years.

Somewhat inexplicably, he entered into a conflict with his father.

He was cast out of — or left — the reigning house.

He wandered in the wilderness — a dark forest, the desert — where he gained a true sense of himself.

He was tempted by sirens, bewitching female figures who tried to lure him away from his path.

He resisted.

A stranger — usually an older man or woman — befriended him.

The stranger helped to show him the way.

The hero-to-be was challenged by a dragon. It was his first major test.

He subdued the dragon and won the "treasure hard to attain," a virgin, a magic lamp, a wishing ring.

Augmented with the "treasure hard to attain," the hero-to-be returned from the wilderness to face his final test: the decisive encounter with the father-figure. The father might welcome him, he might oppose him, but in any case the hero-to-be had to take the father's place. The father represented the conscious world of everyday affairs — but an old consciousness, an outmoded consciousness. By replacing the father with himself, the hero-to-be turned the old consciousness in a new direction, he manifested the new consciousness through his own being and, in so doing, he became the hero.

The hero represented the new consciousness. He appeared whenever the society was ready to change. He did in his own life what society was ready but still unable to do by itself. He showed the way so that others might follow. Disciples were gathered around. They were initiated into the secrets the hero had discovered in the wilderness. They helped to spread the new word. The cycle was completed.

Jerry was striving to complete the hero cycle. He wanted to embody the hero in a McLuhan age. He was going to become the Man on the White Horse.

Even the color that was used in the image had a significance.

White was the symbol of purity. It was also the color that reflected all the other colors of the spectrum. White was the perfect medium for mirroring the hopes and desires that ordinary mortals projected onto the hero figure.

It was a fearsome power Jerry was striving to obtain! I wondered whether I was going off my rocker. But there they were, Jerry's own words about the Man on the White Horse. Jerry was thinking about him even if the rest of us were not.

I talked to a member of the Brown administration about what I was thinking.

"Do you think I'm going buggy?" I asked her. "Is Sacramento getting to me?"

"But he *is* the man on the white horse," she said. "It's perfect." Only she wasn't worried. "His saving grace is, he isn't committed to doing anything," she said. "He'll just let the reins go free and ride around in a circle. He doesn't want to hurt anybody."

That was the bottom line so far as she was concerned. Jerry didn't want to hurt anybody. I wondered. I hoped she was right.

Chapter Nineteen

HOW TO BECOME A HERO IN TWO EASY LESSONS. THE
PARADOX OF THE ZEN ARCHER AND THE ADVANTAGES OF
SYNECDOCHE. THE GOVERNOR BUILDS HIS POPULARITY
TO NEW LEVELS.

NINETEEN SEVENTY-FIVE was a hard time for heroes.

The previous two presidents had been forced out of office.

The President prior to them had been assassinated.

Between 1966 and 1971 the proportion of the population
having "a great deal of confidence" in public officials declined
by half, according to the public opinion polls.

As of 1975, public confidence in the executive branch of
the federal government was at an all-time low.[53]

Political party identification was dropping off.

The media appeared deeply committed to an opposition
role.

It seemed as if Jerry was spitting into the wind when he
talked about the Man on the White Horse emerging.

The situation was so grim that a Harvard government professor published a report in May 1975 that concluded that
the American people were bent on cannibalizing their leaders.

The professor, whose name was Samuel P. Huntington,
conceded that Nixon and Johnson had made some errors in
judgment that were sure to antagonize the American people,
but he felt the problem went much, much deeper. America,
in his words, was suffering from a "distemper of democracy."

The people were almost like mad dogs howling at the palace gates. "People no longer felt the same obligation to obey those whom they had previously considered superior to themselves," Huntington intoned. More people wanted to participate in the system than the system could accommodate. Expectations were being raised. Institutions of higher learning were turning out more activists all the time. Politicians were beset by a rash of contradictory demands that they couldn't begin to satisfy. In an environment of "excess democracy," politicians were bound to have clay feet. They were bound to come up short. There was no more time for heroes, alas.

It was a significant analysis. Samuel P. Huntington was not just your run-of-the-mill political scientist. A former chairman of the Harvard Government Department, he was co-editor of *Foreign Affairs,* he contributed articles to *Public Interest Magazine,* which Jerry and I both read, and his pessimistic report on "the distemper of democracy" was prepared for the prestigious Trilateral Commission, which included among its members David Rockefeller, chairman of the Chase Manhattan Bank; Cyrus Vance, a secretary of the army in the Johnson years; and Jimmy Carter, former governor of Georgia.[54] If a man like Samuel P. Huntington was talking about the almost irreversible decline of political leadership, why, then, who was to say otherwise?

It was a testimony to Jerry's political genius that he saw opportunities where experts like Huntington saw only problems.

There was, first of all, the turmoil of the previous ten years. Huntington looked at it and feared the chaos would continue. Jerry, on the other hand, concluded exactly the opposite. People were tired of the stress and strain; they were exhausted; they wanted to let someone else do the driving for a change. They were ready, even eager, for a hero to emerge. There were so many bogeymen around, it was intolerable to think of the political world as being populated with nothing but Richard Nixons; and as for the revolution of expectations that had occurred during the 1960s, the economy was trailing off, and people were already lowering their expectations. Huntington was dead wrong when he suggested that the masses would continue to devour their leaders.

And that wasn't all. There was another reason as well why the Man on the White Horse could emerge in the 1970s. While Huntington assumed that Nixon and Johnson would have lost legitimacy no matter what they had done, Jerry perceived that these politicians were manifestations of an outmoded consciousness that was increasingly out of touch with the popular will. If only a political leader emerged who spoke the same language as the people did, there was no telling what he could do! Indeed, he would be all the more powerful because he would contrast with the prior, discredited political leadership. He would follow the advice uttered by Prince Hal in Shakespeare's *King Henry IV, Part 1:*

> I know you all, and will a while uphold
> The unyok'd humour of your idleness:
> Yet herein will I imitate the sun,
> Who doth permit the base contagious clouds
> To smother up his beauty from the world,
> That when he please again to be himself,
> Being wanted, he may be more wonder'd at,
> By breaking through the foul and ugly mists
> Of vapours that did seem to strangle him.
> If all the year were playing holidays,
> To sport would be as tedious as to work;
> But when they seldom come, they wish'd for come,
> And nothing pleaseth but rare accidents.
> So, when this loose behaviour I throw off,
> And pay the debt I never promised,
> By how much better than my work I am
> By so much shall I falsify men's hopes;

149

And like bright metal on a sullen ground,
My reformation, glittering o'er my fault,
Shall show more goodly and attract more eyes
Than that which hath no foil to set it off.
I'll so offend to make offense a skill;
Redeeming time when men think least I will.[55]

The prior sins Jerry was considering were not his own, personal sins, of course. They were the sins of politicians as a class. But apart from this qualification, the path Jerry determined to follow was the same as that described by Prince Hal, the future king.

The trick in negotiating the transformation was in finding the right language, and in undertaking this task, Jerry was privy to a secret that Huntington gave no indication of being aware of.

The secret was the Principle of the Zen Archer.[56]

The Principle of the Zen Archer was: Hit the target by not aiming at it.

Build up your authority by exercising less authority.

Assert your leadership by exercising less leadership.

Gain power by eschewing any interest in power.

The principle was so obvious, it escaped the experts' attention.

Thus, while Huntington called for the maximum leader to deal with the "distemper of democracy" by taking the initiative and asserting his authority, Jerry would do the opposite. He would dilly-dally around for a while and do nothing, and he would let the popular desire for a resolution of the problem reach such a fever pitch of intensity that people would plead with him to make a decision.

Likewise with the dangers of citizen activism that Huntington kept referring to. Whereas Huntington suggested that, somehow, citizen participation needed to be reduced, Jerry would encourage it, he would invite the public interest groups into the endless corridors of the bureaucracy and ask them to participate in interminable meetings and discussions.

The result, again, was paradoxical: The activists became so ensnarled in the jungle of the bureaucracy that they were no longer able to fight Jerry on the outside, where it counted, in the courts, the media, the election campaign.

So too it was with the press, which Huntington felt was unreasonably critical of political leaders. While Huntington wanted "to assure to the government the right and the ability to withhold information at the source," Jerry recognized that such a policy would only make the information more interesting and more incriminating, so he did the opposite. He threw open the floodgates of information and buried the newsmen under so much trivia, they couldn't see straight.

It was another example of the power of paradox.

One gained authority by doing nothing.

One exhausted the activists by inviting them in.

One quieted the press by giving them more information than they could handle.

More was sometimes less, and less was sometimes more, but less was almost never less and more was almost never more because that was the old politics.

One hit the target by not aiming at it.

One dealt with reality by ignoring it.

One dealt with reality by substituting symbols.

The symbols were the bow on which the Zen Archer drew his arrow.

The symbols were the arrow, too.

The symbols were the target as well.

The symbols were the means by which the Zen Archer transformed himself into something other and transported himself into another dimension.

Poor Professor Huntington, he didn't realize the symbols were the key because he was still dealing in the hot, print-oriented world. He was like the Nowhere Man in the Beatles' movie *The Yellow Submarine,* fussing, worrying, running about, saying "so little time, so much to do." He was, alas, a pre-McLuhan man in a McLuhan age.

Jerry, on the other hand, was hip, with it, cooled out, a first-class citizen of the new electronic global village, and he saw the symbols as the way out of the seemingly insoluble problems the professor was describing.

Jerry called the way out "synecdoche."

A classical Greek word revived for modern usage, synecdoche was Jerry's ace in the hole.

Synecdoche meant, quite simply, "the belief or practice in which a part of an object or person is taken as equivalent to the whole, so that anything done to, or by means of, the part is held to take effect upon, or have the effect of, the whole."

Or as Jerry defined it more succinctly for reporters later on in his term: "It's when you use a part for the whole — it's a figure of speech — like shaking one hand and giving the illusion you're shaking a million."[57]

Jerry assured the reporters he wasn't going to engage in synecdoche — but of course he had been doing it all along.

The synecdoche strategy Jerry devised in the early months of 1975 went something like this:

Granted, we can't please all the people if we develop programs that help certain groups but inevitably disadvantage other groups. If we give homeowners tax relief, for example, we will have to raise the taxes on business or cut the medical program for senior citizens, and if we slap a tax on big horsepower automobiles in order to conserve gasoline, the support we gain from the conservationists will be more than counterbalanced by the opposition we generate from the big car owners. But what if, at the very beginning of our administration, we adopt no programs of significant size and instead restrict ourselves to symbolic gestures that portend something more? Taxes won't have to be raised, the government won't increase in size, the big interest groups won't be antagonized — and at the same time the voters will feel we are moving in the right direction.

The principle of synecdoche was based upon the perception Bob Gnaizda once stated to me as we were walking over to the Governor's office: "You know," he said without the slightest hint of irony in his voice, "people really don't expect very much of us. All they ask is that we don't make the problems worse and that we try."

Jerry would try, all right; he would use the part as if it were the whole. Thus, instead of increasing welfare benefits for 100,000 black mothers, he would appoint a black judge to the Court of Appeals. Rather than authorizing a substantial reorganization of the prepaid health program, he would inveigh against state subsidies for bureaucrats' briefcases. In lieu of shaking up the schools in order to develop better reading programs, he would make public appearances with rock bands. (Kids liked rock bands better than schools anyway.) Instead of planning major reductions in the property tax, he would save a few dollars by flying tourist class on Pacific Southwest Airlines. Instead of favoring a tax on gasoline-gobbling automobiles, he would drive a compact car. He would do in the microcosm of his own life what it was too risky to do in the larger world. And so, in the calculus of synecdoche, personal example replaced program, appointments were used as well-meaning gestures while systematic reforms were delayed, and style substituted for substance.

Escapism prevailed.

Escapism wasn't an entirely new development in the American culture, of course. In the 1930s, the country decided to go to the movies instead of have a revolution. But what was different about Jerry and California and the 1970s was that the symbolic manipulation was more pervasive, and it was generated more in the political arena. In the 1930s, Hollywood was Hollywood and Washington was Washington and almost never did the twain meet, but by the 1970s politics and entertainment were merging. First there was Reagan, the entertainer turned politician, and now there was Jerry, the politician turned entertainer.

Synecdoche made perfect sense in the McLuhan age, when television enlarged — and made lifelike — everything it portrayed on the screen. Television was a personality medium; it focused on the individual who epitomized the mass. TV visuals could take account of no more than ten to twenty people on the screen; any larger number would be lost in the background. There was no difference between a $100,000 and a $100,000,000 government project except three zeroes, and the television viewers didn't notice the difference. They were watching the facial expressions of the newsman who was making the announcement. With the electronic media, the world was reduced to a box, and what went on in the box was reality.

It was like when I was a little boy. On the blotter of my father's desk rested a glass bell that contained a miniature winter scene and a tiny snowman inside. I would pick up the ball and shake it, and simulated snowflakes would fall on the tiny snowman. It was a perfect little environment, complete in itself, and I would gaze at it for hours. Even if it was a hot, muggy, summer day outside, I could make the snow fall on the snowman inside the glass ball.

"Look, Dad, it's snowing in July," I would say.

"Yes, Jim, I can see, it's snowing in July," my father would reply.

It was still snowing in July. Jerry was just doing on a grander scale what I had done with my little glass ball. And what Jerry practiced to perfection, others in the Brown administration would copy, at first with some hesitancy and then with more assurance. It got to the point that those of us in the inner circle of the administration could do synecdoche in our sleep. Mario Obledo didn't bother working on a jobs program for the unemployed; he simply went to a local unemployment office one day a month and talked to people about their problems. Bob Gnaizda sponsored a couple of commemorative days for blacks and Mexican-Americans and Filipinos. The Filipinos were additionally honored when the bright green Health and Welfare Agency sign was translated into Tagalog, a primary dialect of the Philippines. The American Indians were remembered when a number of their ancestral photographs (the Edward S. Curtis series) were hung on the walls of the Health and Welfare Agency. I remember thinking at the time, Well, native Americans, we can't give you any jobs, we can't give you more food stamps, but we want you to know, we have your pictures hanging on our walls and we're thinking of you...

Synecdoche was not only rationalized in terms of television, it could also be justified in terms of accepted business and political practices. During the 1960s, the Great Society had created programs on a mammoth scale that aborted as soon as they were implemented. (They weren't just disasters; they were colossal disasters.) We, the careful generation of the 1970s, would be more circumspect; we would develop small models of our programs and road-test them before they went into mass production. And we would conduct market research in the political arena as well. The little programs were trial balloons. If, after they were introduced on a small scale, they picked up widespread support, they could be enlarged quite easily, assuming the money was available. After all, the symbol of the programs had already been introduced into people's minds; all we would be doing later on was adding a few zeroes. One of Jerry's advisers called it the foot-in-the-door approach. We were like door-to-door salesmen giving away free samples. If the samples caught on, great, the public might be willing to subscribe to a complete set of encyclopedias. And if not, well, too bad...

We didn't talk much about the second possibility within the Brown administration. Nor did we consider the obvious danger of the synecdoche strategy: that Jerry might legitimize himself so much with the little symbols that he wouldn't have to do anything more. The symbols might become a diversion, an end in themselves; they might give people a false sense of security; they might become a rationalization for callousness and indifference.

In the 1960s, synecdoche was called "tokenism." In the 1970s, synecdoche wasn't called anything pejorative; it was often the operating principle of government.

Cesar Chavez was the first person who educated me about the abuses of synecdoche. It was sometime in 1968, if I remember correctly. Bob Gnaizda and his legal associate Marty Glick were representing a group of farmworkers who had been precipitously fired by a Salinas lettuce grower. Bob and Marty contended the firings occurred because the farmworkers were supporting the farmworkers' union. The grower disagreed. A Catholic priest was brought in to interview the growers' employees, and one of the growers' foremen, a good Catholic, told the priest that the firings had been solely because of the union connection. The priest signed an affidavit, which Bob and Marty presented to the grower. The grower capitulated and not only agreed to hire back the men but also to submit to arbitration if, at any time in the future, he tried to fire the men again. Bob and Marty were jubilant. The victory went to their heads. In a press release, they said that the settlement amounted to "a little National Labor Relations Act for farmworkers." Cesar hit the roof. Bob and Marty's press release would make the urban liberals think his organizing efforts were unnecessary, he said. They were undercutting the union. The union was the only answer for the farmworkers. Bob and Marty were letting their egos interfere with the farmworkers' efforts.

It was a good lesson — but history had a way of repeating itself. One day in the winter of 1975, Bob staged a memorial ceremony for Leonard Carter, the western regional director of the NAACP who had died the previous year. Bob and Mario Obledo had worked closely with Leonard during the early 1970s. Bob wanted to do something to honor Leonard, so the conference room of the Health and Welfare Agency was to be dedicated in Leonard Carter's memory. Officials of the NAACP were invited to the ceremony; about 125 people were present; Leonard's wife and teen-age son were the guests of honor. After Mario displayed the silver plaque that was to be placed next to the conference room door, Leonard's son delivered a few words of thanks. I remember thinking at the time, what an eloquent statement it was. The son began by thanking Mario. He acknowledged Bob's close relationship with his father. He said he and his mother were privileged to be present at the ceremonies. His father had worked for many years without recognition, fighting not just for the rights of black people but for all the poor and the oppressed, he said. Despite differences he had had with his father about how fast the black liberation movement should proceed, he had respected his father, he respected what his father had done, and he hoped the work would be continued. But, he added — and here there was a slight pause — it was not enough to hold dedication ceremonies. There were many people without jobs, without food. He trusted the dedication ceremony would not be used in place of the more fundamental reforms that had to be instituted in the society.

I looked over at Bob. Bob looked away. Bob knew — I knew — that the Leonard Carter dedication ceremony was the only program for black people that Bob and Mario were working on.

The kid was very sharp. The Leonard Carter boy had picked up on the dangers of synecdoche. But as of the winter of 1975, he was a voice crying out in the wilderness. The synecdoche strategy was working like a charm. The public wasn't requiring anything more of Jerry. In the spring of the same year, the California (Field) Poll reported that 86 per cent of the voters sampled approved of the job Jerry was doing.[58] It was the highest approval rating in the history of the California Poll. Jerry was confounding the experts; he was showing them how to become a hero. I thought of the advertisement for correspondence school piano lessons that appeared in the comic books we read when we were kids: "They laughed when he sat down, but when he started to play . . ."

Jerry was playing all right, he was playing his way right into an 86 per cent approval rating. He was a regular Rachmaninoff on the political keyboard.

Chapter Twenty

THE BEST DEFENSE IS A GOOD OFFENSE. THE GOVERNOR
OBFUSCATES SOME MORE. THE GOVERNOR IS SCOLDED BY
ROSE BIRD. THE GOVERNOR LAUNCHES A VERBAL COUN-
TERATTACK AND TALKS ABOUT PUTTING BLACK KIDS IN
A MILITARY COMPOUND.

I CAN STILL SEE him coming down the hall of some state
agency, flanked by aides, bursting through the door like a
karate chop. The occupants would quiver and flutter like a
covey of quail taken by surprise. That was the whole point.
Take them by surprise. Don't let them get set. Don't give
them the chance to lay any demands on you. Keep moving.
Conduct the encounter on your terms. Break people's rhythm.
Speed things up. Change the subject. Create a small
disruption. Ask questions and more questions. Keep the ball
in the other guy's court. Put him on the defensive. If he per-
sists in rallying, break off contact. Resume the game with
somebody else. Remember, always remember, the best defense is a good offense.

One morning, I recall, Jerry zeroed in on a secretary who
said she was leaving the department in two weeks. Why was
she leaving? Jerry wanted to know. Hadn't her supervisor
tried to persuade her to stay? Wasn't the department a good
place to work? The woman tried to explain she was leaving
for personal reasons, but Jerry wouldn't let go. Her plans
were like a Mount Everest that had to be conquered! The

woman's supervisor became panicky. He had prepared a special talk for the Governor. Time was running out. He had no chance to plead for more money. Jerry looked at him and moved away to another part of the room. "You," he said, pointing to a middle-aged man in a white shirt, "what's your title around here?" Jerry said the word "title" with a little laugh, as if all titles were ridiculous. The man's answer caught in his throat. I followed the path of Jerry's still-outstretched forefinger. Like a laser beam, it was pointed to a spot about three inches below the man's belt buckle. Ah, yes. I knew how the man felt. Jerry had done it to me on occasion, and invariably, one's immediate desire was to double up and cup one's hands over one's groin. Talk about putting people on the defensive! Jerry was at it once again.

Jerry regarded the man for several seconds without saying anything, as if to measure him fully, and then walked out of the room. He had spent fifteen minutes in the department, and the state employees hadn't asked him a single question. Afterward, a friend of mine in the administration said, "He's always been ahead, all his life he's had a lead to protect. He spends much of his time keeping people from getting close."

I couldn't disagree. However, the evasions were sometimes easier to see when he was dealing with other people than when he was dealing with oneself.

There was the employment issue, for example. Was he playing around or was he serious? The logic of synecdoche suggested that the farmworkers might be enough to make him a hero, but Gnaizda kept on saying that any day now Jerry would hold the big meeting on the employment program. I couldn't tell. Jerry had sent me so many different signals over the past two months. The first jobs memo was "too short," he said; the second was "too long, too complicated." One morning we set aside some time to talk about the program, only to end up discussing the Zen Center vegetable farm Jerry and Gnaizda had visited on a previous weekend. Another day in early May, Jerry telephoned with the request that I look into the feasibility of expanding the Ecology Corps, which Reagan had started. "Maybe that's the way to go," Jerry said, "developing jobs for teen-agers." Jerry also wanted to know about David Commons. "What's this I hear about Commons working for you?" he asked. I said Commons helped me out of a jam with the building trades; I had hired him as a consultant. "Commons makes enough money as it is clipping coupons," Jerry replied. I said if he didn't want me paying Commons, I would terminate the contract immediately, but I still wanted to use him as an adviser. Jerry indicated he had no objection. I hung up the phone.

We were going on detours, driving around in circles. Jerry admitted that the major economic initiatives had to come from the federal government. At the same time, he didn't want any of his appointees traveling to Washington to lobby. "Washington's the wrong symbol," he told me in February when he personally canceled a trip I had scheduled to the nation's capital. "People are sick of the federal government. Stay in California. Find the answers out here."

It was something of a dilemma. We couldn't find the answers to the unemployment problem without involving the federal government, and we couldn't involve the federal government without calling up a symbol that Jerry found politically offensive. I finally decided the only possible solution was a two-step approach: a model state program, followed by a call for federal action. It sounded sensible and Jerry agreed to the first part in principle, but who knew if we would ever reach the second stage? As of April, the joke around Sacramento was that Jerry had not yet extended diplomatic recognition to the federal government, and by May, I noticed, the more the grapevine buzzed with talk about Brown-for-President in 1976, the more Jerry studiously avoided any mention of Washington. It was paradoxical, if indeed he was planning on running for President. The greater his desire to go to Washington, the less we could consider Washington in our programmatic plans.

In frustration, I threw the *I Ching,* or *Book of Changes,* as it is sometimes called, just to see what would happen. The throw I got was a little eerie, unsettling. Out of sixty-four possibilities I could have come up with, I drew fortune sixty-two, "The Preponderance of the Small." It read as follows:

> ... Perseverance furthers,
> Small things may be done; great things
>   should not be done.
> The flying bird brings the message:
> It is not well to strive upwards,
> It is well to remain below.
> Great good fortune ...

This was the first part of the fortune. The passage then continued with "The Image" and the commentary on "The Image":

> The Image
> Thunder on the mountain:
> The image of Preponderance of the Small.
> Thus in his conduct the superior man gives
>   preponderance to reverence ...
> In his expenditures he gives preponderance
>   to thrift ...
> ... the superior man ... must always fix
> his eyes more closely and more directly on duty
> than does the ordinary man, even though this
> might make his behavior seem petty to the
> outside world ...
> But the essential significance of his attitude
> lies in the fact that in external matters
> he is on the side of the lowly.[59]

The fortune seemed like a confirmation of what Jerry was doing. But then again, it wasn't totally unambiguous. The unemployed could be characterized as "the small," "the lowly." At some point in the future, the fortune seemed to be saying, their time would come.

Toward the end of May, I journeyed to San Francisco to

have breakfast with John Dunlop, the secretary of labor in the Ford administration, and Don Vial, the new state director of industrial relations. Dunlop was in a jovial, even an exuberant, mood, and he regaled Don and me with the story of how, when he arrived in Washington and saw the mammoth office reserved for him, he felt so overwhelmed that he set up his desk and bookshelves in a small room next door. He used the big office only for ceremonial occasions, he said. He also told us how he flew home to Belmont, Massachusetts, every weekend to spend a few peaceful hours with his wife.

I was most impressed. What a breath of fresh air this man was! Despite the importance of his position, he still attached a high priority to his family, and he didn't put out a press release every time he rejected the pomp and circumstance of government. Perhaps there were advantages in proving oneself in academic life or business or law before one entered government service. Dunlop seemed so much more secure than the young men and women who were crowding their way into Sacramento. He seemed to be saying, in effect: "I have certain standards. This government job isn't the be-all and end-all of my life. If I can't perform it and remain true to myself, I'll leave."

I told Dunlop the story of the Jobs March and the portable toilets.

He and Don Vial were much amused.

Dunlop said he hadn't realized things were "so different" in California.

I said yes, I thought they were.

We talked for a while about business matters. Don Vial said the new Occupational Safety and Health Act was causing some problems, and I described the inadequacies of the Employment Service, which was under the joint jurisdiction of the U.S. Department of Labor and the State Employment Development Department.

Dunlop said yes, maybe we could work out a "redesign" of

the Employment Service and try it out in a single state like California. Would I be interested in coming back to Washington for several days to work on it with him?

I said I would, except that I was having difficulties getting out of the state. I related the story about the February trip that Jerry canceled. Maybe, I said, I would have more luck if the Department of Labor paid my plane fare. Would he be willing to approve the expenditure?

Yes, Dunlop said, he would.

"Are you sure?" I responded. "You know, a round-trip ticket is about as expensive as leasing six portable toilets for an afternoon. Do you think I'm worth six portable toilets?"

"Ah, yes," Dunlop replied. "In economics, we have a principle to deal with that problem. It's called the theory of marginal utility. Let's see," he mused, "using the theory of marginal utility, I would say you're worth six portable toilets . . . but not seven."

He laughed heartily.

I laughed.

Vial laughed.

I had discovered my true worth! — from a Harvard economics professor who was secretary of labor, no less — six portable toilets but not seven . . .

We concluded the meeting on that note. It had been a nice respite.

Meanwhile, back in Sacramento, events were proceeding apace. Jerry had agreed to convene a meeting on the unemployment problem. "We'll go for as long as it takes," he told me. I would bring in the EDD research staff and whatever other consultants I needed. We would talk the problem through, from soup to nuts.

Two days before the meeting was to be held, Mario Obledo and I were standing in Jerry's office. "Maybe what we should do," Jerry said, "is cancel the whole cost-of-living increase for state employees and use the money to hire the unemployed. That $240 million could create a lot of jobs."

Obledo was enthusiastic about the idea. "Yes, Governor," he said, "that's what we should do. The state employees aren't worth the money they're receiving anyway."

I, however, sensed a problem. The $240 million cost-of-living increase was set forth in black and white in the Governor's budget. Rose Bird, who was Jerry's chief negotiator with the state employees, had already agreed to the $240 million increase in principle. If Jerry pulled back at this late date, there would be cries of bad faith, as well as a strike. Oroville Dam would probably shut down. Electric lights would go off all over California. The unemployment insurance clerks would walk off the job. The people who were out of work wouldn't receive their bimonthly checks. Jerry couldn't be serious about the proposal. It was the old game of confusion he was playing.

I decided not to participate in the game. The day before the jobs meeting was scheduled, I met with Rose to fill her in on what was transpiring. Yes, she agreed, it was a frivolous proposal, but she had better attend the meeting anyway. Although she was supposed to appear at a legislative hearing on the farm labor bill, she could slip away for a few moments.

I told her I wanted no part of the $240 million.

She smiled a little. There was no conceivable possibility of my getting it, she said.

She seemed quite exhausted.

The jobs meeting commenced much like the Catherine Jermany interview. Jerry asked rhetorical questions; he didn't wait for answers; he talked about the state of the world; he filibustered. And then Rose entered the room.

What was this about the $240 million? she asked.

Yes, Jerry said, he was thinking about using the money for a jobs program. Some of the state employees were earning too much as it was. There might be better uses for the money and he ...

Rose didn't let him finish. She read him the riot act. The

Brown administration had already agreed to the $240 million increase, she said. She had been negotiating on that assumption for weeks. Jerry knew it, the state employees knew it, the only question remaining was how the $240 million would be divided up among the state employees. Jerry couldn't go back on his word. Nobody would believe him again. The state employees needed the pay increases, even the people earning $20,000 a year needed the money. The cost of living was going up. Many of the state employees had families. Jerry had no idea what it was like to support a family on $15,000 or $20,000 a year.

Rose went on and on. She really ground him down.

I looked around for Obledo. He was nowhere in sight.

I looked over at Jerry. He wasn't making a sound. He was just sitting there, taking it, his head hanging like a little boy whose mommy had caught him raiding the cookie jar.

It was a strange moment, *another* strange moment in the life and times of the Brown administration.

Mama Bird and Jerry Bird. The mama was chastizing the baby for having dirtied the nest.

A bizarre thought came into my head. All of our mothers were sitting around the conference table. My mother. Jerry's mother. Mario's mother. They were drinking tea and chatting amiably, and although they didn't know much about the workings of government, they were making fast work of the jobs program. Yes, this was a good idea. No, they didn't like that. Yes, they would do this now and that in six months, if the money was available. There was no nonsense, no games. They didn't know enough to go through the elaborate digressions that we, their sons, involved ourselves in.

Rose had concluded now. The matter was resolved. The $240 million digression was dead.

She turned on her heel and walked out of the room.

Nobody said anything.

The discussion finally resumed, desultorily at first and then with more animation. We were back to the world of reality, talking about the problems of black kids. "If only we can find jobs for black kids," somebody said. "The unemployment problem boils down to the problem of the black kids, 40 per cent of whom are unemployed."

Jerry broke in. "What about Camp Roberts?" he asked.

The people in the room looked confused. Camp Roberts was an old army base in San Luis Obispo County that wasn't being used.

"You know what we should do?" he said. He looked a little churlish, as if he had something to prove. "We should take 20,000 black kids and 20,000 white kids and put them together in Camp Roberts. The black kids can teach the white kids how to fight and the white kids can teach the black kids how to read."

Jerry gesticulated. "It's perfect," he laughed, gazing around the room.

Nobody else laughed. I looked over at Al Saldamando, the legal counsel at EDD, who was sitting across from me. He grimaced. Bob Rosenberg, who was sitting cater-cornered to me, rolled his eyes. They couldn't believe it. Jerry was making a blatantly racist remark.

I tried to figure out what he was driving at. Rosenberg hadn't seen him in action before. I had. The Camp Roberts image was so vivid. Forty thousand kids. They would be wearing uniforms, no doubt. A fence was already constructed around the entire facility. There would be a curfew, rules and regulations, and counselors to enforce the regulations. The counselors would be dressed like guards. The guards would sit in little wooden shelters on cold winter nights. The little shelters would look like sentry houses, watchtowers; the whole place sounded like a detention center, a concentration camp.

Black kids in a concentration camp?

(Yes, but it would be an *integrated* concentration camp.)

He wasn't serious!

He was being outrageous.

He was throwing outlandish images at us, blowing our minds.

He wasn't ready to make a decision yet, but he was unwilling to say so directly, for some reason.

Jerry was evading me once again.

Chapter Twenty-One

THE AUTHOR MEDITATES UPON THE GOVERNOR'S RELUC-
TANCE TO UNDERTAKE AN EMPLOYMENT PROGRAM. THE
GOVERNOR URGES THE AUTHOR TO BE MORE ESOTERIC AND
CONSULT *The Whole Earth Catalog* FOR GUIDANCE. THE
AUTHOR DOES SO WITH SOME MISGIVINGS.

IT WOULDN'T BE FAIR to suggest that Jerry was the only
politician who was dilly-dallying around about the unemployment issue.

He was just more forthright about articulating his uneasiness than the others were.

For three months now, it had been the same. I would go
up to the legislature to talk about various ways of generating
jobs; I would get platitudes and pleasantries in return. I
would inquire about the possibility of letter-writing campaigns and trips to Washington; the legislators would tell
me how busy their schedules were. I formed the distinct impression that people were willing, even eager, to do something, but they wanted somebody else to make the first move.
They were prevaricating.

What were they all so wary of? The difficulty was not
with the end we were trying to achieve. Everyone agreed,
work was a wonderful idea. The problem was, rather, with
the means by which the meritorious end was to be achieved.
This was where the uneasiness arose and the politicians
started looking down at their shoes and coughing in their

hands. There was no consensus, and because of the size of the stakes involved, nobody wanted to experiment. The employment problem was like a gigantic gorilla in the rain forest. There was no telling what the gorilla would do if the white hunters tried to capture him. "My God, Captain, do you see the size of that footprint! I'd rather not go in there, sir, if you don't mind." The employment problem was the King Kong of political issues. The politicians weren't necessarily able to say how or why the issue was dangerous, since many of them weren't very sophisticated about matters of economic theory, but they knew in their stomachs it was. Their highly developed survival instincts told them that much.

What was to be done? Reagan dealt with the problem by forming an Ecology Corps. Beginning in 1971, small numbers of unemployed youth were rounded up in the cities, shipped off to "ecology centers" in the mountains, handed picks and shovels, and told to fight fires. The operation never exceeded 500 "corpsmen" at any one time. Little, if any, training was provided. Of the 2600 young people who "graduated" from the program, few obtained jobs in private industry. (It was the rare corporation that was fighting fires in the Sierra Nevadas.) According to one state official who evaluated the program in 1975, "significant" numbers of seventeen- and eighteen-year-olds dropped out of the program because they were homesick. In reality, the Ecology Corps was a dead end. As a symbol, however, it was very effective. Black and brown youths were being removed from the cities where they, or their ilk, were causing trouble. They were quarantined in remote areas of the state and housed in a militarylike setting, organized, disciplined, contained. Whereas in the 1960s black and brown youth had rampaged through the central cities, starting fires, now they were being paid to put fires out! Uniforms had even been provided, green uniforms. The black power of the 1960s would give way to the green power of the 1970s. The black teen-agers would be surrounded by trees, deep in the primeval forest, out of sight, out of mind. Reagan's dream was reminiscent of Jerry's Camp Roberts fantasy. The fact that they both reached the same conclusion indicated how safe youth programs were politically.

I resolved to improve on Reagan's model. There were a number of changes we could make that would make the program less racist in its imagery and more real in its operation.

First, we would move the program into the cities, where it would reach larger numbers of young people at less cost. The state would not have to pay room and board; the homesickness problem would be avoided.

Second, we would vary the kinds of jobs provided, build in a training component, upgrade the skills of the program participants, and give them some choice as to what they could do.

Third, we would dovetail our youth program with adult public service projects so that if the youth program enrollees were unable to find private sector jobs later on, they would still have a place to go.

Fourth, we would hire unemployed union members as work supervisors in order to win union support for the experiment.

Finally, and perhaps most important, we would try to work through private nonprofit corporations as much as possible in order to avoid an expansion of the government bureaucracy. It was bad enough that the government was going to be paying the bill; it was even worse if we expanded the government bureaucracy unnecessarily. The bureaucracy was too much like a dinosaur: slow to act, impervious to change, with a brain the size of a grapefruit. The nonprofit corporations were more flexible; they also could spin off profit-making adjuncts. At some later date we could open up the jobs program to the private sector.

It all made sense. The only problem was that I had been proposing variations of this strategy for the previous three months, and Jerry hadn't approved anything I'd given him. Finally I decided that because Jerry was so enamored with symbols, I had to come up with a new image for public service employment.

But what might the new image be? I thought through all the conversations I had had with Jerry over the previous eight months. What, if anything, did he want? There was an afternoon in October 1974, I remembered. We were sitting on the couch in Jerry's living room, talking about the problems of old people. "Do you know what I want to do?" Jerry asked. "I want to bring the generations together," he said, answering his own question. "You ought to look into it. Old people could help out in day-care centers, young people could take care of shut-ins. We could pay them a little bit every week."

Then there was another afternoon in May 1975. Jerry's father had turned up with Eddie Albert, the movie actor, who hoped to persuade Jerry to support the urban gardens project Eddie Albert was working on in Los Angeles. The idea was springing up all over the country, Eddie Albert said. Vacant land was being made available in the cities. People were supplied with seeds and tools; they learned the virtues of self-reliance, cooperation, thrift. The projects reminded him of his own boyhood in Indiana. Jerry seemed enthusiastic. He also wanted to get his father and Eddie Albert out of his office. "Look into this," he said as he turned Eddie Albert over to me and guided us out the door. "We might be able to build a jobs program around it."

The incident was one of many. The ideas cascaded out at times. Jerry was full of suggestions. He wanted to do something original, unique. The Zen Center in San Francisco was a model for him. Jerry talked about the Zen Center a lot. Richard Baker, the center's director, was a friend of Jerry's. On weekends, Jerry went to Green Gulch, the cooperative farm the Zen Center maintained in Marin County. Jerry liked to sit in the sun there, relax and talk to people there. He felt at ease in the austere, quiet environment, which seemed to remind him of his days in the seminary. On one occasion, after Richard Baker and I and two of Richard Baker's friends had been sitting in Jerry's office, Jerry described to me how the Zen Center was trying to "clean up" a black neighborhood by setting a good example. The Zen Center's building, which was located in the middle of the neighborhood, was kept in immaculate condition, and a grocery store, stocked with produce from Green Gulch, was opening up down the block. "Maybe that's the way to go," Jerry said. "Cooperative ownership; everybody works, nobody makes much money."

There were other conversations in February and March and April in which Jerry urged me to consult E. F. Schumacher and *The Whole Earth Catalog* for innovative ideas. At first I didn't respond very enthusiastically to his suggestions, which seemed farfetched, but Jerry kept talking about the do-it-yourself notions in the two books so often that finally I capitulated. One weekend I sat down and studied the most recent version of *The Whole Earth Catalog* from cover to cover.[60] It was incredible. There were notations on the amount of drinking water a toilet wastes every time it flushes (four to five gallons), the perniciousness of industrial growth and capitalism (E. S. Schumacher again), mail-order chickens, dwarf fruit trees, tepee makers, tepee poles and the erection thereof, whipmaking, glassblowing, the manly art of knitting, how to take the worry out of being close, doing away with Christmas presents, living poor with style, breath coordination, the atlas of sexual pleasures, daily life in revolutionary China, motorcycle repair, guerrilla television, post-scarcity anarchism, stone-age economics, no more public school, psycho sources, serious games, an atlas of fantasy, the book of the weird, time tripping, the complete out-of-door job, business and professions book, pioneer life in Western Pennsylvania, the beginner's guide to dousing, basic drug manufacture, the botany and chemistry of hallucination, and an R. Crumb cartoon of a pointy-eared monster with polka-dot pants, masturbating. *The Whole Earth Catalog* was certainly a far cry from Dayton, Ohio, where I had grown up. There wasn't a single word about baseball in the whole book.

But perhaps I was too much of the prosaic Midwesterner at heart.

I began working on describing the jobs program in *Whole Earth Catalog* terms that Jerry would like. "People are encouraged to be more self-sufficient," I wrote. "They also help each other." "Senior citizens are employed as teachers' aides in child-care centers." "Unemployed teen-age girls work as shoppers' aides for bedridden senior citizens." "Six to seven Vietnam veterans are trained and employed as security guards for senior citizens who are being mugged and robbed in San Francisco's Tenderloin district." "Construction workers and teen-age youth repair Los Angeles schools damaged by vandals." "Unemployed laborers work with Indian youth to build a hiking trail." "Teen-age girls and boys work on venereal disease control for a neighborhood health clinic." It was all there, not a program so much as a series of newspaper headlines. I was losing my virginity politically, playing synecdoche at long last. I decided I wasn't too proud to play synecdoche if we could use the symbols to bootstrap our way into a real jobs program later on. The important thing was that the symbols lead somewhere. I even threw in a quotation from E. F. Schumacher. Every observation Jerry had made over the previous six months I regurgitated back to him, packaged and symbolized in his own likeness. It seemed a little unnecessary to me and slightly hokey, but if those were the cosmetics he wanted...I was willing to stand on my head to get a jobs program.

David Commons was very enthusiastic about the revised memo when I showed it to him, and Bob Gnaizda said he agreed with it "almost 100 per cent." "Mario liked it too when he read it," Bob told me later. Bob said he thought a few changes should be made to involve profit-making corporations in the first stage, but basically he was ready to go with it. "It's just Jerry's style," Bob observed. I hoped so. I had gone through conniptions trying to cast the obvious in esoteric terms.

Chapter Twenty-Two

THE GOVERNOR DANGLES A JOBS PROGRAM IN FRONT OF
THE AUTHOR AND THEN PULLS IT AWAY. THE AUTHOR
BLOWS HIS STACK.

THE NEWS WAS too good to be true.

"You're kidding," I said to Alice Daniels, Jerry's deputy
legal counsel, who was calling from the Governor's office.
"He's playing around again."

"No, Jim," Alice replied with some conviction. "I really
think he's serious this time. It's the chance you've been waiting for. Jerry told Gray Davis to work on it full time.
You're supposed to tell them how to spend the money on
jobs."

Alice wasn't talking about pennies from heaven. Fifty
million dollars was the figure mentioned, $50 million for
jobs. The money was to be taken from the Law Enforcement
Assistance Act (LEAA) program, which Jerry had previously
publicly characterized as "gibberish and mishmash." Instead
of spending the money on armored cars, walkie-talkies, television surveillance systems in parks, and on a lot of other
technological gimcrackery that seemed to be of little use in
decreasing the crime rate, Jerry was apparently proposing
that we go to the root of the problem and hire unemployed
teen-agers in high-crime neighborhoods. The suggestion was
so audacious in its concept and scope, it took my breath away.
Jerry was thinking about an approach, which, almost liter-

ally, would turn the guns (and armored cars) into plow-
shares and would dramatize, as never before, the underlying
connection between unemployment and crime. I took my hat
off to him. He was brilliant. The only question was whether
the police would go along. Alice felt they would. So did
Gray Davis, Jerry's executive secretary, when I talked to him
the same day. "We think we can handle the police. Don't
even worry about it. Jerry wants you to tell us how to spend
the money."

It was an exhilarating prospect. EDD already had the job
proposals on the drafting board; all we needed to do was
plug them into Jerry's crime prevention program. The EDD
staff was ecstatic when I told them the news. Although we
had been disappointed before on jobs proposals that Jerry did
nothing with, this time *felt* different. Jerry was more specific
about what he wanted; he had a particular plan in mind, it
appeared. The money was available, and the critical tie-in
had been made between unemployment and crime. The Governor's office was working with a sense of urgency they had
never shown before. The farmworker issue, which had occupied Jerry's attention for months, was almost resolved, and
the newspapers were saying he had scored a brilliant victory,
which he had. The Man on the White Horse had finally
emerged for all to see, resplendent, commanding. Perhaps
now for the first time Jerry had the time and the confidence
to grapple with the unemployment problem. I was willing
to suspend my disbelief.

We began working day and night, talking to criminolo-
gists, union leaders, and government officials who knew the
ins and outs of the LEAA funding game. All the initial signs
were favorable. Jack Henning, the secretary-treasurer of
the state AFL-CIO, and Jimmie Lee, the statewide head of the
building trades, were favorably disposed. Jerry Whipple, the
leader of the UAW on the West Coast, was willing to spon-
sor a car-repair project for teen-agers. The word from the
LEAA experts was that the Law Enforcement Assistance Ad-

ministration, which disbursed the funds from Washington, would agree to almost anything in order to avoid a controversy; they were in trouble with Congress. Even the key police chiefs in the state might be inclined to support the project if Jerry approved their pet projects and agreed to continue local control. After all, wasn't it the Los Angeles police chief, Ed Davis, who over the previous two years had spoken out again and again on the dangers of juvenile delinquency? If Davis, the most influential law enforcement officer in the state, could be won over — if the conversion of the LEAA money could be described as his brainchild, for example — we were home free.

When it rained money, it poured, it seemed. During the course of our work on the LEAA program, Bob Rosenberg came in with the news that, as a result of the revisions we had made in a special work incentive program for welfare recipients that EDD was administering, $5 million had been saved. Did I realize what that meant? he asked. The money could be used to fund some of our model jobs projects! We didn't have to ask Jerry for state money! A state jobs program could be funded completely with federal dollars!

It was a sunny day in Mudville. Casey was at the bat. I felt sure he would drive the runners home. A bandwagon effect was developing all over Sacramento, and state officials were rushing to climb on board. As of early June 1975, the Business and Transportation Agency was working on its own job proposal while the Department of Conservation was exploring the feasibility of expanding the Ecology Corps. Allard Lowenstein, the former congressman who had led the dump-Johnson movement in 1968, was going to be working in the Governor's office during the summer. He was primed to persuade Jerry to lead a youth movement that would declare as its first priority a jobs program for teen-agers. I couldn't have been happier. The air was filled with excitement and possibility. At one meeting, which was held in the Governor's office shortly after I finished my *Whole Earth*

Catalog revision of the jobs program, Jerry said money was no problem. He was willing to put state money into the jobs project if necessary. The state was going to be running a surplus in excess of $400 million; most of this amount was being held in reserve for pet projects Jerry had in mind. He wanted to make some dramatic moves. There was even a secret fund stashed away in the state health department budget. The legislators thought the money would be needed for medical care for the aged, but the costs of this program wouldn't run as high as they anticipated or as the administration was letting on. Jerry said I should think about tapping as much money as I needed. I couldn't believe my ears. Did he mean a sum as large as $50 million? I asked. He seemed to nod assent. A hundred million? I asked. He nodded again. He didn't appear to be disagreeing with the figures I was citing. I asked once more. This time I posed the question to Bob Gnaizda as we were going out the door of Jerry's office. "Use the $100 million figure," Bob replied. "Work on that assumption."

I did. We were going full tilt by now. With the $5 million Rosenberg had saved, we began drafting contracts that would be entered into with community-based, nonprofit corporations. One of the organizations we talked to was TELACU, the East Los Angeles Community Union. TELACU was a beautiful organization. Originally financed by the United Automobile Workers, TELACU had administered teen-age job projects for several years, as well as a credit union. They seemed to have the administrative competence and the financial stability to be able to expand. I approved a $1 million jobs contract for them. The project was to be jointly sponsored by TELACU and the Los Angeles Building Trades Council. Unemployed building tradesmen would work with low-income teen-agers. An abandoned East Los Angeles jail would be converted into a community center, thereby fulfilling Jerry's dream of turning the instruments of repression into symbols of peace and understanding. David Commons even suggested we erect a sign at the job site stating that the work was proceeding under the auspices of the Governor of California. I thought it was a fine idea. The money we were talking about would carry us far beyond the dangers of symbolic manipulation. The $155 million — or $5 million from WIN, $50 million from LEAA, and $100 million from the state surplus — would generate 54,000 six-month jobs, or enough work to employ one out of every four young people in the state who were unemployed. The money wouldn't last forever, of course, but by the time it ran out, the federal government might be pressured into doing more about the problem. These 54,000 jobs would give Jerry a lot of moral credibility when and if he flew to Washington to lobby. He wouldn't even have to raise state or local property taxes in order to start the program.

The news from Washington was also reassuring. The previous year, a black congressman from Los Angeles, Augustus F. Hawkins, had introduced a bill, entitled the Equal Opportunity and Full Employment Act, which required the federal government to insure a job for every American who was willing and able to work. Now, in the late spring of 1975, the Hawkins bill was picking up support. The Black Caucus in the House of Representatives endorsed it, as did a number of other congressmen and senators. There was talk that Hubert Humphrey, one of the most respected Democrats in the Senate, would agree to cosponsor it. Although the bill, as then drafted, was likely to prove inflationary and although it contained some disquieting references to centralized economic planning, it was nevertheless a step in the right direction because, at the very least, it raised the issue of full employment for national consideration. The Hawkins bill also opened up some negotiating room. If Jerry — or other politicians — came in with proposals that seemed less drastic, they would appear all the more moderate in their approaches.

The late spring of 1975 was characterized by a combination of immense possibilities and enjoyable trivia. One weekend Bob Gnaizda scheduled an outing for Jerry and the rest of the cabinet. A group of activist thinkers was to be flown in from the East to talk about the Brave New World the Brown administration could begin in California. Ralph Nader had agreed to come; so had Jim Ridgeway, Dick Barnett, Gar Alperovitz, Jim Hightower, Marcus Raskin, and a number of others who had written about the evils of corporate America. East would meet West, the new thinkers would interact with the new politicians, and it would all happen in lovely Belvedere, a suburb perched high atop a hill overlooking the San Francisco Bay.

The prospects were intriguing, to say the least. Imagining Jerry and Ralph Nader in the same room, debating the evils of the bank holding companies, was a little like Godzilla meeting the Deep Sea Monster in a Japanese science fiction movie. There was even to be a sports period late Saturday afternoon. Gnaizda was setting up the weekend like a summer camp. A recreation group affiliated with *The Whole Earth Catalog* was scheduled to lead us in what were called "New Games," or noncompetitive athletics. The feature was "the Earth Ball game." A gigantic, inflated ball was lifted into the air and moved aimlessly about. Since the ball was very big, it could be kept in the air only if it was supported by all the members of the group working in a cooperative fashion. It was supposed to be a metaphor for the interdependency of all life forms and the need for cooperation on a global scale that the *Whole Earth Catalog* people were preaching.

Very nice. I looked forward to the spectacle of Jerry and Ralph Nader and the rest of us pushing the giant Earth Ball about in the air. Alas, it was not to be. The Friday before the weekend was to transpire, a Sacramento reporter got wind of the plan, and misreading the agenda item entitled "New Games," asked Jerry whether he was attending a weekend conference where they were going to play "Nude Games." Jerry blanched white, of course, the idea of nude encounters being anathema to him, and so he said he didn't know about any nude games and he wasn't going to any conference of any description. The categorical denial was enough to satisfy the reporter's question, and Jerry changed the subject.

Now it would not, I think, be fair to say Jerry had fibbed to the reporter. Jerry did not, in fact, intend to participate in nude games, and because he lived his life in a state of constant contingency, he probably decided, as a result of the reporter's question, not to attend the conference. In any case, the matter was resolved with Jerry escaping by the skin of his teeth. But because Jerry decided to absent himself at the last moment, half of his cabinet followed suit, and the East-West encounter commenced with something less than its anticipated drama.

Jerry's absence proved to be only part of the problem, however. There was also the question of what to do about servants. It would have been expecting too much to have required us to fix our own food and wash our own dishes, I suppose, the principles of the counterculture having permeated only partway into our consciousness, and so it was decided that we would maintain some of the forms of the new consciousness while dispensing with the rest. Casual clothing was authorized; servants were to be furnished as well. This did not end the matter, however. Indeed, the problem, in all its complexities, had just begun. Black or brown persons, or women of any racial complexion, might have needed the work most, but the spectacle of underprivileged people waiting on members of a group that, with one exception, was all white was most unfortunate, to say the very least. Indeed, the prospect of this occurrence was enough to cause even the least sensitive of us some uneasiness. And so a compromise was reached, a felicitous compromise, I might add. The initiates of the Zen Center were commandeered for the task. Since they were all white, there was no danger of racial tension, and since they were voluntarily poor, there was no possibility that we would be said to be exploiting them. They would be doing what they wanted to do, which was to be of

181

service, and we would be doing what we wanted to do, which was to be served, and everything would be quite beatific. We could munch our pâté, French bread, and Camembert by the San Francisco Bay without the slightest feelings of remorse while we talked about the problems of worldwide hunger.

The afternoon proved to be a delightful experience after all. The food was simply marvelous, better than expected. Our host's elaborate mansion was filled with exquisite Chinese antiques. In the distance, below us, the sailboats went hither and yon between Sausalito Harbor and Alcatraz. And meanwhile, the shaven-headed initiates from the Zen Center scurried about with understanding unobtrusiveness, attired in their Japanese slippers, Indian shirts, and white, baggy, drawstring trousers. They even bowed slightly when we looked at them. A new style was developing, it seemed. In the 1960s, rich New Yorkers invited to their fashionable East Side apartments Black Panthers who delivered merciless harangues against the evils of wealth while the hors d'oeuvres were served by Puerto Rican maids. Tom Wolfe, the celebrated journalist of the time, referred to the practice as "radical chic." Now, in the 1970s, Zen initiates served the hors d'oeuvres while the guests were left in peace. There were no blacks to disrupt the festivities, the contradictions were less obvious, and everyone felt oh so much better about things. I suppose Tom Wolfe would have called our scene "Zen chic." It certainly was our answer to the servant problem. One could hire an ashram for the weekend to cater the food.

On Sunday morning, Jerry appeared. Ralph Nader had left the previous afternoon; the "New Games" never got off the ground; no reporters were in sight; the coast was clear. Most probably, I suppose, Jerry's curiosity got the best of him. In any case, it should be emphatically stated that Jerry's appearance did not mean he was acting inconsistent with the truth he had told the reporter the previous Friday afternoon, for as Jerry once said when asked about two other apparently inconsistent positions he had taken: "Then was then and now is now." Exactly. He was utilizing Zen logic. According to this view, each point in time is unique, and what and how we are at one point is, in reality, different from what and how we are at another. Life is a continuum, so to speak, consisting of a series of moments in which we live constantly in the Now. The Now is not only the doorway to higher consciousness, it is also useful in more temporal ways. A Now politician, for example, can never be accused of prevarication, deception, inconsistency, or lack of sincerity. He just is. He thinks. He acts. All thoughts and acts are separate. The thoughts and actions have to be accepted for what they are, pebbles in the stream of life. And so, to illustrate: Before the reporter asked Jerry whether he was going to the weekend encounter, Jerry thought he was, which was his Now state of mind; but when Jerry heard the question, he decided he wasn't, which was also his Now state of mind; and after the reporter went away and Jerry reflected on the weekend, he determined to go, which was also his Now state of mind. There was absolutely no inconsistency, and if, after the meeting was over, the same reporter had asked Jerry whether he had attended the conference after all, Jerry could have answered quite truthfully that he had and he hadn't (he had on Sunday and he hadn't on Saturday) and let the matter go at that.

The Sunday Jerry participated in the conference was the scene of the Great Potato Chip Debate. The altercation commenced when Jim Hightower made a disparaging remark about Pringle's potato chips. Pringle's potato chips weren't even potato chips, Hightower said. They were ground-up, processed potato stock of doubtful nutritional value which people paid exorbitant prices for because the potato chips were packaged in air-tight containers that looked like tennis ball cans. Well, it so happened that just before Hightower made his comment, Jerry had not been getting much attention, and so he created a little scene. What was wrong with Pringle's potato chips? he asked. *He* liked them. Moreover, lots of people liked them. So what if they were more expensive and not very nutritional. What *was* a potato chip, anyway? Who could say? Were the experts assembled in the room so high and mighty that they could define what a potato chip was? He, for one, wasn't convinced. He wasn't convinced about anything. What was reality, anyway?

It was a good question. It was always a good question, especially if one spent a lot of one's time manipulating the appearance of things and guarding against the manipulations of others, as Jerry did. Jerry was concerned, even obsessed, with the question of reality, I think, because its alteration was so much a part of his life. What the Great Potato Chip Debate was really about was the right of a corporation or a politician to engage in "hype." Hype was a word from the advertising and entertainment industries that meant the conscious and premeditated alteration of appearances for the sake of material gain. Hype was not only a word; it was a concept, a whole philosophy. It was where a lot of the action was in California, especially in Southern California. One heard a lot about hype in Southern California, where Jerry's media whiz, Tom Quinn, grew up and where Jerry reached maturity. Whole magazines were devoted to the propagation of hype, whole industries were based on the use of it, and politics was no exception. Hype was the staff of life, the magical ambrosia. The bread, one could take for granted. The critical question was: How was the bread packaged? How did the politician present himself to the world? How could he, the potato chips, and the bread seem more than they actually were? All people were commodities in this line of thinking, and all commodities could be sold with hype. Hype was what tied it all together. It was the unifying principle in life, and the dynamic force as well. The reality changed far less than the appearances did. The appearances changed almost every day. The appearances started dressing up the reality; then they altered it; then, finally, they devoured it. After a while, there was nothing left of the old-style reality. Appearances *were* the New Reality, and if you tried to hold on to the Old Reality in spite of it all, you were unhappy or went crazy or did both.

The East Coast intellectual-activists couldn't have been expected to agree with the New Reality, of course. They were committed to the plain, literal meaning of the printed word and world, and they made their living by it. Even Nader, the only television personality in the crowd, talked like a book when he was in front of the cameras. Jerry didn't, which was one reason why he was Governor of California and Ralph Nader wasn't. The California hype was what the Belvedere weekend ended up arguing about. Watch out, America: The California hype was moving East. Jerry did it, Reagan did it in spades, and Nixon did too, after a fashion. Three of the most influential political figures of the decade came out of the California hype, influenced it, and rose to power on the basis of it. There must have been something to it. We were, indeed, in the Age of Television. Jerry had an advantage over the East Coast people he argued with. He not only had Zen logic and a television presence, he wasn't committed to anything beyond himself. The East Coast people were. Therefore, Jerry was more flexible than they were. He could take any side of any question and hype it up or down.

Meanwhile, back in Sacramento, events were proceeding apace. The news, such as it was, still seemed to be good. At the same time, however, a few storm clouds could be seen gathering on the horizon. David Packard, a multimillionaire industrialist and the leading Republican fund raiser in California, mailed out an appeal for funds that asked whether businessmen could receive a fair hearing from the poverty lawyers and other unusual sorts Jerry had appointed to public office in Sacramento. The Packard letter caused Jerry some unhappiness. Then, a subsidiary of the *Wall Street Journal* released a study that alleged that, of the fifty states, California was third from last in providing a "pro-business climate." The study caused more consternation still. Then, on June 3,

1975, I addressed a memo to Jerry reporting that, "according to EDD's May, 1975, estimate, the 1975 year-end balance of the UI (Unemployment Insurance) Fund will be about $520 million, $150 million less than EDD's January, 1975, estimate." (The unemployment rate had run higher than our statistical experts had estimated.) "If, as it now appears," I continued, "the Fund continues to decline at this rate during 1976, the Fund will be bankrupt near the end of 1976."

Bankrupt was not a nice word. It also wasn't a nice prospect. Although we could borrow the necessary funds from the federal government, as New Jersey and six or seven other states had done, we would, I pointed out, be forced to declare bankruptcy first, which would undoubtedly "tarnish the Brown administration's reputation for fiscal responsibility." Also, I added, the federal government would require us to begin paying back the loan in 1979, when another recession might be under way. I recommended raising the money ourselves by levying an additional tax on the employers who paid money into the UI Fund. The extra tax could be accomplished in one of three ways, I said: Either the tax rate could be increased, or the wages that the employers paid taxes on (the wage base) could be increased, or a combination of these two methods could be used. I recommended the second approach. In any case, I concluded, $600 million would have to be raised.

My memo was not received with much enthusiasm in the Governor's office. Jerry had been saying for months that there would be no general tax increase; now I was telling him businessmen had to be taxed an extra $600 million. Although the two statements could be squared logically since the tax on the businessmen was not a *general* tax increase, we were nonetheless going to be violating the spirit of Jerry's promise. David Packard might write another letter.

There was another problem with my memo, I learned later. When Jerry read my statement about the Brown administration's reputation for fiscal responsibility being "tarnished," he was outraged. According to Bob Gnaizda, who was present at the time, I had trespassed on sacred ground. I had made reference, albeit indirectly, to It: the Image, the Image that was daily, even hourly, being crafted in the Governor's office. The reference was to a taboo subject. One never referred to It in Jerry's presence, not unless one were Tom Quinn. *It* was sacrosanct. *It* was an effective means of manipulation only so long as one did not call attention to It or acknowledge It was being manufactured. The operative principle was quite simple: The people don't mind being helped along in their thinking so long as we don't tell them that's what we are doing.

Jerry didn't talk to me for two weeks after my memo was delivered. In the meantime, however, the LEAA portion of the jobs program was running into trouble. Gray Davis, the chief honcho on the enterprise, had failed to lay the necessary groundwork with the police chiefs. Some of them were raising objections to the conversion scheme. Jobs for juvenile delinquents might be all well and good, but what about the issue of local control? they asked. And what about their pet projects?

Soon after these questions were raised, Jerry decided to backtrack. One afternoon, when I called Alice Daniel to find out what was happening, she indicated that Jerry was thinking about giving all the money back to Washington and letting Washington worry about the police chiefs. "Sure," she acknowledged, "I know Washington will fund the chiefs directly and keep the program as it is, but think of what a dramatic gesture it would be for Jerry to refuse the funds." I said I didn't like the gesture much, and Alice agreed with me. She said she'd try to do what she could. I held my breath. It was a depressing situation. Once again, symbols seemed to be winning out over substance. I sensed what Jerry might be thinking. If he had to raise the UI Fund taxes, he could compensate with the LEAA turnback and preserve some of his credibility with conservatives. The police chiefs wouldn't squawk; there would be one less bureaucracy for them to deal with. In all likelihood, the newspapers wouldn't raise embarrassing questions since the final result, the direct funding of the police chiefs, wouldn't become apparent until months later, when everyone had forgotten about the issue. The only ones who would get hurt were the black kids, who didn't have a group lobbying for them. It was more of the same.

The next day, the final verdict was rendered at a meeting in the Governor's office. Alice said the whole experience was depressing. Jerry brought Jacques Barzaghi in to play the role of spoiler. Jacques did as he was expected, asking rhetorical questions and agreeing with alacrity whenever Jerry suggested they give the money back to the Indians. No one could agree on anything positive to do with the money, Alice said. Finally, Jerry decided they wouldn't return the money to the federal government and they wouldn't spend the bulk of it on jobs, either. They would just leave the program where it was, eliminate 265 of 280 positions in the state LEAA office, transfer the remainder of the employees to the state finance office, and let the police chiefs fight it out with Washington. Approximately $1.5 million would be set aside for a symbolic youth employment program. If the press asked any questions about whether the reorganization was a publicity stunt, Jerry could always point to the $1.5 million and talk about the great work the kids were doing. "Jerry just got bored with the issue," Alice said. "He didn't want to deal with the problem anymore."

Around nine o'clock in the evening of the day the final verdict was reached, I heard a knock on my apartment door. A state policeman was standing in the hallway with a note from the Governor's office. The note said I was supposed to report to the state's LEAA office at eight o'clock the following morning and inform the employees that they were being laid off. The episode was all over but the funeral, it seemed, and I was to be the chief pallbearer. The situation was filled with irony. The employment development director was now in charge of layoffs. Talk about the misuse of language! Over the previous six months, Jerry had created absolutely no new jobs. He had, however, eliminated 250 positions, and I was to be the instrument of his policy. I supposed I was selected in order to cast events in their most positive light. If the employment development director was the bearer of bad tidings, the poor souls might think more about the new positions they could look forward to.

The meeting the next morning was worse than I had expected. News had already filtered down to the LEAA employees; I was only confirming what they already knew. Several women were crying. The men's faces were grim or totally devoid of life. A feeling of latent hostility was in the air. Several of the people I spoke with seemed less upset over losing their jobs than over the humiliation the incident had caused them. Jerry had really done a job on them in the media, suggesting that not only was their program worthless, but that they were worthless too. One woman made the point very graphically. "I've been made to feel meaningless," she said. She did not need to explain what she meant, and I did not attempt to tell her how she and the other employees had been used as foils for the Governor's publicity operation. It was almost total luck of the draw. Jerry could have picked on somebody else to illustrate the wastefulness of bureaucracy, but he had chosen them. He had milked them and the LEAA issue for all it was worth, and then when the publicity value of the issue was exhausted he had tossed it — and the LEAA employees — aside like so much refuse.

As I left the LEAA office that morning, I realized I was furious. I didn't agree with most of the goals of the LEAA program, but these people had been treated shabbily. What finally set me off was the woman who said she felt meaningless. Jerry and Gray hadn't had the guts or the decency to drive out to the office and tell the employees why they were letting them go. They weren't taking responsibility for their decision on a human level. The people were being treated as if they were symbols. It would have required such little effort to have treated them like human beings. A few words of reassurance would have sufficed. The employees were not to blame, Jerry and Gray could have said. The program was at fault. Maybe the employees would have felt better. But Jerry and Gray didn't say the words. They didn't say any words, face to face. Instead, they cut and ran. The LEAA reorganization was a hit-and-run job, pure and simple. In college we had a word for what Jerry and Gray had done. The word was "chickenshit."

I drove back to my office on Capitol Mall and called the Governor's office. Jerry and Gray were unavailable. Still steaming, I walked over to Bob Gnaizda's office. Since Bob was involved in Jerry's media operation, I felt he was somewhat responsible for what had happened. I let him have it. I was sick and tired of the publicity stunts, I said. I wanted some straight answers for a change. If Jerry didn't want a jobs program, he should say so. If he didn't like me or what I was doing, he should tell me, man to man. I was through playing ring around the rosy with a lot of ass-kissing sycophants. All we were doing was misusing language. The idea of the employment development director being put in charge of layoffs was absurd. If I was going to be working in Sacramento to lay people off, Jerry could damned well say so and give me an appropriate title, like "unemployment director." I would even do layoffs, I said, if a meaningful jobs program was in the works. I was willing to be the good soldier all the way, but I didn't want to operate under false pretenses.

I must have talked for ten minutes nonstop. Bob didn't say a word. He just sat in his chair, his legs crossed, his arms folded, his head slightly tilted and bowed, looking chagrined. Finally, I asked him if he had anything to say. He shook his head no. I walked out.

The rest of the week I had time to reflect upon my situation. I wasn't receiving any calls from the Governor's office, that was for sure. After a day or so of stewing about, I realized that my position was less august then I had believed it to be. The $37,200 salary, the fancy title, the big office, the special parking place, and the power I had over the lives of 15,000 EDD employees — that stuff was just so much window dressing. In reality, I was a glorified errand boy. My role wasn't to make employment policy or even to influence it very much. I was supposed to make a few suggestions, be available when called, carry out orders, and put a good face on a bad situation. If Jerry was the Man on the White Horse, I was the stable boy. When the horse made a mess, I was expected to clean it up. When the horse was moved to a new stable, I was supposed to lay down a bed of straw for him. It wasn't my prerogative to say where the horse was kept or what kind of food he ate or even what time he left the stable. If he stayed, I stayed. If he dumped a load on the floor, I reached for my shovel.

The horse was a metaphor for the system. And I wasn't the only hired hand who was doing the cleaning up. The director of the welfare department, the health director, and the prisons chief were stable boys too. We were all supposed to shovel up the problems the system dumped on the floor. Unemployment? Onto the shovel and into the garbage can. Mental illness resulting from economic dislocation? Onto the shovel and into the garbage can. Black kids who stole? Into the garbage can. The prisons were a garbage can. So were the unemployment insurance offices. The pathetic state hospitals the health department maintained were too. We were all stable boys, and the high salaries and fancy titles we were given were nothing less, nothing more, than a few pieces of silver designed to persuade us to shovel harder and faster and pretend we were doing something else.

It was the pretense of our work, not the reality, that in the final analysis humiliated me the most. We fooled ourselves into thinking we were something other than what we were.

Perhaps the illusion was necessary for us to do our work with any amount of conviction, I didn't know, or possibly it was required if we were to persuade others that nothing could be changed; but whatever the case, the illusion we lived under weakened us at the same time it gave us the sensation of power. We didn't even know what we were doing or what we were. What a pathetic situation to be in.

Chapter Twenty-Three

BOB GNAIZDA DESCRIBES HIS STRAW HAT AND HIS SUCCESS
IN DEALING WITH THE DOCTORS. THE AUTHOR NOTES
SIGNS OF DISINTEGRATION WITHIN THE BROWN ADMINIS-
TRATION. TWO BAD OMENS APPEAR. BOB GNAIZDA IS
REALLY SAYING THAT THE AUTHOR IS NOT FIT FOR STATE
SERVICE.

THE REST OF June was little more than a series of impressions, fragmented, discordant, dreamlike. I bumped into Bob
Gnaizda in front of the EDD building one noon. Neither
one of us mentioned the LEAA encounter. Bob was wearing
a straw hat. Yes, he chortled, it was a new hat. Mario was
wearing one too. We talked about the hat. There was little
else to talk about, it seemed. Bob said he had just returned
from a meeting with the doctors. It was a smashing success,
he said. He had finally figured out how to hold meetings,
he confided. You didn't give them too much. You made
them think that everything you gave them they were lucky
to get. Bob had an arrangement with Mario. Mario wouldn't
come to the meeting. It was a waste of time. The meetings
were all a waste of time, Bob said. Bob would tell the doctors
that Mr. Obledo was busy, but that if they were very lucky,
he might be able to come in for a few minutes at the end of
the meeting. And then at a prearranged signal Mario would
walk in. The doctors were so pleased, Bob said. They were
more appreciative than if Mario had been there the whole

meeting. They asked fewer questions, besides. Bob laughed, the slightly hysterical, machine-gun laugh. He was thinking about doing the same thing himself, he said. He would have an aide there to open the next meeting. The aide would announce that Mr. Gnaizda had been detained in an important conference with the Governor but would do his best to join them. Then Bob would appear. The people would be so appreciative. And so on and so forth. The government was a charade. . . .

I was talking to a secretary in the Governor's office who was telling me what had happened to a friend of hers who also worked in the Governor's office. The friend, returning home from work late one evening, had found her apartment in a shambles — the bed unmade, the closet full of dirty laundry, and no clean pantyhose for the next day. She hadn't eaten since breakfast, she realized. She started frying some bacon for a bacon and tomato sandwich. Then she decided to wash her dirty pantyhose in the bathroom sink. Then she remembered her bed wasn't made, and she wanted to go to sleep in a nice, neatly made bed. As she was bending down, smoothing out the bottom sheet, she smelled something burning. It was bacon. She ran into the kitchen. The bacon was ruined. She threw the burned bacon into the garbage can and prepared herself a tomato sandwich. She was just beginning to eat the tomato sandwich when she remembered she had forgotten to pour soap into the sink. She walked into the bathroom. The stockings were soaking in the dirty, tepid water. She picked up the box of soap and began to cry. Her life was in confusion. Everything was unmade. It was eleven o'clock at night and she was too tired to take care of herself. She realized her whole day had been like that. Every day was like that. She would begin working on something only to be interrupted. Do this, she would be told. Do that. The signals constantly changed, the interruptions were continual. Her life was in fragments. She had no peace.

I thought about my own personal life. It wasn't much

different. "Don't accept a job in the Governor's office," Lennie Ross had told me before I went to Sacramento. "Working with Jerry every day is..." He didn't need to finish the sentence. We had both worked in the campaign. Jerry was a great fellow to eat dinner with, but not to work for. It was humiliating sometimes. Hurry up and wait. Sit around and hope for a decision that was never made. Lennie, a former Quiz Kid, was smart: He followed his own advice and accepted an appointment to the Public Utilities Commission, which was based in San Francisco. I had gone to Sacramento anyway.

I also thought of Paul Halvonik, who was a better sport than I about the hurry-up-and-wait business but who was still gritting his teeth. His magnificent sense of humor was wearing thin. He had moved a piano into his room in the Governor's office, and when he was especially frustrated with Jerry he would sit down and play. He would play and play. It was better than playing charades with doctors, I decided.

One morning in early June, a friend of mine in the legislature said, "I'm living on junk food and junk sex, and neither is very nourishing." He hit the nail on the head. People in the Sacramento power scene were too much into using one another to be able to feel much love or sensuality. It was sad. There was little nourishment on a human level. People couldn't afford to feel close to one another or express feelings. Feelings were too dangerous. Anything you expressed could be used against you. The outside world had to be kept at bay. What was it Lord Acton, the British historian, said? "Power corrupts and absolute power corrupts absolutely"? I had often wondered what he meant by the word "corrupt," but now I thought I knew. The corruption began when the inner self atrophied. I wondered whether I too was becoming affected. It was almost as if there was a chain of abuse within the hierarchy of government. We allowed ourselves to be abused by those above us, so we handed it out to those below, and they, in turn, acted similarly with their subordinates, and their subordinates did so with their subordinates — and where did it all end, this alternating cycle of submission and humiliation? Probably with some janitor who went home at night and beat his wife. It was almost certain: The humiliation games became less and less abstract as we moved down the chain of command.

One friend of mine from San Francisco said she had the impression that each of us in the higher reaches of the Brown administration were living under a bell jar. Jerry would pick up several of the bell jars and we would dance around for a little while, and then he would put it down again and we would subside. Sometimes several of us got trapped under the same bell jar; other times we were quite separate. For a while, a few of us tried to tap on the glass and make signals to the others, but no one seemed to notice. If Rose Bird was having difficulties, that was *her* problem. We went about our own separate business and tried to relate to Jerry, the only one who tied it all together. He was the apex of the whole system, and somehow, the stronger he got, the weaker we got. Jerry explained the process very graphically to me in October 1974. "When something good happens, I take all the credit. When something bad happens, my appointee takes all the blame." That was how the ship of state was supposed to proceed, apparently, with each of us locked in our separate water-tight compartments. If a torpedo hit, the area was immediately sealed off. Bob Gnaizda made the same point in another context. "Don't write any more memos that are addressed to the Governor by name," he said. "Jerry wants deniability." I hadn't heard the word "deniability" since Watergate.

On June 15, I decided to stay for six more months and see what developed on the jobs front. There was still plenty to do and — who knew? — the necessary pressure for a jobs program might develop. Around the eighteenth of June, my chief administrator, Marian Beecham, reported that a plan was under way to consolidate the employment, welfare, and health department computers into one gigantic computer center that would be controlled by the Health and Welfare Agency. Although the plan was being described as only "tentative," and although the employment, welfare and health directors were supposed to be "fully consulted" before any final decision was made, Marian said the fix was on. She was on the planning committee and even she wasn't getting all the details. As best she could determine, the strategy was for second-level computer bureaucrats to rubber-stamp the agency's proposal, prepare a final report that didn't use the word "consolidation," and submit it to the directors without prior warning and without a request for their concurrence. The whole issue would be finessed, in other words, and the critical decision-making level, the director's level, would be leapfrogged.

It was enough to make a person paranoid. I called Jerry Lackner, the health director, who said he'd never heard of the consolidation scheme and, in fact, didn't even know the planning committee existed. His administrative deputy, it turned out, had "forgotten" to tell him about the committee. The acting welfare director, Jerry Prod, was a little better informed, but not much. Finally, both Prod and Lackner agreed to meet with me to decide what to do, but because neither of them wanted to risk antagonizing Obledo and Gnaizda, they requested we meet after business hours in my apartment. It was a very strange situation. My old friend Bob Gnaizda was so feared in the state administration that we were forced to meet behind his back in order to discuss a matter that vitally affected our departments.

The meeting was held, Prod and Lackner agreed to oppose the consolidation scheme, and thereupon we communicated our position to Bob and Mario. Jerry Lackner was sufficiently apprehensive, however, that when the three of us sat down with Bob and Mario in Mario's office, Jerry's hands were shaking and his voice quavered slightly. What is happening to us? I wondered at the time. A grown man, the head of the largest department in state government, was acting like a frightened schoolboy called into the principal's office. The shaking hands were not a good sign.

Around the same time the computer controversy was unfolding, another bad omen appeared. Marty Glick, Bob Gnaizda's old sidekick from the CRLA days, turned up in Sacramento as the new general counsel of the Health and Welfare Agency. One day about two weeks after Glick started work, I invited Bob Gnaizda to meet a friend of mine, Dick Boone, who was working on a new kind of jobs program for teen-agers. Dick had been one of Bob Kennedy's closest associates; he had helped draft the original War on Poverty program. I said I thought Bob might enjoy meeting him. Bob said fine, he'd ask Marty to come to the meeting too. I said fine and filled Dick in on who Bob and Marty were. Marty, I told him, had represented a lot of Mexican-American kids who were having problems in the schools. There was one case in particular that stood out, the *Diana* case. A little Mexican-American girl named Diana had been assigned to the mentally retarded class because she didn't perform very well on the IQ test. Marty, suspecting the test was linguistically and culturally biased, took on the case and finally compelled the state Department of Education to revise the testing procedures. Diana was retested in Spanish. She scored significantly higher than she had the first time, and she and several other Spanish-speaking youngsters were returned to the regular classroom. It had been a great victory, I said to Dick as we were walking over to Bob's office.

The meeting with Bob turned out to be something of a disaster. Armed with a pencil and legal pad, Bob began by asking Dick whether he had written any books on the subject he was working on. Then, after Dick had replied in the negative, Bob imported into the room a tall, discourteous assistant with a black cowboy hat who, for the rest of the meeting, proceeded to sit at the conference table and read the newspaper, his hat still firmly implanted on his head. At one point in the interview, which was beginning to sound like an interrogation, Bob rendered one of those hard-line, categorical opinions that were widely favored but seldom acted upon in the early days of the Brown administration. "Education," Bob intoned, sounding just like the Governor, "is almost totally useless." And so saying, he peered intently at Dick to see what his reaction would be. Dick recovered nicely, however. Knowing something from me about Marty Glick's litigation background and knowing further that Marty had accepted a teaching appointment at Stanford after he had left CRLA, Dick turned to Marty and said, "Marty, I would be surprised to hear you agree with that." Marty didn't hesitate a second. "Oh, yes," he replied, displaying his small, slightly indented front teeth, "I think education is less than useless."

"Boy," Dick said to me later, after we had left Bob's office, "I haven't seen hostility like that since Washington." He shook his head sadly. "Do you know what the scariest part of that whole meeting was?" he asked. I shook my head no. Perhaps I was becoming desensitized. "It was that guy Glick," Dick continued. "Do you realize that in response to Gnaizda's cue he just disowned the last seven years of his life?" He shook his head again. We were almost across the street by now. "Glick must really want something from Gnaizda," he mused. "I wonder what it is?"

The next day I bumped into Alice Daniel in front of the capitol steps. "You'd better have a talk with Bob," she said. "He's telling Jerry you're not suited to serve in the Brown administration."

Chapter Twenty-Four

THE AUTHOR'S JOB MEMO IS LEAKED TO A HOSTILE NEWS-
PAPER. ALL HELL BREAKS LOOSE BUT ONLY TEMPORARILY.
THE CONTROVERSY IS REVIVED. THE AUTHOR RECEIVES
SOME ADVICE. THE FINAL RESOLUTION OF THE CONTRO-
VERSY IS DESCRIBED.

IT WAS Götterdämmerung time. On June 19, the most
recent version of my jobs memo was leaked to the right-wing
Oakland *Tribune,* which ran this front-page banner headline:
EXCLUSIVE — BROWN'S SECRET WORKER STATE
So as to leave no room for ambiguity, the headline was
printed in red ink, and the subhead read: "The Secret Job
Revolution."

The lead to the story was equally unequivocal: "A secret
agenda for creating 100,000 jobs as the first step in a worker-
controlled, virtual economic revolution in California is under
consideration by Gov. Edmund G. Brown Jr.'s administration."

The remainder of the story described the specific proposals
I had made to Jerry, based on his Zen Center model. Read
in another context, the proposals might have seemed relatively inconsequential, but considered beneath a headline and
a lead that suggested Chairman Mao was arriving momen-
tarily, the proposals could only sound revolutionary. The
word "revolution" was even used twice in the first two
column inches of the story. Whoever had leaked the memo

had really meant to do a hatchet job. More than any other major newspaper in the state, the Oakland *Tribune* would be certain to react with hostility to any employment program that did not rely exclusively on subsidies to big business. The bacon was in the fire.

Within two hours after the paper appeared on the newsstands, the telephone in my office was lighting up like the Keno board at Las Vegas. Was there a secret plan? the reporters from the other dailies wanted to know. When were we going to introduce Chinese-style communes in California? I was tempted to respond, but Bob Gnaizda called with the request that I sit tight and say nothing until he took care of it with the Governor. He would get back to me, he said. I remember thinking at the time how calm and collected he sounded.

Who had leaked the memo? My guess was one of the disgruntled Reagan holdovers at EDD, but both David Commons and the Shadow disagreed when I spoke with them later. They thought the source of the story was Bob Gnaizda. Bob Gnaizda? I responded somewhat incredulously at the time. We had had our conflicts, but he was still my friend. "Are you sure of that?" David Commons asked me. David didn't think Bob was my friend, and he felt furthermore that this little operation had Bob's fingerprints all over it. The person who had chosen the Oakland *Tribune* had to have some media sophistication, and he also had to have access to the memo. Moreover, he had to wish me ill. Bob qualified on all three grounds, David said.

I wondered. Bob *had* been acting strangely since our blowout over the LEAA money, and there *was* an incident five years before, when Bob had engineered an artful preemptive strike against one of CRLA's most vociferous opponents. But why should he leak the memo without Jerry's authorization? And why should Jerry authorize the leak when the newspaper article put him in a bad light? It didn't make sense to me. The Shadow said it might make perfect sense. "You watch," he warned. "Jerry can back away from that memo in any of three different ways — and you'll be left holding the bag."

He was right. When the reporters called Jerry later on the nineteenth to ask him what he thought of the jobs proposal, he denied knowing anything about it. Maybe, he suggested, the plan was never presented to him because the agency it came from didn't think much of it. "I don't like plans," he added. "I don't deal in plans. That is just a bunch of paper. Don't be mesmerized by phrases; the reality is that we have 1 million people out of work. We have to find a way to put people to work. I'd give just as much weight to your [the reporters'] proposals."[61]

The reporters were satisfied. Jerry had turned aside the proposal adeptly, with a mere flick of the wrist. And to make sure the press stopped bothering him, he made one other comment that was very interesting. "I have no doubt the state cannot finance it," he said of the proposal. The jobs program I had suggested would mean an increase in taxes, he alleged, and he had already pledged no tax increase.

The discussion was ended. Jerry had made no mention of the $400 million surplus, and the press did not ask him about it. They all rode off on the false issue of the tax increase, which was a red herring thrown across their paths at an opportune time. I thought of Jerry's previous colloquy with the reporter regarding the Nude Games and the Belvedere weekend. He was using Zen logic again. Before the Oakland *Tribune* article appeared, his Now frame of mind was that $100 million of the surplus might be available for jobs; after the story appeared, his Now state of mind was different, and it was all consistent. There was no surplus now for jobs — the surplus itself disappeared in a cloud of contingency — and at least for the time being no more visits were scheduled to the Zen Center and no further references were made to E. F. Schumacher and *The Whole Earth Catalog*. The artful dodger was at it again, bobbing and weaving, covering his right flank.

The Shadow thought I should counterattack. "Leak back

on him," he importuned. "Leak back on him. Put out the word about the $100 million he promised you. Make the surplus the issue. You and the legislators have a common interest in the surplus. They don't like the fact he's squirreling it away any better than you do. You've got some potential allies over there. Use them."

I said I didn't think it was the appropriate move. Even though I hadn't been particularly enamored with Jerry of late, my job was to protect him, not undercut him.

"Oh, my God," the Shadow exclaimed, "you really are a boy scout, aren't you." He was very exasperated. "Look," he said, "your first duty is to survive. This is a survival issue now. You can't do a damned thing for Jerry or the unemployed or anybody else if you don't survive."

I didn't agree with him. I didn't like the palace politics that were developing within the Brown administration. It seemed to me that I lost a great deal if I started playing those games at this late date. Moreover, I had no hard evidence that Jerry had ordered the memo leaked.

The subject was closed. I resolved to hunker down in the trenches, say nothing, absorb whatever bad publicity was generated, and wait. My own sense was that the controversy would blow over. After all, Tom Quinn had practically confessed to political blackmail two months before and he was still alive and well. All I had done was present a jobs program for the unemployed.

The Shadow had one further comment. It was the next to last conversation I was to have with him in Sacramento. "You know what Jerry may be trying to do," he said, somewhat reflectively. "He may try to use this controversy to divert attention from the $600 million he's got to hit the businessmen for on the Unemployment Insurance Fund. I mean, it makes sense, right? He's in trouble with business right now and he's going to alienate them further by breaking his no-tax pledge, so why not use you as a cover? When he rejects your radical-sounding proposal, he sounds conservative, and at the same time he quietly introduces the tax increase, which nobody notices because they're too busy watching you. It's perfect, moving right and left at the same time."

I was intrigued by his theory. I also wanted to know something else. What did he think of the latest jobs memo? Had he read it?

"Oh, it was nothing very special," the Shadow replied. "Except for the language, it was a retread of a lot of ideas that have been discussed before. The rhetoric was wrong, though. I mean, if you're going to conclude that business can't do the job, which you obviously have, you should throw in some language praising business; and conversely, if you were going to develop a program that helped business, you should add some language criticizing them. The point I'm driving at is that in politics the language should always ride off in a different direction than the program it's describing. I mean, that's what Jerry may be doing on the Unemployment Insurance Fund. He's smart. You could learn from him."

The Shadow was stating an old law of politics that I had been growing aware of but was also resisting. In politics, language often didn't communicate meaning; it disguised it. The words were the bauble the politicians dangled in front of the baby's face while they changed his diapers. I was learning the lesson the hard way. I was the bauble being dangled in the public view.

The press soon seemed to lose interest, however. Indeed, the jobs controversy died down almost as quickly as it had erupted. The June 20 edition of the Los Angeles *Times* devoted a brief, four column inches to the issue, on page 3, and the San Francisco *Chronicle* paid even less attention to it. Neither news story made the jobs program sound very radical. On June 25, the Sacramento *Bee* carried a story reporting that in 1970 the Reagan administration had considered a jobs proposal very similar to mine. Although the proposal was subsequently killed by the Reagan administration's hard-liners, it was certainly not outlandish, the *Bee* reporter indicated. In fact, the article suggested there had been much to recommend the proposal.[62]

I breathed a sigh of relief when I read the *Bee* article. The jobs controversy had been put in context. Jerry had not been damaged. I seemed to be home free.

I was mistaken. On Monday noon, July 7, an item appeared in the Sacramento *Bee* that reported that the administration was asking the state's major corporations for recommendations on how to bolster California's economy. During the course of the article, a comparison was drawn between the Brown administration's "responsible" leadership and my "wild-eyed" schemes.[63] Since the article contained a few facts that could have only come from the Governor's office, I knew the Governor's office was the source of the story. They were reviving the controversy!

At three o'clock the same day, a meeting was scheduled at the Health and Welfare Agency to discuss the computer consolidation proposal. A preliminary report had been prepared by the Policy Advisory Council, the committee composed of the departmental computer experts, and the position recommended by health director Lackner, welfare director Prod, and myself had apparently been accepted by the council: namely, that no final action would be taken until the directors had had ample time to study the proposal. Consequently, when I went to the meeting I fully expected nothing more than an explanatory session. I was in for a rude awakening. Not only were the directors to be excluded further from the decision-making process, the Health and Welfare Agency representative indicated, the final decision might be made within the next several days. I was outraged. The next day, July 8, I composed a strongly worded letter to Bob and Mario. The key section of the letter was as follows:

> Had not there been previous attempts by Dr. Earl Brian [the secretary of the Health and Welfare Agency under

Reagan] to consolidate all of the Agency's computers in one massive center, the subject of how computers are integrated ... might not be so sensitive, but the history is there, and on at least two occasions the Legislature included in the budget act prohibitions against the consolidation of departmental computers within the Health and Welfare Agency.

There were good reasons for these prohibitions, I believe. The consolidated data processing center established in 1972–1973 in the Business and Transportation Agency (sometimes called the Teale Center) proved to be so costly and produced such conflicts among departmental users that the Legislature did not wish to reproduce the Teale experience in another place. Although the thinking of "third generation" computer experts emphasized the advantages of a single mega-computer processing and controlling all data, the views of the "fourth generation" (which we are now in) stress the lower cost and greater flexibility of smaller, decentralized computers tied together in a single network. There is also the civil liberties issue. If all information were organized in one place, there would be a data bank which could put together a complete dossier on every aspect of the lives of every person in the state receiving SSI (supplemental security income), AFDC-FG (aid for families with dependent children, family group category), AFDC-U (aid for families with dependent children and an unemployed parent), Disability Insurance, Unemployment Insurance, Medi-Cal and various other benefit programs reaching more than six million persons. Once sensitive data was centralized ... it would be much more vulnerable to access by persons with improper motives, including disgruntled employees, special interest groups and organized crime.

I should have added power-mad bureaucrats and politicians to the list of "persons with improper motives," but I was in a hurry. The letter went on for several more pages and concluded with a request for careful review, full consultation with the departmental directors, and a delay in the decision. The critical paragraph in the letter dealt with the civil liberties issue. I wanted to head off a 1984 situation. The 1984 problem seemed so obvious to me. I had assumed Bob and Mario would understand. They had both handled civil liberties cases before coming to Sacramento. But now, I was beginning to wonder. Perhaps power caused people temporary amnesia. One thing was certain, though. The rhetoric of the Brown administration was going off in a different direction than the reality. The rhetoric said: Small is beautiful, decentralize, make the political leaders accountable. The reality was somewhat different. Not only in regard to the data processing issue but also in reference to a number of other administrative matters as well: big was beautiful; power was continually being centralized within the administration; fewer and fewer people were making decisions; and a great deal of effort was expended in insulating the Governor from criticism and reducing his accountability.

Quite conceivably, centralization and hierarchy were inevitable concomitants of late-twentieth-century government. A problem arose. The Governor wanted information fast. The officials who tried to do his bidding discovered some of the information was hard to obtain. He yelled at them when they came back empty-handed. They quite naturally reacted by trying to centralize the information-gathering network within their jurisdictions, and some of the brighter ones, like Gnaizda, perceived that in government information was power, it was the only kind of power that could be readily obtained by appointed officials who had no political base of their own.

And so it went. The need to protect Jerry's image was another reason why power had to be centralized. If different departmental heads could go off on their own and do and say different things, inconsistencies would undoubtedly arise, and Jerry would appear as if he were not in control. He did not want this kind of impression to be communicated, understandably, and so the reins of control were tightened and the span of supervision was narrowed. The first time a departmental director issued a press release that caused the Governor unhappiness, a directive went out from the Governor's office that in the future all press releases had to be cleared with the Governor's press secretary. Then, when a departmental director took the initiative on something Jerry didn't like, the order went out that nobody could do anything until the matter was cleared by the agency secretaries, who reported directly to the Governor. Again, the directive was completely understandable in the context in which it was issued, but once issued, it remained for all situations, and because, again quite understandably, the Governor's appointees didn't wish to incur the Governor's displeasure, they erred on the safe side and refrained from taking *any* significant action, and because, furthermore, this particular Governor made it his business to be interested in small issues as well as big ones (since small issues might still have great symbolic significance), the administrative part of Brown's administration finally, almost inevitably, came to a creaking standstill, and nobody took initiatives on anything without first checking with the Governor. Trips to Washington were delayed until the Governor gave his approval. Appearances before legislative committees were put off until there was a frantic, last-minute discussion in the Governor's office. The investigation of the prepaid health scandal was put in the deep freeze; Jerry didn't seem to be interested. The reorganization of the Department of Industrial Relations was postponed for six months; Jerry refused to delegate authority to Rose Bird to authorize the change. My memo regarding the impending bankruptcy of the Unemployment Insurance Fund sat on Jerry's desk for three weeks with no action being taken; Jerry was miffed with me. At times, the government seemed almost paralyzed because of the needs of Jerry's media operation.

The concern with image led not only to the centralization of authority, but also to a flight from responsibility. The Governor had to be insulated from bad news. "Deniability" was being stressed on all memos that were written for his attention. The underlings within the administration were organized in separate compartments, and sometimes the left hand didn't know what the right hand was doing. As a result, the image prospered while the day-to-day administration suffered. And so did the concept of accountability. The Zen logic that was used, the frequent shifts and double shifts Jerry negotiated, the constant air of mystery he maintained, the practice of keeping the legislators in the dark on important matters until the last possible moment — all of these tendencies reduced Jerry's accountability in the end. He was asking us to lower our expectations, yes, but in a different way than we had first realized.

After the computer controversy, I decided that the talk about "small is beautiful" was protective coloration. The reality was that the centralization of government was growing every day. It had grown under Reagan, who had the image of a small government man, and it was growing even more under Jerry, who played the image game even harder than Reagan did. The image had to be protected, that was the bottom line, and centralization that was discrete and occurred behind the scenes afforded the image more protection.

On Wednesday, July 9, Mario Obledo and I hosted a luncheon meeting for several of the state's labor leaders. David Commons was also present. Mario hadn't had any contacts with the labor leaders before, so he had been after me to arrange the get-together. I finally agreed. The meeting proceeded without incident. A few pictures were taken of us sitting around the table at Posey's, a popular Sacramento restaurant.

On Wednesday evening Mario and I negotiated another meal with labor representatives. This time the featured guest was Jerry Whipple of the UAW. At one point in the dinner conversation, Mario made some comment to Whipple about there being as much unemployment as there was because people weren't willing to work hard enough. I looked over at

Whipple to see his reaction. He practically choked on the piece of food he was chewing, but he kept his cool. I think from that point on he wrote Mario off as something of a fool. Mario had just put the wrong record on the phonograph. The speech about workers not working hard enough was the line he was supposed to use with conservative businessmen, whom he was very good at playing up to.

On the way out of the restaurant, Mario said he wanted me to come back to the Health and Welfare Agency and talk over a few matters with him. I agreed. We let ourselves in through the back door and sat down in one of the secretarial offices. "Jim," Mario said, "you have lost your effectiveness in the Brown administration. It's my belief you should submit your resignation to the Governor." He shifted uneasily in his chair. I didn't say anything. He obviously felt he was in a very difficult position. Outside the room where we were sitting, his daughter was playing. I had wondered why Mario had brought her to the dinner, it having been the first time in six months that I had seen one of his children, but now I suspected the reason. He had been afraid of talking to me alone. The child was intended as a kind of shield. Perhaps if she was playing nearby, I wouldn't get mad at him the way I had with Bob.

The poor man! I suddenly felt sorry for him. Here he was performing this difficult task, which he didn't relish doing. He really had a good heart. He was just afraid, afraid of incurring the Governor's disapproval, afraid of not completing the Horatio Alger dream he had fashioned for himself, long before in that little Texas town he grew up in. The difference our backgrounds had made in our personalities was never more manifest. I had grown up in comfortable surroundings; I could afford to say no and get angry. He couldn't. He was the poor boy made good, and he had to follow orders to do better. My unwillingness to submit to Jerry's games must have seemed to him like the height of upper-middle-class arrogance and self-indulgence. He, by contrast, was willing to put the bit in his mouth and go where his rider told him. Who knew? Perhaps someday he would be able to shake off the reins and be his own man. But I doubted it. I felt Mario had made a bad bargain. He was allowing Jerry to do to him what the Indians feared the tourists would do to them when they pulled out their cameras. Jerry was robbing Mario of his soul.

I finally responded to Mario's request. My answer was very brief. I'd think it over and let him know, I said. He nodded. He seemed relieved that the ordeal was over.

I informed my staff at EDD the same night. They were shocked, more shocked than I was, I think. I had sensed it coming. David Commons, who had attended both the luncheon and dinner meetings that day, had one ascerbic comment: "That dinner with Whipple was really like the last supper, wasn't it?" he said.

The next several days were spent waiting. I wasn't absolutely convinced Jerry was behind Mario's request, but if he was, I was determined to flush him out of the bushes. He was going to have to assume responsibility for a change.

On Monday, July 14, Bob Gnaizda called. I didn't return the call. He telephoned again and left a message. It was quite urgent we get together and talk, the message said. I threw it in my wastebasket.

On Tuesday, July 15, Mario and I met again. Mario wanted to know what my decision was. I said I thought we should take a walk in the garden behind the capitol. While we were strolling among the rhododendron bushes, Mario started pressing me. What had I decided? What had I decided? I told him I was still thinking about it. He didn't seem very pleased. He looked a little bit like a man who was being subjected to the Chinese water torture. Finally, as we were bidding each other good-bye in front of the Health and Welfare Agency building, he made one last try and, almost as if he were attempting to reassure me that everything would be all right once I resigned, said, "Jim, I've decided who I want to replace you." Who? I asked. "Marty Glick," he said. I shook my head and walked away.

On Thursday, July 17, Bob Gnaizda and I had lunch together at Posey's. We reminisced about old times. Bob tried to be conciliatory. Around midway through the lunch, however, he said, "You really have no choice." I probed to find out whether Jerry was behind the demand. Bob gave a guarded response. I sensed he was trying to protect Jerry, who wanted to stay uninvolved. I asked a few more questions. Bob laid it on the line. I wasn't cut out for government, he said. I was unmanageable. There was probably something wrong with me. I was a little neurotic. I would do all right on a regulatory board, though. Or as a judge. He thought I would make a good judge. I just looked at him. I was having trouble finishing my turkey sandwich. I knew he didn't have a very high opinion of the judiciary, but this was too much. I was too neurotic for state government but I would make a good judge. I mumbled something inconsequential about being glad to know what he thought. Little more was said during the rest of the luncheon. We got up, paid the bill, walked out of the restaurant, and began the long, slow walk back to the mall in front of the capitol. As I turned to cross the street to my office, Bob called out. "Wait," he said. I waited. "I love you," he said.

The rest of the afternoon was spent in phone calls to interest groups I had worked with in the past: the labor leaders, the NAACP, one or two women's groups. By four o'clock, there were supposed to be thirty telephone calls and telegrams pouring into Mario Obledo's office. We decided to focus the pressure on him. Jerry would still be kept out of it. I would honor my commitment to myself not to put pressure directly on him. David Commons reported that Jerry Whipple had told him that the Governor said he had no intention of firing me. Jerry Whipple supposedly told Jerry Brown what a good guy I was. Jimmie Lee also made a call to the Governor's office, and John Cinquemani of the Los Angeles Building

Trades did too. I was gratified by those two calls. Lee and Cinquemani didn't have to walk the extra mile for me. By five o'clock, the report from the Health and Welfare Agency was that Mario was not accepting any more phone calls. His pinball machine had gone on Tilt. David Commons was convinced Jerry wouldn't fire me. "He doesn't have the heart for it," David said. "I know him, I know him well; he doesn't like to fire anybody."

The morning of Friday, July 18, broke hot and humid. David was staying at the apartment the UAW lobbyists used while they were in Sacramento. I walked over there about eight o'clock in the morning. The birds were chirruping in the trees. It was a lovely, early summer day in the San Joaquin Valley. David was still in his underwear. "You've got to see Jerry this morning before Gnaizda does," David said. David had learned that Bob had an eleven o'clock appointment with Jerry. David called over to the Governor's office to try to get me in before ten. One of the secretaries he spoke with, a member of the informal network that, during the campaign, was known as the Irish Mafia, said she would do her best for me. She called back ten minutes later and said I should be in the anteroom to Jerry's office no later than ten o'clock. I blew her an imaginary kiss. She was a good sort.

At ten o'clock sharp I walked into Jerry's office. Jerry was sitting on the couch. He began the conversation by trying to be philosophical. All jobs were temporal, he said. Mine was no exception. We all had to go sooner or later. I didn't say anything, but I thought to myself: Okay, I choose later rather than sooner. Jerry talked about the jobs program I had drafted. Many of the suggestions were all right, he said, but the rhetoric was wrong. He sighed. He realized that running the jobs through nonprofit corporations was more effective, he said, but having the government hire the kids directly was safer. There was more control. He looked at me with some friendliness, as if to indicate he knew I was right about the usefulness of the nonprofits but not about the politics.

214

Mario Obledo came into the room, walking quickly and appearing a little flustered, as if he had been summoned at the last moment. He was carrying his straw hat. Jerry got up from the couch and excused himself. He had another matter to attend to, he said. Mario and I walked into the little room behind Jerry's main office. He was quite upset. Why had I called out all the telegrams? he asked. He had had no peace. At first I thought he was going to become angry with me, then I realized he was frightened. He just wanted to know. I mentioned the luncheon with Bob and how I had not appreciated being called a neurotic. Mario said "Oh," and his face softened. He shook his head as if he didn't like the word either. And then he started pleading with me. Please, couldn't I go quietly. He would go quietly if he were in the same situation, he said. He felt I should do the same. He was concerned about my family. He felt I should be taken care of. He didn't think a man should be thrown out on the sidewalk with no income. He would do what he could. I thanked him. We walked back into the main office.

Gray Davis was there now, seated in a chair. We chatted about the problems of government. The Los Angeles *Times* had recently broken a story indicating that Lieutenant Governor Mervyn Dymally was mixed up in some kind of scandal involving the misuse of Ford Foundation money.[64] The Governor's office was going to "cut off Dymally like that," Davis indicated, and so saying he chopped his right hand down like a guillotine. I looked down at the space in front of Davis's chair. Dymally's imaginary head was rolling around on the floor. Davis talked about other matters. Marc Poche, Jerry's liaison man with the state senate, entered the room and sat down. They both commiserated with me and asked me to accept the inevitable. I sat there and waited for Jerry. I wanted to hear Jerry say the magic words.

After a while, Jerry walked into the room. He looked slightly put out. I had not disposed of myself yet. "Look," he began. His tone was harsher now, more impatient. The press had got wind of the situation. Reporters were beginning to call the Governor's office. He didn't want the uncertainty to drag on. A decision had to be made. He wanted a decision. I thought for what seemed like an eternity. I didn't want to cause him inconvenience, but I didn't appreciate being ganged up on. The pressure in the room seemed almost unbearable. They were putting the pressure on. I told him I'd think about it and get back to him at three o'clock that afternoon. Jerry sat up suddenly on the couch. He seemed flabbergasted, as if he hadn't heard me correctly. "Why wait?" he asked. He was very impatient now. I said I wanted to talk to my staff. They had served loyally through thick and thin. I felt I owed them some consideration. Jerry shook his head in amazement. "What does your staff have to do with it?" he asked. "This is between you and me." I said I begged to differ. Maybe we were different in that respect. He shook his head in disgust. "You and I just aren't on the same wavelength," he exclaimed.

The interview was over. I walked back to my office. The staff felt I should refuse to resign. If Jerry didn't like the job I was doing, he should say so publicly and accept responsibility for the decision. I wasn't entirely convinced, but there was one argument that swayed me. During the course of the luncheon with Gnaizda and during the meeting in the Governor's office that morning, the possibility had been raised that I could be appointed to another position, such as a judgeship or the Agricultural Labor Relations Board, which were outside the Governor's direct chain of command. I decided that although I might be *worth* only six portable toilets, I didn't want to put a price tag on my head, like a judgeship.

My mind was made up. At three o'clock I returned to the Governor's office with a letter I had prepared for Jerry. As I was walking down the hallway to Jerry's antechamber, Tony Kline, the Governor's legal counsel, intercepted me. I wondered whether he was authorized to make the offer of the judgeship. I decided he wasn't. Tony and I walked into his office. We exchanged pleasantries. I sensed he was trying to feel me out as to what my decision was going to be. I refused to tip my hand. After ten minutes of waiting around, Tony left the room and Jerry appeared, looking quite stiff and uncomfortable. I glanced down to see if his right pant leg was trembling. It wasn't. I think he was almost as intimidated by the encounter as I was, however.

"Jerry," I said, "I respect you a lot, but I must decline to accept your invitation to resign. Here is a letter explaining my reasons."

I handed him the letter. He looked at the envelope but didn't open it. I gathered he was somewhat at a loss to know what to do next. I was as well. Finally, we walked out of the room together. He proceeded one way down the hallway and I went the other way. As I was opening the door to the reception area, one of the members of the Irish Mafia handed me a handwritten note: "We love you. We're 10,000% with you." It was a nice gesture.

At eight o'clock Friday evening Jerry called me at my apartment to say he had decided to replace me with Marty Glick. A letter would follow confirming the decision. The letter was delivered about half an hour later, scrawled in Jerry's own, slightly illegible handwriting. It was all over. We had made a run for the money and lost. The rest of the EDD executive staff decided to resign the following day, en masse. I wasn't sure they were making the right move, but they were adamant. Glick wouldn't be fun working for anyway, one of the staff members said. I didn't bother to correct her. Whatever her state of mind, Glick wouldn't tolerate her presence for more than two weeks.

Jerry's press release on the firing was issued the evening of the nineteenth. Apparently he and his assistants had written it before he called me. "Jim is a man of high ideals with a commitment to serving people," Jerry announced. "But despite his considerable talents, I don't think he can adequately manage such a large department of state government and effectively help meet the state's responsibilities to the 1 million unemployed people in California."

All things considered, I felt it was a generous, almost

affectionate statement. I wasn't a bad fellow, just administratively incompetent. There was no difference of opinion between us regarding the unemployment issue. Apparently Jerry wanted to do something about the unemployment problem and I didn't.

I sensed he wanted to keep his options open, alienating neither left nor right.

On Monday, July 21, when I held my farewell press conference in the state capitol, I tried to return the compliment. Jerry was a fine person, I told the assembled reporters. We had had a disagreement about how hard and fast to push a jobs program. I wanted to go further than he wanted to. And so on and so on. As I was talking, I could hear the newsreel cameras whirring in the background. One of the reporters asked me whether it was true that the administration of the Governor's office was highly disorganized. I mumbled something in reply about the Governor encouraging a give-and-take process that was intended to elucidate different points of view.

I was still protecting Jerry, it turned out! For the previous year, I had considered my relationship to him something like that between an attorney and his client. Now I was discovering, standing in front of the reporters that morning, that I was having a hard time breaking myself of the habit. Jacques Barzaghi came to me afterward and thanked me for being nice to Jerry.

The same morning, Marty Glick gave his first interview. "I don't come in with any agenda whatsoever," he said. "I really don't have a plan at the moment. I don't think the job in EDD is to reorder society." Nevertheless, he added, he believed the Governor would approve financing for jobs programs whose merit could be proven.[65]

The following week the debate heated up somewhat. Derek Shearer, an associate of mine at EDD, wrote an "op-ed" piece in the Los Angeles *Times* that quoted Jerry on his Camp Roberts remark.[66] According to two of my old friends in the Governor's office who still kept me informed about what newspapers criticized him for obfuscating the issue. However one described it, a tax was a tax was a tax.

In December 1975, Alice Daniel resigned her position in the Governor's office. She later accepted a job in Washington, D.C., as general counsel for the Legal Services Corporation, which funded legal aid for low-income people.

Bob Gnaizda left the administration in February 1976.

Mario Obledo stayed on and survived.

Marty Glick stayed on and prospered.

Paul Halvonik resigned his position in the Governor's office in June 1976 to become state public defender. According to the grapevine in the Governor's office, which I was still privy to, Paul was supposed to serve in the position for a year or less and then be appointed to the State Court of Appeals. At last report, however, he was still waiting for his judgeship.

Don Burns, Jerry's close friend and secretary of the Business and Transportation Agency, resigned his position in December 1976 to enter private law practice in San Francisco. When questioned by reporters about his reason for leaving, Don denied having had any difficulties working for Jerry. He just wanted to make more money, he said.[68]

Rose Bird remained as secretary of the Agriculture and General Services Agency until February of 1977, when she was appointed chief justice of the California supreme court.

Tony Kline remained in the Governor's office as legal counsel, working closely with Jerry.

Gray Davis did so as well.

David Commons was supposedly on the outs with Jerry for some time after my firing but maintained contact through Tom Quinn, who, as head of the state Air Resources Board, received more publicity than any state official except Jerry.

Richard Maulin was reappointed chairman of the state Energy Commission, despite some ongoing differences with Jerry.

Bob Rosenberg accepted a job with the state senate as special consultant on unemployment problems.

was going on, the alarm bells sounded immediately. Jerry didn't appreciate publication of a remark that sounded as if he harbored hostilities against blacks.

On Tuesday, July 29, I met in Los Angeles with two Los Angeles *Times* reporters. The very next day, July 30, Jerry made a surprise appearance at the *Times'* editorial offices, where he began to shift ground somewhat. Whereas in the press release announcing my firing he had recognized the state's responsibility to meet the needs of 1 million unemployed people, now he indicated that the state could do little for the jobless. "Unemployment is basically a national problem," he told reporters Harry Bernstein and Kenneth Reich. He did not say whether he would authorize Glick to begin lobbying in Washington. He did state that the jobs memo published by the Oakland *Tribune* was not a significant factor in his decision to fire me.[67]

I wondered. Several months after the firing, my old friend and legal counsel at EDD, Al Saldamando, telephoned. "Guess who I saw today," he said. I said I couldn't. He chuckled. "Jerry," he exclaimed. "Man, he spent a long time talking to me about you. I think he felt a little guilty. He went on and on about what a bad administrator you were and I just looked at him, as if to say, 'Aw, come on, Jerry,' and finally, you know what he said?" I said I didn't know and Al replied, "Jerry said, 'It was that guy Commons. That was the real reason. Commons made me nervous working with Lorenz.'"

So now I knew. Maybe. Commons, the substitute father for both of us, had been more of a problem than I had realized. I should have known. What a fool I was. I had worked hard all those years in college and law school and law practice. I had filed big lawsuits. I had started California Rural Legal Assistance and other organizations. I had made it almost all the way to the top of state government by the age of thirty-six. And what had I succeeded in doing? I had succeeded in becoming involved in a sibling rivalry with the Governor of California.

Chapter Twenty-Five

LIFE GOES ON. SOME OF THE GOVERNOR'S FRIENDS LEAV[
THE ADMINISTRATION. OTHERS REMAIN. THE GOVERNO[
BECOMES A NATIONAL CELEBRITY AND CONTINUES TO
DEAL IN SYMBOLS. THE GOVERNOR SEES THE PLIGHT OF
THE JOBLESS WITH HIS OWN EYES BUT THEN GOES SEARCH-
ING FOR WHALES.

AROUND THE TIME I was fired, acting state welfare director Prod was relieved of his position. Jerome Lackner, the
other departmental head who had met with me on the
computer problem, was allowed to stay on. His department,
however, was put in a kind of receivership, with two deputy
directors loyal to Gnaizda installed in charge of administration.

The computer consolidation proceeded as originally
planned by Gnaizda and Obledo. In the summer of 1975,
responding to Obledo's request, the legislature removed the
language in the budget act that prohibited computer consolidation in the Health and Welfare Agency.

The recommendations I made regarding the Unemployment Insurance Fund were followed. The taxable wage base,
the amount of wages the employers paid UI taxes on, was
expanded, and approximately 600 million additional dollars
were generated for the fund. At first Jerry tried to contend
that taxes weren't being raised since it was the taxable wage
base, not the tax rate, that was being increased, but several

Jacques Barzaghi was placed in charge of the Ecology Corps.

The name of the Ecology Corps was changed to Conservation Corps.

The name of the scandal-ridden prepaid health programs was changed to Medical Service Institutes.

Few, if any, substantive modifications were made in the operations of either program.

I, meanwhile, returned to San Francisco and entered the real estate business.

When superficial acquaintances who had read about the jobs controversy asked me what I was doing and I told them, they seemed surprised, as if they half-expected me to be a local organizer for Mao Tse-tung. Most times, I didn't even bother to explain the difference between appearance and reality in politics.

About two months after Bob Gnaizda left Sacramento, he telephoned and invited me to have dinner with him. Somewhat curious about what he would say, I accepted.

When we sat down at the table together Bob was not at a loss for words. "I've decided to forget the bad times and remember the good ones," he began.

We proceeded from there, talking somewhat guardedly about the old days I gathered from the bits and pieces of information Bob gave me that although he still had great affection and respect for Jerry, he had been too frustrated working for him to stay on. Toward the end of his sojourn in Sacramento, Bob had been put in charge of the medical malpractice controversy that was then raging. He was unable to persuade Jerry to make a decision, however. It had been a maddening experience for Bob, apparently. "Jerry's a great guy when you don't need anything from him," Bob explained, "but when you have to get a decision..." He shook his head in frustration and grudging admiration. There was nobody better at avoiding decisions than Jerry.

I saw Bob on one other occasion, several months later.

Sitting in the Shandygaff Restaurant on Polk Street in San Francisco, surrounded by the hair stylists and fashion designers who frequented the neighborhood, we talked at length about what kind of President Jerry would make. Bob, who was convinced Jerry would climb to the top of the pile one day, felt Jerry would be a great President. (I nearly asked Bob if he was prepared to support Jerry "almost 100 per cent.") "I know he's a lousy administrator," Bob said, "but he won't start any wars." I faintly recollected hearing that kind of statement before, from the secretary in the Governor's office who said she supported Jerry because he wouldn't hurt anybody.

We talked on. Bob was in somewhat of a quandary about what to do. He wanted to resume public interest law work but felt inhibited about suing the state on any important matter because he was afraid of embarrassing Jerry. The conflict was made more acute because Bob understood Jerry's weaknesses so intimately and the workings of state gorvernment so well. How could he exploit this inside information when he had gained it as a result of his friendship with Jerry? He was not sure he could. If he used the information and attacked the Brown administration, he would feel disloyal, and if he refrained from doing battle, he would be deprived of his favorite target, the State of California. It was a terrible dilemma for him. Bob finally mentioned something about the possibility of suing the federal Social Security Administration, but this, I recognized immediately, was no solution. The federal Social Security Administration was small fry compared with the State of California. Thanks in part to the media campaign Jerry had been running, the State of California was front-page news across the country. Bob, moreover, had earned his considerable reputation as a public interest lawyer by suing the state and ridiculing it in the press. If he had to restrict himself to the mundane operations of the Social Security Administration, he was relegating himself to a backwater, and Jerry, in effect, had deprived him of his favorite metier. What a horrible price to pay for friendship with a political leader, I thought at the time. At least I didn't have that problem. One of the advantages of being fired was that you didn't have to agonize over being coopted.

The luncheon with Bob occurred at a time in my life when the political goings-on in Sacramento seemed light years away. I was getting involved in other things: real estate investment, writing, and spending time with my two children, Shanna and Aaron. Aaron was just learning to talk. He could say two words: "no" and "uh-oh." With that vocabulary, I decided, he could do very well in state government.

Occasionally I wondered about my conflict with Jerry. Would events have turned out differently if I had written another memo or had steered clear of David Commons or had held my temper with Gnaizda? I was inclined to think not. Although I might have stayed on in Sacramento longer, I wouldn't have had any more success persuading Jerry to approve a major jobs program. The problem, in the final analysis, was not my personality or Jerry's or Gnaizda's or David Commons's, idiosyncratic though those personalities may have been. The problem was, there was no pressure for a jobs program.

Jerry described the problem very graphically about two weeks before I was fired: "Listen," he said, almost tauntingly, "I'll believe I have to do something for the unemployed only when I see them rioting in the streets." He was being his usual hyperbolic self, of course, not really wishing for a riot, but only saying that pressure was necessary in order to transform a social problem into a political issue. There was no Cesar Chavez on the unemployment issue. The big unions lobbied hard only for their members. The black kids standing on the street corners were not members of the Carpenters or Operating Engineers or the other unions Jimmie Lee represented. Nobody had been representing the black kids in Sacramento, not the NAACP or the Urban League or the black ministers or the black legislators. It was strange. After

225

all the civil rights ferment in the 1960s, the 1970s were characterized by an eerie, deadly quiet. The blacks were not pushing. There was, in Jerry's opinion, no black leadership in California. That was one reason why, in December 1974, he had decided to "tilt" toward the Mexican-American community. He didn't fear the blacks the way he did the Mexican-Americans and Cesar Chavez. The blacks had no Cesar.

How Martin Luther King was missed! Jerry and the other new politicians of the 1970s would not have been able to get away with ignoring the blacks if Martin Luther King had been around. For the first time I understood the great man (or woman) theory of history. The great person really did make a difference, especially if he (or she) was on the outside of government, pushing in. There was such a great misunderstanding about politics. Most people thought the major decisions were made only on the inside, by the big politicians who were in the public spotlight. Most people were wrong. The politicians like Jerry followed much more than they led; they sniffed the wind, they put their ears to the ground, and then they straightened up and announced their decision as if they had known it all along. The art of politics was in convincing people you were leading when actually you were following. The modern politician was a kind of walking Gallup Poll, unwilling to make any move until he checked the popular pulse and cleared the decision with the key interest groups.

The situation was not so surprising if one thought about it for a while. An American politician wasn't an emperor; he didn't make decisions unilaterally, from on high. Democracy was a two-way street. The pressure had to come in in order for the decisions to go out. It took two to tango: the politicians and the pressure groups. The politicians arbitrated and modulated the various pressures that came in. The pressure groups created the necessity for making the decisions, like the wind that made the sailboats go. If a politician went out and did something on his own, one or more pressure groups would chop him to pieces. "He didn't *have* to do that," they would say. "He's doing that of his own volition." The politician was then considered a troublemaker, a rabble-rouser, an ideologue. He lost his appearance of neutrality, which was crucial for him. Even if a politician was as prejudiced and partisan as all get-out, he had to *seem* neutral. After all, according to the high school civics books, the politician was the representative of *all* the people in his district. The pressure generated on him was an important part of this charade, if nothing else. When the politician moved farther right on the political spectrum, he had to be able to say to the groups on the left that he had had no choice, overwhelming pressure was being generated on the right; and when he moved farther left, he similarly had to point back over his shoulder, to the furies on the left. The justification for his action always was: If I didn't do what I did, something worse would have happened; better half a loaf with me than no loaf with somebody else. It was always the same. When the politician huddled in the center of the political spectrum, that meant the pressures from right and left were about equal.

Sometimes, ingenious politicians like Jerry tried to levitate above the pressures, but it was only an illusion they cultivated to reduce the amount of pressure brought to bear on them, which was sometimes excruciating. The working formula was clear: Symbols plus no pressure equaled synecdoche; symbols plus pressure equaled program. The farmworkers got a collective bargaining bill because they exerted pressure; the black kids got a symbolic Conservation Corps because they didn't.

I often wondered why the blacks didn't generate more pressure. I never came up with a completely satisfactory answer. Jerry certainly poked and pressed them enough, testing to see if they had any mettle. There was usually little, if any, response. In January, after the major appointments had been announced and the only black chosen was put in charge of the General Services Administration (a few of the cynics in the administration called him "the head janitor"), I held my breath to see if there would be any protest from the black groups and black legislators. There wasn't any to speak of. In February and March and April and May, when Jerry went out of his way to ostracize Mervyn Dymally, the black Lieutenant Governor, I waited for the protest. There wasn't any, either — and how incredible the silence seemed. Dymally was the first black ever elected to statewide office in California. If the blacks were going to allow him to die on the vine, they were telling the world they were weak and disorganized. Finally, in June the NAACP entered a complaint with Jerry. The complaint, though politely worded, was enough to cause Jerry to decide tentatively to include Dymally in the cabinet meetings, but alas, the NAACP failed to persist in their pressure, and when Dymally got into trouble with the Los Angeles *Times*, the Dymally-integration scheme was quietly dropped.

The pattern of lost opportunities was repeated over and over again. When Jerry attacked the administration of the LEAA funds and raised the possibility that the money could be used for unemployed teen-agers, there was no communication from the black groups. When the state Department of Finance confirmed the fact that the year-end surplus might be in excess of $400 million, there was, again, no statement from outside. According to my calculations, if the surplus had been distributed according to the votes for Jerry in the 1974 election, the blacks should have gotten at least $100 million for their programs. The issue was never raised, so far as I knew. In the winter of 1975, when Willie Brown, the brilliant black assemblyman, was considering making another run for the assembly speakership (he had lost twice before to Jerry's ally Leo McCarthy), he could have exacted a considerable price for not running, such as a tenfold increase in the Conservation Corps. He chose to make a third try for the speakership instead — and lost. One of the state's most talented legislators was out of commission for the rest of the year, relegated to a tiny office with one secretary.

One day in the late spring I asked one of Jerry's aides why the black legislators weren't pressing harder. If they had ever organized themselves as a group and demanded a jobs program for the hard-core unemployed, they probably could have gotten it. The aide replied that the legislators were too interested in making it on their own. This one wanted a judgeship out of Jerry; *he* wouldn't make any waves. That one had credit card problems. This one wanted to chair a legislative committee. That one was thinking about leaving the legislature. Jerry's comment about the lack of black leadership seemed to be confirmed.

I suppose I should have asked Jerry's aide why the Mexican-American legislators and urban white legislators weren't doing more. But so much of the Mexican-Americans' energies were going into the farm labor bill, and the whites had to worry about Jimmie Lee and the building trades. The hard-core unemployment problem, for better or worse, was a black problem. And as Jerry said, blacks were "the wrong symbol." The first part of the 1970s was, drawing on Daniel Patrick Moynihan's memorable words, the time of "benign neglect" for blacks. The blacks, according to this theory, terrified white voters too much to remain in the center of the stage; they would do better to retire to the wings and keep quiet for a while.

The theory was less than fully convincing, as far as I was concerned. In politics, nobody got anything but symbols if they remained quiet. The Moynihan thesis sounded more like wishful thinking or the attempt to rationalize what was already happening, namely, the wholesale discouragement of the civil rights movement after Nixon came to power. The American people were tired of street marching, true enough; but this fatigue did not need to prevent blacks from agitating for jobs. The blacks could have conformed to the quieter style of the 1970s and pressured as Cesar Chavez did, marching behind a religious symbol. In the final analysis, symbols were a function of pressure more than a cause of it. If a movement was viable, it would select the right symbols for itself. That the black community was able to find no attractive images to express its needs suggested that there was a power vacuum.

Was it unfair to single out the black legislators for criticism? Probably. They too were insiders now. If they wanted to run for higher office, as many of them did, they couldn't sound too much like firebrands. The agitation had to come from outside the government. The agitation didn't develop outside the government for one very simple reason, however. It was too easy for younger, ambitious, middle-class blacks to make it on the inside. The political process *was* opening up to them, and if the large majority of blacks had to remain outside, underfed and unemployed, that might seem a temporary problem that would be corrected as soon as the middle class gained a foothold in the system. The incentives were all on the inside: steady work, newspaper publicity, good pay, business connections, and honorary degrees from universities. Being an outside organizer, by contrast, was tough work. The pay was skimpy, the hours long, the membership of the community organizations usually uninterested in the idealism the organizers tried to convey. There were few organizers who could aspire to Cesar Chavez's charisma. Perhaps if the system had allowed less upward mobility, more would have tried to become Cesars, but at a time of opportunity for the black middle class, why bother? There was more to be made on the inside by going along. Even effective organizations like the East Los Angeles Community Union fell into this line of thinking to some extent. If they were asking the government for million-dollar contracts, they couldn't very well build pressure the way traditional organizers like Cesar and Martin Luther King and Saul Alinsky had been ready to do. That was why Cesar always refused to take money from the government. He told me once that it was impossible to make a fist and open your palm for money at the same time. The roles were just inconsistent. If you were an organizer, you were a warrior. The insiders were the dealers and peacemakers. In order for the insiders to make the peace, the organizers had to make war first. The farm labor bill would never have occurred if Caser had not waged an all-out battle for ten years before. The same was true for a jobs bill. What I needed more than anything else in Sacramento was a black Cesar. The black Cesar did not arrive in time, which was the main reason I was fired.

Perhaps the ebb and flow of pressure was cyclical, like the tides. In the 1960s, black pressure waxed; in the 1970s, it waned. Cesar and Ralph Nader continued throughout, but they were exceptional. Ordinary mortals were subject to the moods and limitations of their times; it was only the extraordinary individual who rose above the times and influenced the period according to his own likeness. The fact of the matter was, the early 1970s was a time of retreat. The mass demonstrations disappeared; the encounter groups appeared. People left the picket line and jumped into the hot tubs. EST sessions sprang up. So did meditation, organic gardening, yoga, Tai Chi, Rolfing, massage, transactional analysis, and Zen bread making. Almost every mundane activity that became a fad was described and justified in terms of individual growth. This activity was supposed to develop a sense of self, and that activity, a higher consciousness. The 1970s were the "me first" decade. The macrocosm of the world would be played out through the microcosm of the individual. People would retreat from the larger, messier reality in order to reenter it at some later, unspecified date, presumably transformed. For the majority of the population, Jerry was the appropriate symbol. He was perhaps the best reflection of the decade, a mirror of the times. He first popularized the concept "small is beautiful." He was the "me first" politician for a "me first" decade. If some of his style — or "New Spirit," as he called it — seemed oddly adolescent, well, then so was the decade as a whole. America had always been a young country, living for the present and looking to the future more than it reflected upon the past, and now, in the 1970s, America was experiencing the first awareness of its own limitations. This growing, still unformed awareness was analogous to adolescence, when the young person experiences but does not fully accept the limitations of adulthood. The mad search for an identity, the continuing uncertainty about who one actually was, the dogmatic self-assertions followed by the inchoate questioning, the desire for authority alternating with the rebellion against authority, the inflation of the self, the mock humility, the desire for illusion, the treatment of private experience as if it were totally representative of the outside world and were, indeed, the outside world — all of these tendencies were characteristic of Jerry, of adolescence, and of a large portion of our American experience in the 1970s. The only thing that was certain in this period was that we would grow out of it.

Meanwhile, the farmworkers went on picketing, perceiving quite correctly that they wouldn't capitalize on the collective bargaining bill by attending yoga classes.

And Jerry continued to play the symbols game. In August 1975, responding to the controversy over my firing, he made a well-publicized tour of a wilderness area where the Conservation Corps might initiate new projects and hire additional workers. For the most part, the press treated the tour as if it were synonymous with an expanded jobs program, praising Jerry for good intentions.[69] During the remainder of 1975, no further action was taken by the state regarding the Conservation Corps. The press puff had been enough, apparently.

On December 5, 1975, when the state unemployment rate was in excess of 9.8 per cent, the Brown administration made an important announcement. The nativity scene that had been displayed on the capitol lawn for three decades of Christmases would be relegated to a vacant drugstore. The administration had decided that the tableau amounted to a monument to one type of religion and violated the constitutional separation of church and state. Religious music of all types would be permitted, however. Christmas carols would be piped through the loudspeakers that supposedly helped calm the squirrels on the capitol lawn.[70]

Jerry was still dazzling them with trivia.

Around the same time, the Governor's office revealed that the Governor had refused an eleven-year-old girl his autograph. The girl, from Rome, New York, had written to all fifty governors to ask for their signatures. Only Jerry had refused. Subsequently, however, he relented and penned the following note: "Yes, Linda, there is a Governor in California. Your letter and perseverance have reached him. Good luck on your project and may it be but a beginning." The incident was worth two newspaper stories, the first indicating Jerry's frugality and mystery, the second, his generosity.[71] Possibly newspaper readers were too fascinated by the plight of the eleven-year-old girl to note that on January 1, 1976, two laws Jerry had signed the previous month would go into effect. The first legalized homosexuality; the second, marijuana smoking.[72]

On January 7, 1976, Jerry delivered a brief "state of the state" speech in which he called for a $10 million fund to create jobs to clean up the environment. The fund, which would be part of the Conservation Corps, involved only $5 million in state spending and opened up less than a thousand new jobs.[73] Several days later, I talked to Rosenberg on the phone. "Let's see," he said, "at this rate we should have full employment in California by the year 3976." A state legislator, Terry Goggin, was no less critical. The Conservation Corps, he said, "is a drop in the bucket."[74]

On March 5, the San Francisco *Chronicle* reported that the number of unemployed people in California rose above the 1 million mark the previous month for the first time since June 1975.[75] The very same day, a Sacramento reporter disclosed that the Governor was fasting for periods of forty-eight hours or more. When the Governor wasn't starving, the reporter said, he was eating junk food like ketchup and french fries. No mention was made of Pringle's potato chips.[76]

On the evening of March 12, Jerry called four reporters into his private office, where he sipped fruit juice and talked of many things. One thing he touched upon was his decision to run for President of the United States.[77] The announcement had been planned for months but was made in a typically casual, offhand manner, recalling the observation of McLuhan: "In the cool TV age, the office must chase the man . . . Anyone *seeking* office is far too hot for the new cool electorate."[78] Not surprisingly, Jerry announced no platform and no program. He would let his audience fill in the gaps, thereby allowing them the sensation of participation. The same evening he gave a talk to five hundred Democrats at the Peacock Golf and Country Club in San Rafael, California. When one county supervisor asked him what he was going to do about nuclear safety regulations, the audience hissed so loudly at the question that the Governor was not required to reply. A few minutes later Jerry said, in response to another question, "I don't duck things . . . I postpone them for further reflection." And when another member of the audience asked, "Now that you're a presidential candidate, how without a [unemployment] program do you put these people to work?" Jerry replied, "I'm going to deal with it one day at a time." The audience seemed appreciative.[79] As McLuhan was to note in another context: "The Forsythe shirt ad shows a field of daisies. There is no sign or mention of shirts. You simply look and feel as fresh as a daisy."[80]

Later on in the campaign, Jerry criticized Jimmy Carter for vagueness on the issues and announced his own foreign policy program, which he called "planetary realism."[81] He did not define the phrase "planetary realism." Like punishment that was "swift, sure and just," the buzz phrase from the previous campaign, "planetary realism" seemed to have something for everybody. "Planetary" was right out of *The Whole Earth Catalog;* it would please the young people and ecofreaks. And "realism" was for middle-class people in Omaha who had their feet on the ground.

On Friday, March 26, the San Francisco *Examiner* reported that three Democratic assembly chairmen, invited to Governor Brown's office for a chat the day before, walked out when the Governor kept them waiting half an hour. "If the Governor can keep Democratic chairmen waiting in his office at his pleasure, then he is controlling us," said Assemblyman James Keysor, chairman of the Elections and Reapportionment Committee. "I was p———d off," said Charles Warren of the Resources, Land Use and Energy Committee. "I had work to do."[82]

On March 29, the administration announced a $25 million jobs program. Although the press release stated that the jobs were to be created in private business, the details of the appended job package indicated nonprofit corporations were defined as private businesses.[83] Jerry had just dressed my old jobs program in new clothes, it appeared. Several days later, San Francisco *Chronicle* columnist Abe Mellinkoff noted:

> The plan itself unfolds in flashing acrylic, bright enough to dazzle the fast reader and surely to confuse the unemployed worker...It promises to create 3000 jobs but that figure barely bears the mark of truth for most of the money — $15 million — has already been sent down from the Ford administration in Washington to hire the unemployed. Assuming the new combined program — spending both old Federal money and new State money — works, there will be only 1200 new jobs, the other 1800 being provided for under the previous Federal plan. No, the pea is under that walnut shell over there.[84]

The $25 million program, it turned out, was opposed by the building trades unions and died a quick death in the legislature. The employment director had forgotten to consult with Jimmie Lee before he unveiled the program, and Jerry didn't bother to lobby for the proposal. Jerry was off campaigning in Oregon, Nevada, New Jersey, and Maryland.

The Maryland scene was described by Joe Klein, a *Rolling Stone* correspondent:

> It was a sensation rather like floating. Completely out of hand, but almost serene, almost euphoric. There was so much noise, it was quiet. Everything seemed to be moving in slow motion and we had no real control over our bodies ...It was Jerry Brown's first crowd in Maryland — the sort of crowd that makes a candidate believe that anything, even the presidency, is possible... Jerry Brown wandered aimlessly through Maryland, knocking them dead. He arrived (via tourist class on a commercial flight, of course) accompanied only by a glorified baggage handler and a press secretary whose sole function appeared to be shrugging his shoulders and saying he could never tell what Jerry might do next.[85]

Later the press would dub Jerry the "un-candidate." The crowds loved the new casualness. Jerry was doing what he had started to do in the 1974 gubernatorial campaign, only now he had the method perfected. The buzz words rattled off, polished one- and two-liners. He told his audience about the bill he had signed that would reduce the amount of water a toilet flushed. The crowd, which was mostly composed of young people, ate it up. He seemed so down to earth, so irreverent. There were only a few occasions when he ventured onto uncertain ground. One evening at Johns Hopkins University, a young man in the front row asked Jerry what he thought about the last two chapters of E. F. Schumacher's book, the ones where he called for a gradual conversion to a system of decentralized socialism, with the workers and the communities controlling the factories.

"Could you repeat that?" Jerry asked, although the question was entirely audible. "I'm not sure I understand."

The student repeated the question.

"Well, I'm not sure I know what you're referring to," Jerry said. "Those last chapters are kind of vague."

It was an interesting response, since the last two chapters of *Small Is Beautiful* are probably the most specific of the whole book. Most of the audience wasn't following the colloquy, however. They had come to see Jerry and Keith Carradine and Ronnie Blakely, two of the stars of *Nashville* who served as Jerry's warm-up act.

One student, though, picked up the drift of what was going on. "I think it's kind of strange that these stars from 'Nashville,' which was a movie about a politician with no program exploiting rock stars, are allowing themselves to be exploited by a politician with no program," the student was quoted as saying.[86] The student was zeroing in on the politics of hype.

The rest of the spring primaries Jerry participated in were a rerun of the Maryland experience. There was hype and more hype. The audience had never seen anything like it before. Or maybe they had. Jerry was playing to the young voters, the generation that had grown up with TV, the generation that would be almost a majority of the country in another eight years. It almost seemed as if he were running for the 1984, rather than the 1976, election. He didn't even bother to file for the Oregon primary, although he had time to do so after he announced his candidacy. I suspected he felt he was more interested in embarrassing the other candidates with a big write-in vote than he was in running the risk of winning (or losing) as a conventional candidate. A reporter friend of mine who covered the Oregon primary said it was almost frightening how much unquestioning fervor Jerry evoked in his audiences. The students who crowded around him didn't seem to care about program or experience. They liked Jerry's buzz words. Jerry had "good vibes." They were impressed that Cesar Chavez's farmworkers were working for him. If Cesar was on board, how could there be any doubts? The months of planning and practicing had paid off. Jerry had them eating out of the palm of his hand. I thought of the comment he had made in October 1974: "A politician can do anything he wants so long as he manipulates the right symbols."

Watch out, America, the California hype was on the way, rolling across America. The results were staggering. Jerry, the last-minute candidate, beat Jimmy Carter in Maryland, 49 per cent to 37 per cent. He won Nevada. He scored a record write-in vote in Oregon. He took California in a landslide. He was all vagueness and possibility. On May 31, *Time* magazine reported he had endorsed the Humphrey-Hawkins full employment bill but in a characteristically amorphous way. "Humphrey-Hawkins," Jerry said, "is a symbol, a commitment. Commitments are important."[87]

Although this general commitment was all the unemployed got from Jerry in the late spring of 1976, it seemed to be enough. On June 9, several days after the California primary, the San Francisco *Examiner* reported:

> The issues of jobs and unemployment helped Gov. Brown sweep to an impressive victory over fellow Democrats Jimmy Carter and Frank Church, according to an Examiner election poll.
>
> Nearly 1,000 voters from the Bay Area's five major counties were surveyed by the Examiner at 33 precincts after they cast their ballots. They were asked whom they voted for and what issues they felt to be most important in the presidential race.
>
> The issue mentioned most by all voters was "integrity and accountability in government"...
>
> Only the supporters of Gov. Brown placed higher importance on the issue of unemployment. The governor's call for full employment has apparently struck a responsive chord in the electorate.[88]

The same week the San Francisco *Chronicle* reported that, since beginning his presidential campaign travels on April 28, Jerry had paid four one-day visits to Sacramento.[89] The story was somewhat surprising in light of a statement Jerry had made on March 21: "I am putting in a good working day and evening and I'll continue doing that." He had left himself an out, however: "If we analyze this out on a 40-hour week, assuming I get the nomination in the election, I will come very close to putting in a four-year term (in 19 months in office)."[90] The press was being treated to a little Zen logic. The Now was almost infinitely expandable.

The California public didn't seem to care about the absences. Even the blacks were going along with Jerry. During the spring campaign, I read the newspapers eagerly to see how he was going to deal with the blacks. It wasn't an easy task, shunning a group for months and then noticing them all of a sudden when you needed their help, but Jerry pulled it off, and very ingeniously too. He started with the black legislators in Sacramento, who he may have felt were the most obvious symbol of the black community and who also had the most to gain by going along with him. According to a newspaper story printed on April Fool's Day, a press conference was scheduled. All but two black legislators were present. In his remarks to the reporters, Jerry made two concessions to the blacks. He promised to meet more frequently with them. (Little did they realize he would be in Sacramento only four days over the next two months.) And he modified his remark of February 1975 about the welfare mothers having to "tighten their belts." (That remark had rankled a number of black legislators.) "In a period of belt-tightening," Jerry said, "those with the biggest belts ought to tighten them first." Although he didn't explain what he meant by "belt-tightening," and although he made absolutely no programmatic concessions to the black legislators (the surplus was not mentioned in the press conference), the legislators seemed satisfied and offered him their wholehearted support.[91] I could almost hear Jerry saying after the meeting, "They're only words," meaning that all he had done was to rescind a previous statement that didn't mean anything anyway.

About a month later, Jerry journeyed to Charlotte, North

Carolina, to appear before a caucus of black political leaders, which numbered some 900 strong. His approach with the out-of-staters was most interesting. While in California he had been taking every opportunity to put down the 1960s, he now extolled the 1960s as the Golden Age and claimed he was part of this great tradition. "I represent the generation that came of age in the civil rights movement, in the anti–Vietnam War movement," he cried. His audience did not seem terribly impressed. One or two black officials asked why he had ignored his black Lieutenant Governor. Jerry brushed the charge aside. Why, if he were elected President, he pointed out, he "would appoint him" (and here he gestured toward Dymally, who was sitting in the room) Governor of California, the first black governor in state history! Jerry could still not bring himself to refer to Mervyn by name. A magazine reporter wrote later that Jerry was guilty of a little illusory giving. Under the California constitution, the Lieutenant Governor *automatically* succeeded to the governorship when the governorship was vacated.[92]

Shortly after Jerry's return from the Charlotte meeting, he administered the coup de grâce to the doubts the black community was harboring concerning his candidacy. What a masterful stroke it was. Only Jerry and one or two other politicians in the country could have thought of the maneuver, I believe. He assembled the segment of the black community that was least threatening to white voters — the black ministers — and quoted the Bible to them. "He who is first shall be last and last, first," he intoned. "So the last shall be first, and the first last, for many be called, but few chosen." The quotations from Saint Mark and Saint Matthew brought the house down. The hundred or so black clergymen who were gathered together at San Francisco's Fairmont Hotel loved the reference to the Scriptures.[93] Jerry was speaking to them in their own language. The special identity black people felt — an identity that archetypically was expressed by the Bible — was being recognized. They and their congregations were no longer invisible men and women. It made no difference that Jerry made no programmatic concession to them; the words were enough. The biblical quotation even had a double meaning. Jerry was camping it up again. The talk about the last being first might refer to the black community — or it might refer to Jerry's own candidacy, since he had been the last major candidate to enter the presidential race. The audience could take the words any way they wanted. Jerry was having his own private joke — and he was tantalizing them with delicious ambiguity.

On September 20, 1976, the prepaid health scandal blew up in the Brown administration's face. According to the San Francisco *Chronicle,* the prepaid health plans were termed "a nationally publicized disaster." Other programs were also under investigation by at least a dozen attorneys and auditors for the state attorney general's office, a U.S. Senate subcomittee, the General Accounting Office, and the federal Department of Health, Education and Welfare. Investigators were probing corruption in San Francisco's homemaker chore programs for the elderly. Critics said the state wasted many months before implementing a law providing for the screening of schoolchildren for diseases.[94] On November 11, new federal guidelines were announced that would require the state to make drastic cutbacks in the prepaid health programs.[95] The same month, a new scandal broke out in the state's mental hospitals. Some 139 patient deaths had occurred in the previous three years, a grand jury announced. The state had failed to adequately investigate the causes of these mortalities. On Sunday, November 14, Jerry paid a surprise visit to the Metropolitan State Hospital in Los Angeles.[96] He was playing a little synecdoche, apparently. Two weeks later, Democratic state senators Alfred Alquist and Arlen Gregorio told reporters that Governor Brown had been warned two years before about the state mental health system being a "potential time bomb," but nevertheless he had vetoed legislative efforts to increase hospital staffing. Alquist said he believed that most, if not all, of the 139 patient deaths would be blamed on inadequate staffing.[97]

The public hardly seemed to notice the health department scandal, however. The younger voters were still talking about Whale Day, which Jerry had staged in Sacramento on November 20. The whales were a perfect symbol. The environmentalists and under-thirty generation were up in arms about their impending extinction; at the same time there was absolutely no action Jerry could take to save them, the whales being beyond the three-mile limit. They were a safe issue. Jerry could have taken some action to save the three-toed salamanders, which were being liquidated in Santa Cruz County, but this would have meant instituting building moratoriums and alienating the building trades unions. Jerry chose the whales instead. He had first run across the whales while he was campaigning in Oregon the previous spring. The college audiences had gone wild every time he brought them up, so he kept the reference in his standard repertoire. Whale Day was apparently intended to solidify his hold on the younger voters. Joni Mitchell, the singer, was persuaded to appear at the rally. The celebration was a great success. Several days later, a friend of mine called from the state health department. "Just think," he said bitterly, "if we change the name of the Medi-Cal program to 'Medi-Whale' or 'Moby-Cal,' the Governor might give *us* some attention for a change."

The health department wasn't the only segment of the state government suffering from neglect. The previous month, the Legislative Audit Committee reported that over the preceding twenty-three-month period, the Governor had failed to expend 67 per cent of the total federal discretionary money allocated to him for job development.[98] Jerry had apparently forgotten about the money for the unemployed.

On January 10, 1977, Jerry submitted his third budget to the legislature: $15.2 billion of expenditures were called for, or $2.6 billion more than the amount requested the previous year, and approximately $4 billion more than Jerry's first budget in January 1975. Some $400 million of the new money would go for property tax relief for homeowners. Another $220 million would be used to comply with the state supreme court's *Serrano* decision, which required equalized funding of public schools. A surplus of $846 million was set aside. And $2.6 million would be used to augment the budget of the Conservation Corps.[99]

I added up the figures. Pursuant to the housing finance bill that the legislature passed and Jerry signed in 1975, the building trades stood to gain $450 million over a three-year period, or approximately $150 million a year. The teachers would benefit by a minimum of $220 million a year as a result of the equalized school financing — and some Sacramento observers estimated the sum would more likely be in the neighborhood of $1 billion per year. (Jerry's request was a bare-bones figure.) The homeowners, few of whom were perennially unemployed, would make $400 million. The black kids, by contrast, would end up with $6 million more than they had received under Reagan, or eight tenths of 1 per cent as much as the other groups. Jerry had not even been in favor of the *Serrano* decision the time I talked to him about it, having characterized the ruling a waste of money. Nevertheless, he had done nothing to reverse the decision. The black kids were still standing on the street corners.

Around the time Jerry submitted his budget to the legislature, the San Francisco *Examiner* ran a story about a housing project called the Pink Palace, where the residents were terrified to go outside because there were too many juvenile delinquents, dope addicts, and other criminals roaming the neighborhood. Several days after the article appeared, Jerry paid a surprise visit to the Pink Palace. The trip was supposed to be secret, but somehow the reporters were tipped off while he was conversing with residents.

"I have come to see for myself the conditions which exist and what is going on," he was quoted as saying as he sat in the $84-a-month, four-bedroom apartment of a woman with five children. The *Examiner* ran the story on page 1 the following day, along with a picture of Jerry standing in front of a pile of trash.

According to the newspaper account, Jerry stayed at the project overnight. Some of the tenants were incredulous that he would be visiting their homes. Asked if he would like to meet the Governor, one wool-capped man replied: "The Governor of what?" After an introduction, the two shook hands.

"What's happening?" the Governor asked. "It's terrible," said the man. "I'm healthy, but I need jobs. Jobs."

The newspaper reporter said Jerry nodded.

He was more vocal, however, when he was asked what he could do to solve the problems of the neighborhood. He needed help from the schools, churches, police, sociologists, psychiatrists, and the tenants themselves, he said. He was particularly harsh on the professionals, who rarely lived in the community where they worked. "They can go home at night and forget about it," he complained, adding that any sense of urgency slipped away.[100]

The following day the Governor journeyed to San Luis Obispo County to watch the migration of the whales.

Two weeks later, an aide in the Governor's office was quoted by the press as saying that the Pink Palace visit "was one of the most cynical things we've ever done."[101]

244

Chapter Twenty-Six

THE AUTHOR COMES TO THE END OF THE JOURNEY. THE
QUESTION IS ASKED WHETHER THE GOVERNOR OF CALI-
FORNIA SHOULD BE JUDGED HARSHLY. THE AUTHOR DE-
CIDES NOT BECAUSE OTHERS ARE RESPONSIBLE. THE
GOVERNOR'S INFLUENCE ON JAMES EARL CARTER DE-
SCRIBED. MARSHALL MCLUHAN IS VINDICATED. THE
AUTHOR WORRIES ABOUT THE FUTURE. THE GREAT RIVER
REVISITED. HUCK FINN AND TOM SAWYER ONCE AGAIN.

IN THE LAW, the judge's decision always follows the rec-
itation of the facts.

In the movie world, the great Hollywood director Frank
Capra once said, you can preach to people *after* you entertain
them.

But what judgment?

What sermon?

The Pink Palace escapade was a bit much even for Jerry,
who seemed inclined to toy with the wrath of the gods every
once in a while. But even so, would it be fair to summon
Jerry before the bar of justice and single him out for blame?

I think not. Jerry was the mirror of the society in the mid-
1970s. He was giving us, the voters, what he thought we
wanted. And he was usually correct in his estimates. Even
in November 1976, almost two years after he had succeeded
to the governorship, he was scoring a 78 per cent approval
rating in the California Poll, a level of popularity unprece-

dented in California history.[102] If we didn't like what we saw, we had only ourselves to hold accountable. We were looking at our own reflection in the mirror. If we wanted Jerry to cut out the reliance on symbols, he would oblige. If we wanted him to pay more attention to black people, he would do so. He had no commitment one way or another. He didn't care. The sole concern he had was expressing the popular will successfully enough to be reelected Governor in 1978 and President in 1984. Jerry was the totally democratic man. Like the proverbial weathervane, he turned in whichever direction the winds blew him. For as he himself said to me one day long before we were to reach a parting of ways: "Popularity is the only currency of the realm around here."

Meaning the Governor's office.

Meaning the presidency.

If one had any doubt whatsoever about the viability of Jerry's method, one need only consider the performance of one James Earl Carter after the November 1976 election. The President was playing the same kind of symbols game Jerry Brown was. Indeed, there were people in Sacramento who said the President was copying the Governor of California. And wasn't imitation the sincerest form of flattery? In Jimmy Carter's inaugural address, he even called for a "new spirit." Toward the end of 1976 and the beginning of 1977, the New Spirit seemed to be mostly visual symbols appropriate for television viewing. Jimmy Carter fishing in his pond. Jimmy and one of the furniture movers carrying Amy's dollhouse across the front lawn. Rosalynn worrying about whether she should wear her old dress to the inaugural ball. Amy's first day in school. Amy's new dog. Jimmy telling his cabinet members to drive smaller cars. (He didn't say anything about Plymouths.) Jimmy turning the heat down to 65 degrees. (What an appropriate symbol for someone who wished to "cool off" the country; McLuhan must have been pleased.) Jimmy wearing a coat-sweater when he talked to the press about the natural gas shortages. Jimmy wearing blue jeans in the White House. Jimmy putting out a press release about wearing blue jeans in the White House. The casual method was always calculated, just the way Jerry's was. (If nothing else, the 1970s cultivated self-consciousness to an extraordinary degree.) Several days after Jimmy Carter appeared on television in a coat-sweater, Jerry showed up at a press conference in one of his own, apparently in order to dramatize the need to conserve fuel. The good players learned from each other. Television was an instant form of communication. Sometimes the symbols that were televised were helpful in implementing policy and sometimes not. In either case they poured forth from the White House in such profusion that some of the Washington reporters joked about Jimmy Carter still running for the presidency. They didn't understand. In the Age of Television, an incumbent had to run for office every day of the week.

The symbols continued. Jimmy invoking the ghost of Roosevelt in his first fireside chat. Jimmy holding a press conference at Warm Springs, Georgia, where Roosevelt died. (Jimmy Carter understood full well about the past being a mother lode of symbols.) Jimmy asking his appointees to spend more time with their families. (Was this request an indirect slap at Jerry, whose odd working hours made a normal family life almost impossible for *his* appointees?) Jimmy calling on his aides to get married. (Was this another slap at Jerry?) Jimmy disapproving of people living in sin. (The New Spirit was noticeably, almost self-righteously moralistic.) Jimmy getting down on his knees to talk to schoolchildren. (What a marvelous gesture of humility that was.) Jimmy speaking in sign language to the deaf-mutes. (For television viewers, hand signals were more expressive than the spoken word.) Jimmy appointing a triple amputee head of the Veterans' Administration. (Eighteen months earlier, Jerry had selected a quadriplegic as head of the California Department of Rehabilitation.) A picture of the triple amputee appeared in Saturday papers throughout the country. Almost every day of the week, the White House staged a "visual" for the cameras. Unquestionably the visual symbols stuck in the public's mind. Who knew or cared what tax preferences were being hatched in the bowels of the Treasury Department? The visual tableaux that were unfolding in Washington and Sacramento were much more entertaining. It was Jimmy doing this and Jerry doing that. Jimmy, Jimmy, Jimmy, Jerry, Jerry, Jerry — even the names were diminutized to make the political leaders seem less threatening. By February 1977, everyone was agreed: small *was* beautiful.

Of course. The movement had begun in California and spread east. That was because California was the capital of the entertainment world. What played successfully in California in 1974 and 1975 would play to a larger audience in Washington in 1977 — and this media style, in turn, would undoubtedly start appearing in Western Europe and Japan by 1979 or 1980. The symbol was the thing in the 1970s, and California was the vanguard of the symbolized world. Jimmy Carter just adapted the symbols Jerry used and made them more American. There was more use of family in Jimmy Carter's symbols, more reference to the land, more invocation of the virtues of small business. That was because Jimmy Carter's experience was closer to the American archetype than Jerry's was. On reflection, it was inconceivable that Jimmy Carter would not be elected President in the bicentennial year, that time when, more than any other time, the American people would wish to respect and invoke the archetypes of American experience. Just as Jerry Brown was a kind of politicized Kung Fu, so the Carter family was the Waltons incarnated on the political scene. If American television viewers had not watched the Waltons for the three years preceding the 1976 election, they might have found Jimmy Carter less familiar, less acceptable, but the appropriate symbols were already implanted in the popular consciousness. Jimmy Carter was John Boy grown older. The right man coincided with the right symbol at the right time —and so Jimmy Carter was elected.

I rather think Jimmy Carter learned about the mythological process he was involved in as he proceeded through the campaign. His instincts were correct all along, of course, but for a while, before the Democratic convention and then later on during the fall campaign, he seemed to lose effectiveness. He sounded too strident, too aggressive, too "hot" for the television medium. He got rattled. He imparted too much statistical information. There were not enough visual symbols. Perhaps he got tired, I don't know, but I rather think he drew too far away from the strengths of Plains, Georgia. Fortunately for him, he was given the opportunity to recoup. His Republican opponent was far less adept at symbolic communication than he was. Had Reagan, that past master of symbols, been the Republican opponent, the outcome might have been different, but history played funny tricks, Reagan having barely lost out at the Republican convention. And so Jimmy Carter was home free. Later, after the election, when he had time to regain his strength and sense of perspective, he began to act more symbolically. The change in his *modus operandi,* as much as anything Jerry Brown did, indicated once and for all the extent to which a modern politician was required to act symbolically if he was going to gain great success.

Jimmy Carter had learned the hard way about the symbols, just as Jerry had. For Jerry, the object lesson was his father, whom he loved very much and who had been a competent Governor but who was eaten alive by Reagan, the symbolic politician. Jerry would not make the same mistake himself — and neither would Jimmy Carter. McLuhan, the prophet of the television age, was vindicated. The properties of the medium were too powerful to overcome. The aspiring politician had to go with it, not resist it. All the politicians who stressed program in 1976 — Ford, Jackson, Udall, and Harris

— lost. The new politician had to express something else: not program, but personality, character, virtue. The 1976 election was a contest to see who could exemplify the most virtue. Every move, every statement, had to be calculated to achieve that end. Jimmy Carter was incredibly talented at doing so. He had another strength as well. Most of the time he remembered to keep his sentences short. (At least intuitively, he was aware of the overload problem.) He even had a style of speaking that respected McLuhan's advice concerning the importance of the interval. In the middle of a sentence, often, Jimmy Carter would pause and give his viewers a space to participate in. The resulting impression was very effective. As of the winter of 1977, the only mannerism Jimmy Carter had that McLuhan probably would have disapproved of was the constant, indelible smile. Jerry picked up on this weakness as well in the spring of 1976, when, referring to Carter, he asked, "What's behind the smile?" In *Culture Is Our Business,* McLuhan suggested flashing teeth were too aggressive for the new, laid-back medium.[103] The problem would undoubtedly be corrected over time. Certainly there was much in a President's life that Jimmy Carter would have a hard time smiling about.

As for the rest of his demeanor, Jimmy Carter was quite appropriate for the times. The Man on the White Horse (or was it the White House?) was alive and well, riding across the television screens of America. Perhaps Jerry would follow him in eight years. Who could say for sure? Eight years was a long while to maintain a hit on prime-time TV.

Was television the only explanation for the emergence of the Man on the White Horse in 1976? I'm not sure it was. Certainly everyone would point to Vietnam and Watergate and conclude that the country needed some hope for a change. But were even Vietnam and Watergate the full explanation? A few astute political observers felt not. Between the years 1973 and 1976, four works were published that suggested that the desire for a superleader, unblemished by any human frailty, went deeper than this or that misbegotten policy, deeper even than the media. These works were, in order of publication: *The Fiscal Crisis of the State* (1973), by James O'Connor; *Legitimation Crisis* (1973), by Jürgen Habermas; *The Cultural Contradictions of Capitalism* (1976), by Daniel Bell; and "The Democratic Distemper" (1976), by Samuel Huntington.[104] Although these authors reflected almost diametrically opposed political viewpoints (O'Connor, an economics professor at San Jose State in California, and Habermas, a German philosopher, were both Marxists, while Bell and Huntington, professors of sociology and government respectively at Harvard, were both conservatives), they came to very much the same conclusion. Modern government was, in Habermas's memorable phrase, suffering from a "legitimation crisis." The greater the number of problems that arose in the economy and society, the more government was inclined to intervene. The more government intervention there was, the more the credibility and effectiveness of the government were put to the test. The more government failed to meet this test, the more the government lost legitimacy. The more legitimacy the government lost, the less effectively the government was able to intervene in the next crisis. The cycle seemed inexorable and never-ending. Quite understandably, political leaders (and corporate and labor leaders as well) were forced to spend greater and greater amounts of their time justifying what they were doing. The symbols, which none of the four authors talked about very much, were one way of providing this justification.

The O'Connor-Habermas-Bell-Huntington thesis was a provocative one. The thesis, interestingly enough, was also one touched upon by Jerry on July 25, 1976. In the first extensive interview he granted after the Democratic convention, Jerry said: "You have to have purpose ... This is my job. This is my vocation ... [The American people] want to be part of something larger than themselves that conforms to what they understand to be of value and lasting significance. You can't have a world based on legitimacy, if those who are in positions of authority are with no pervasive values that most people agree on."[105]

The key word in the interview was "legitimacy." Jerry was working full time trying to acquire it and hold on to it. So was Jimmy Carter. Conceivably, if enough legitimacy could be accumulated, the Man on the White Horse could lead the people out of the valley of sorrows. In an age of increasing scarcity of natural resources, people would begin to recognize their common interests. There would be more reasonable give-and-take. The symbols were only the means to a greater end. They would show people the way, exemplifying in the microcosm what people would sooner or later come to accept in the macrocosm. Jimmy and Jerry were the embodiments of the new consciousness. They were Moses traveling toward the promised land. If the people would just give them some help, we might all arrive faster, with fewer casualties along the way. It all made sense, what Jerry was talking about and what Jerry and Jimmy were doing, and I was inclined to think they might achieve a certain degree of success.

But ... but ... There was still a but here someplace. Perhaps I was just a worrywart, or perhaps the Sacramento experience had warped my judgment, but looking over the year I spent with Jerry and the eighteen months since then, when I had followed the play in the newspapers, I felt a palpable, somewhat ill-defined uneasiness in the pit of my stomach. Something was bothering me. What was it? Looking into the crystal ball of the future — and whatever else he was, Jerry was a crystal ball — I had seen a possibility that deeply disturbed me. What was this possibility? It wasn't Jerry Brown or Jimmy Carter per se. (I was ready to concede they were both honorable men who would not misuse the considerable power they were striving to obtain.) The possibility was present in the society itself. We were all of us — even Jerry Brown and Jimmy Carter — corks on the great sea of society, and deep down there somewhere, somehow, there was a rip tide building. The rip tide could sweep all of us away before we knew what was happening. The symbols were too powerful. They worked upon us at too unconscious a level, penetrating right down into the base of the brain, below the rational, cautionary faculties. We could get caught up in something and be motivated without knowing why and end up ceding a part of our free will to somebody else. There were tendencies in the society that increased the chances of this possibility. A fuel shortage. Diminishing natural resources. A significant segment of the population that was consistently and unthinkingly overlooked. Growing unemployment. Rampant inflation. Racial strife. Interest groups that disrupted the economy. General misunderstanding. And then?

... the Man on the White Horse who understood how to manipulate the symbols and didn't have the scruples Jimmy and Jerry did. The people would reach out, especially the generations that had been conditioned by the dumb images flashing on the TV screens. Jimmy and Jerry, Kojak and Wonder Woman, Baretta and Batman — the images had all prepared millions of TV viewers for the eventuality, even the inevitability, of the superhero — and now he or she would ride in with the right symbols, the right buzz words, and do anything he or she wanted, and we would all be so appreciative.

The people who would be most susceptible to the Man on the White Horse would be the ones from the broken families. The number of divorces and broken families was growing every year. The father-figure was increasingly absent from the home. If the children from the broken homes couldn't find the father-figure in the home, they would look for him somewhere else — on the television screen, in politics. Politics was the wrong place for the absent father-figure to appear. The political father-figure would be too unreal. The children would understand too little about him. The politicians had too much power already.

I finally understood why, when they wrote the Constitution, the founding fathers provided for checks and balances and an irrevocable separation between church and state. Not only did they wish to avoid any possibility of an official religion being established, they perceived the enormous risk that would be created if the religious and temporal authority were situated in the same person. The temporal authority had too much power already. If it was vested with a religious significance as well, the people might be so overawed by the mystery and omniscience of the high office that they might forget to question, to oppose, to fight back. It was better if the politicians were discouraged from employing powerful archetypical symbols and presenting themselves as quasi-religious, moral leaders. Religion should be kept in the church, the father-figures, in the home, and the symbols, in the entertainment world. It was one thing for Cesar Chavez or Martin Luther King or Mahatma Gandhi to cultivate a religious charisma; they did not have the police power at their disposal. The Governor of California did and so did the President of the United States.

I wasn't daydreaming. Already there were a few indications of what might come in the future. There was first of all Jerry's own testimony in the fall of 1974 about the Man on the White Horse being able to do anything he wanted to if he manipulated the right symbols.

There was second of all the Maryland and Oregon primaries, when Jerry had finally tapped into the unquestioning fervor building up in the populace.

There was also a special series that appeared in the *Wall Street Journal* in the fall of 1976; it reported:

- that the average high school graduate today will attend school for 11,000 hours but will have sat in front of the TV set for almost twice as long and will have been exposed to an estimated 350,000 commercials and 18,000 murders.
- that habitual TV viewing encouraged passivity and loss of creativity.
- that TV viewing encouraged an unrealistic view of the

254

world and the sense that the hero can always solve the
problem, even when ordinary people cannot.

In the early 1970s, the *New Yorker* published a cartoon that
seemed prophetic. A father who was changing a flat tire was
saying to his two children, who were sitting impatiently in
the car: "Don't you understand? This is *life,* this is what
is happening. We can't switch to another channel."[106]

The cartoon was touching on a serious problem.

And what was happening in California in 1975 and 1976
while we were switching to another channel? Often, the
symbols predominated; the reality was overlooked. Reality,
apparently, was too grim, too complicated for the voters to
comprehend. We were given symbols instead.

For example. At the same time Jerry was proclaiming that
small was beautiful and power should be decentralized along
E. F. Schumacher lines, power was being centralized within
the state government and the state Energy Commission and
the state air resources gained the de facto power to control
the nature and amount of economic development in the state.
Was the newfound power of the state Energy Commission
and the Air Resources Board a good idea or not? Unnecessary
or not? Could we have solved the problems of energy deple-
tion and air pollution without vesting such enormous powers
in the government? For the most part, these problems were
not addressed by the general population. The people were
too busy watching the symbols. If one had questioned the
average voter about the most important thing Governor
Brown had done in two years in office, he probably wouldn't
have mentioned the Energy Commission; he would have
talked about the Plymouth.

To cite another example. At the same time Jerry was
extolling the virtues of the Zen Center, large corporations
and large government agencies were assuming more and
more control of the nation's economy, and centralized economic planning was being called for. The pro-planning
group was led by a Wall Street financier named Felix
Rohatyn, who helped manage the New York City fiscal crisis,

who was a long-time adviser to Jerry's father, Pat Brown, Sr., and who was one of Jerry's major contacts with the New York financial community. Was Felix Rohatyn a good idea or not? His proposals certainly would have electrified the staunchest socialist. The issue was not addressed, however. The television viewers were too enthralled learning about the solar heating unit Jerry was installing in his bathroom.

Or to cite a third example. During the period when Jerry was railing on about the evils of bureaucracy and red tape, the Dow Chemical Company was trying to secure approval for a petrochemical plant in Contra Costa County that would have generated several thousand jobs. Dow struck out. Despite the expenditure of two and a half years of time and $4.5 million in planning and design costs, Dow was able to secure only four of the sixty-five government permits required. The red tape proved to be too much, so Dow decided to build its plant elsewhere.[107] Was the Dow plant a good idea or not? It may have been a bad idea, but until Dow pulled out, the governmental planning that was going on was not focused upon. And even after the Dow decision was announced and legislative hearings were held, the debate quickly shifted to the need for "one stop" zoning and the establishment of statewide standards for industrial development. "One stop" zoning was a code word for more centralized planning. Was centralized planning a good idea or not? Once again, the Governor did not address the issue, which seemed to conflict with the small-is-beautiful image.

The examples of decentralized rhetoric and centralizing reality were by no means restricted to California. In 1976, the year of the Bicentennial, when President Ford quoted Tom Paine and declared war on the spread of governmental bureaucracy, the Federal Energy Administration expanded to 4100 employees, including 111 public relations officers who were turning out more than 1500 press releases a year. (Three years before, the FEA didn't exist.)[108] Was there an alternative to this kind of government regulation? The question wasn't asked by the White House.

The examples went on and on. During the 1976 campaign, Jimmy Carter bragged about the reorganization of state government he engineered while he was Governor of Georgia. The reorganization involved enormous centralization of authority and increased the number of state employees by more than a third. Was the centralization a good idea or not? Jimmy Carter did not discuss the question because, for the most part, he was intimating that the power of the government had been reduced.

It was the old familiar story. The image did not comport with the reality. In November and December of 1976, after Jimmy Carter was elected, the symbols disseminated from Plains, Georgia, were all small town, peanut farming, and small, private enterprise. The reality was very different. When the President's major appointees were announced, the vast majority of them came from New York, Atlanta, and Los Angeles and had spent much of their lives working for the federal government or giant corporations. At least six of the Carter appointees were directors of, or provided legal advice for, International Business Machines, the largest data processing organization in the world.

What was going on? Were the facts so disturbing to the American people that our leaders could not bear to tell us what was happening? Were we witnessing the passing of a way of life, which we could not yet bring ourselves to admit? Was the old-fashioned free-enterprise system going the way of the whales? Were the whales such a powerful image because they represented a freedom and natural order that we feared we were losing in our own lives? Was Plains, Georgia, the metaphor that would enable the people to accept IBM? Was E. F. Schumacher the jacket cover but Felix Rohatyn the book? If the answer to any of these questions was yes, then perhaps the symbols we gravitated toward in the bicentennial year described more of what we were leaving behind than what we were moving toward.

I wasn't sure. Arguably, there was no alternative to bigness, centralization, and the corporate state. But of this I was certain: Unless we were willing to deal with the issue of smallness versus bigness in the real world, there was no possibility we would be able to retain the way of life that many of us still cared about.

The symbols weren't enough.

The task of shaping reality according to a more human proportion would take at least a generation. The way would not be easy. In order to increase our chances of success, we would have to take a number of steps that many of us had not thought too seriously about before.

First, we would have to become more aware of the uses and abuses of political symbolism.

Second, we would have to take back control over the symbols and use them for our own ends.

Third, we would have to devise ways of simplifying the governmental processes so that ordinary people could understand government and participate in it.

Fourth, we would have to find ways of dealing with serious problems without always calling on the powers of the government.

Fifth, we would have to encourage young people to remain outside the government, avoid the dangers of cooptation, and work on the process from outside.

Sixth, we would have to be on the lookout for the Man on the White Horse and guard against his coming, no matter how reasonable he might sound on television.

Seventh, we would have to care much more deeply about strengthening the cohesiveness and viability of the family and bring the father-figure back into the family.

Last, we would have to recognize that so long as a significant segment of our population remained without employment and subject to humiliation, the possibility of general and social disorder would remain.

The list wasn't very original. Probably my grandfather Daniel Henry Lorenz would have made most of the same points seventy-five years ago, when he was operating a small grocery store on the corner of Wayne Avenue and Clover Street in Dayton, Ohio. Maybe that was progress. It took me thirty-eight years to learn what he knew by the age of twenty-one. But in any case, now I knew.

It had been a long journey, starting that day in August 1974 when I commenced work for Jerry. Now this part of the journey was almost ended. The voyage had been — how shall I say? — like a trip down a river . . .
                    the great river . . .
                    the Mississippi River.
In my imagination, I was back on the great river now, moving through the heartland of the country, where the truest, most profound American archetypes reside, Huckleberry Finn and Tom Sawyer and Jim, the runaway slave — and somehow the story that Mark Twain composed ninety-two years ago seemed like a metaphor for us all.

Huck was the typical American, a young man who was coming of age in a country that also was coming of age. His trip down the Mississippi was a rite of passage or initiation.

Tom Sawyer didn't travel the whole distance. He took a short cut. Tom was always looking for short cuts and concocting complicated schemes that never seemed to turn out. He was a trickster, and if Huck represented a kind of balance between the feelings and the thinking functions, Tom was mostly intellect, trying to manipulate the world with his brain.

Jim stood for the feeling, intuitive side, the part of the personality that even in Twain's time was beginning to be suppressed as the nation became more industrialized and subject to corporate control. Jim, appropriately enough, was trying to escape to freedom.

That was what the book was about, really, an escape to freedom.

There were many adventures along the way.

When Huck and Jim were south of Cairo, Illinois, for

example, they ran into a couple of confidence men named the Count and the Duke, who had a plan to trick the inhabitants of a small, provincial town. They would announce a theatrical production and charge admission, and then they would only put on a small part of the show; the townspeople who saw it would be so embarrassed about being tricked that they wouldn't tell the others who had bought tickets for the second and third performance, and then, before the end of the final performance, the Count and the Duke would sneak away with all the proceeds.

Well, the plan worked out as expected. But because the Count and the Duke weren't satisfied with the size of their haul, they tried to turn Jim in for a reward. And then things really began to happen. Huck escaped — and ended up at the house of a woman who turned out to be Tom Sawyer's aunt. Jim was captured and locked in the woodshed nearby. Tom Sawyer showed up, and right away Huck said they ought to go down and let Jim out. But Tom said no, that was too easy, they should have a more complicated plan than that and do the escape the way it was done in the Middle Ages, with rope ladders and secret messages and all, and so Huck went along. Jim was agreeable to most anything. He just wanted to get out and was grateful Tom and Huck wanted to help, which they began to do. Huck and Tom smuggled a couple of knives in to Jim and told him to dig his way out under the walls of the shed. Huck was still skeptical but Tom Sawyer reassured him. "It don't make no difference how foolish it is," Tom Sawyer said at one point, "it's the *right* way — and it's the regular way. And there ain't no *other* way, that ever *I* heard of, and I've read all the books that gives any information about these things. They always dig out with a . . . knife — and not through dirt, mind you; generally it's through solid rock. And it takes them weeks and weeks and weeks, and for ever and ever." Huck was satisfied. Just before Jim was able to tunnel his way out, though, Tom Sawyer got bored and decided they were going to have to create a little disturbance to make life more interesting. Tom wrote a letter to his aunt saying there was a desperate band of cutthroats from the Indian Territory who were going to steal the runaway slave. Well, of course the whole place was in an uproar, and it was a wonder anything good happened after that.

And so the story ended. Perhaps the world hadn't changed too much since Mark Twain's time. There were still confidence men roaming the river, and possibly there was a little of Huck and Tom and Jim in each one of us, although sometimes we didn't like to admit to ourselves how much of Jim was present. Jim was still locked in the woodshed, and despite Tom Sawyer's advice about the need for a complicated scheme, maybe all we had to do was walk over to the shed, open the door, and let him out.

It was that simple.

Notes

1. Los Angeles *Times,* September 6, 1974, Part II, p. 3.
2. Ibid., March 27, 1974, Part I, p. 3. Alioto's remark about Jerry campaigning "in the closet" was made at a news conference, after which Alioto added that he considered Jerry's talk to a California Democratic Council convention in February to be "effeminate and deceptive." Alioto did not elaborate.
3. Sacramento *Bee,* January 7, 1975, p. A-1.
4. See *The Random House Dictionary of the English Language* (New York, Random House, 1969), p. 173.
5. San Francisco *Chronicle,* February 24, 1975, p. 23.
6. Sacramento *Bee,* August 10, 1975, p. A-1.
7. The remarks about Jacques and Jerry, which were related to me in the fall of 1974, were set forth virtually verbatim in the Sacramento *Bee,* August 10, 1975, p. A-1. In setting forth the quotation, I have used the Sacramento *Bee* version.
8. For a newspaper account of the debate, see the Los Angeles *Times,* September 28, 1974, Part II, p. 1.
9. Marshall McLuhan, *Understanding Media: The Extensions of Man* (New York, Signet Books, 1964).
10. Ibid., p. viii.
11. For one account of Jerry's colloquy with the press, see the San Francisco *Examiner,* February 28, 1975, p. 8.
12. See, for example, the *Wall Street Journal,* February 25, 1975, p. 1; Marvin Ross, "Economic Conditions and Crime: Metropolitan Toronto 1965–1972," *Crime and Delinquency Literature* (September 1974): 362; Harvey Brenner, *Mental Illness and the Economy* (Cambridge, Mass., Harvard University Press, 1973); Thad Phillips, Harold Votey, and Darold Maxwell, "Crime, Youth, and the Labor Market," *Journal of Political Economy,* 80 (May–June 1972): 491; John Allison, "Economic Factors and the Rate of Crime," *Land Economics,* 47 (May 1972): 193; William Bonger, *Criminality and Economic Conditions* (Bloomington, Indiana University Press, 1969); Eli Ginzberg, *Manpower Agenda for America* (New York, McGraw-Hill, 1968), pp. 124–126; *Report of the National Advisory Commission on Civil Disorders*

(New York, Bantam Books, 1968), pp. 266–277; President's Commission on Law Enforcement and Administration of Justice, *Task Force Report: Crime and Its Impact — An Assessment* (Washington, D.C., U.S. Government Printing Office, 1967), pp. 25, 207–210; Belton Fleisher, "Income and Delinquency," *American Economic Review,* 56 (March 1966): 118, and "The Effect of Unemployment on Juvenile Delinquency," *Journal of Political Economy,* 71 (December 1963): 543; Daniel Glaser and Kent Price, "Crime, Age, and Employment," *American Sociology Review,* 26 (October 1959): 679.

13. Belton Fleisher, "The Effect of Unemployment on Juvenile Deliquency," *Journal of Political Economy,* 71 (December 1963): 543.

14. Harvey Brenner, *Mental Illness and the Economy* (Cambridge, Mass., Harvard University Press, 1973).

15. San Francisco *Examiner,* March 2, 1975, p. 2.

16. Ibid., February 18, 1975, p. 8.

17. See *Handbook of Labor Statistics 1974* (Washington, D.C., U.S. Government Printing Office, 1974), p. 27, Table 1.

18. For confirmation of these figures, see *Economic Report of the President 1976* (Washington, D.C., U.S. Government Printing Office, 1976), p. 196, Table B-22; p. 224, Table B-46.

19. For a critical discussion of the Phillips Curve, see Robert Lekachmen, "Inflation, Jobs, Equity and Power," *Inflation, Unemployment and Social Justice,* Proceedings from the Full Employment Without Inflation Conference (Columbus, Ohio, Academy for Contemporary Problems, 1974), pp. 61–63.

20. See Studs Terkel, *Hard Times* (New York, Avon Books, 1971).

21. E. F. Schumacher, *Small Is Beautiful* (New York, Harper & Row, 1973).

22. Los Angeles *Times,* April 12, 1975, Part I, p. 27.

23. *The I Ching* (Princeton, Princeton University Press, 1975).

24. Dane Rudhyar, *The Pulse of Life* (Berkeley and London, Shambala Press, 1970).

25. Ibid., pp. 31–38.

26. On April 3, 1975, the California Fair Political Practices Commission ruled that John Henning must give up his role as a labor lobbyist and union official who decided which candidates received political contributions. San Francisco *Chronicle,* April 4, 1975, p. 24. My appearance before Senator Cranston was on the day before, April 2.

27. James MacGregor Burns, *Roosevelt: The Lion and the Fox* (New York, Harcourt Brace Jovanovich, 1956). This observation appeared at the beginning of Burns's book: "A prince, wrote Machiavelli, must imitate the fox and the lion, for the lion cannot protect himself from traps, and the fox cannot defend himself from

wolves. One must therefore be a fox to recognize traps, and a lion to frighten wolves. Those that wish to be only lions do not understand this. Therefore, a prudent ruler ought not to keep faith when by doing so it would be against his interest, and when the reasons which made him bind himself no longer exist. If men were all good, this precept would not be a good one; but as they are bad, and would not observe their faith with you, so you are not bound to keep with them."

28. Pat related the Chessman story several times after Jerry was elected Governor. See the Sacramento *Bee,* December 10, 1976, p. A-1.
29. California Unemployment Insurance Code, Section 1264.
30. See ibid., Section 2626.2.
31. *Statistical Abstract of the United States 1974,* p. 336, Table 542.
32. Ibid., p. 340, Table 550.
33. For a description of how, in the media, women were discouraged from working after 1945, see Marjorie Rosen, *Popcorn Venus* (New York, Avon Books, 1973), pp. 201–220.
34. In *The Pursuit of Loneliness* (Boston, Beacon Press, 1970), pp. 62–70, Philip Slater discusses some of the ways Dr. Spock's child-centered, child-rearing philosophy reshaped the consciousness of the 1940s and 1950s.
35. Los Angeles *Times,* April 4, 1975, Part I, p. 1.
36. For an incisive study of the Southern California ambience, see Carey McWilliams, *Southern California: An Island on the Land* (Santa Barbara and Salt Lake City, Peregrine Smith, Inc., 1973).
37. For background on the Red Scares of the post-World War I and II eras, see Frederick Lewis Allen, *Only Yesterday* (New York, Bantam Books, 1959), pp. 31–52; Richard Hofstadter, *The Age of Reform* (New York, Alfred A. Knopf, 1956), pp. 270–300; and I. F. Stone, *The Haunted Fifties* (New York, Vintage Books, 1969).
38. San Francisco *Chronicle,* February 15, 1975, p. 16.
39. Ibid., March 1, 1975, p. 10.
40. Los Angeles *Times,* March 13, 1975, Part I, p. 1.
41. Susan Sontag, "Happenings: An art of radical juxtaposition," *Against Interpretation* (New York, Dell, 1966), pp. 263–274.
42. San Francisco *Chronicle,* March 14, 1975, p. 2.
43. Los Angeles *Times,* March 25, 1975, Part I, p. 1.
44. Ibid., April 3, 1975, Part I, p. 3.
45. For one of the first — and still the best — explications of Camp, see Susan Sontag, "Notes on 'Camp,'" *Against Interpretation,* pp. 275–292.
46. Los Angeles *Times,* April 24, 1975, Part I, p. 3.
47. Ibid., April 25, 1975, Part I, p. 1. The story also describes the telegram to Colonel Rock and Project VIC.
48. Ibid.

49. Ibid., April 30, 1975, Part I, p. 1.
50. Sacramento *Bee,* April 26, 1975, editorial; May 3, 1975, editorial.
51. *King Henry IV, Part 2,* act 1, sc. 2, lines 204–206.
52. Joseph Campbell, *The Hero with a Thousand Faces* (Princeton, Princeton University Press, 1968); Erich Neumann, *The Origins and History of Consciousness* (Princeton, Princeton University Press, 1973).
53. See Samuel Huntington, "The Democratic Distemper," *The American Commonwealth 1976* (New York, Basic Books, 1976), pp. 16–18.
54. Ibid.
55. *King Henry IV, Part 1,* act 1, sc. 2, lines 162–184.
56. See Euger Harrigel, *Zen in the Art of Archery* (New York, Vintage Books, 1971).
57. Sacramento *Bee,* March 21, 1976, p. A-3.
58. Los Angeles *Times,* March 18, 1975, Part II, p. 1.
59. *The I Ching,* pp. 239–244.
60. *Whole Earth Epilog* (Baltimore, Penguin Books, 1974).
61. Sacramento *Bee,* June 20, 1975, p. A-1.
62. Ibid., June 25, 1975, p. A-1.
63. Ibid., July 7, 1975, p. A-1.
64. Los Angeles *Times,* July 3, 1975, Part I, p. 3.
65. San Rafael *Independent Journal,* July 22, 1975, p. 2.
66. Los Angeles *Times,* July 28, 1975, Part II, p. 7.
67. Ibid., July 31, 1975, Part I, p. 3.
68. San Francisco *Chronicle,* December 17, 1976, p. 5.
69. See Los Angeles *Times* editorial, August 11, 1975, Part II, p. 6.
70. San Francisco *Chronicle,* December 5, 1975, p. 5.
71. Ibid., March 6, 1976, p. 6.
72. Ibid., December 30, 1975, p. 6.
73. Ibid., January 8, 1976, p. 1.
74. Ibid., March 15, 1976, p. 6.
75. Ibid., March 5, 1976, p. 24.
76. Ibid., March 5, 1976, p. 1.
77. See Sacramento *Bee,* April 11, 1976, p. A-1.
78. McLuhan, *Culture Is Our Business* (New York, Ballantine Books, 1972), p. 60.
79. San Francisco *Chronicle,* March 13, 1976, p. 12.
80. McLuhan, *Culture,* p. 32.
81. San Francisco *Examiner,* May 10, 1976, p. 1; San Francisco *Chronicle,* April 3, 1976, p. 6.
82. San Francisco *Examiner,* March 26, 1976, p. 8.
83. Ibid., March 30, 1976, p. 1.
84. San Francisco *Chronicle,* March 31, 1976, p. 46.
85. *Rolling Stone,* July 15, 1976, pp. 41–43.
86. Ibid., p. 44.